D0073332

LABOR PRODUCTIVITY CONTROL

LABOR PRODUCTIVITY CONTROL

New Approaches for Industrial Engineers and Managers

John C. Martin

PRAEGER

New York
Westport, Connecticut
London

Library of Congress Cataloging-in-Publication Data

Martin, John C.
Labor productivity control : new approaches for industrial engineers and managers / John C. Martin.
p. cm.
Includes bibliographical references and index.
ISBN 0-275-93663-5
1. Work measurement. 2. Labor productivity. I. Title.
T60.M37 1991
658.5′4—dc20 90-7449

Library of Congress Catalog Card Number: 90-7449
ISBN: 0-275-93663-5

First published in 1991

Praeger Publishers, One Madison Avenue, New York, NY 10010
An imprint of Greenwood Publishing Group, Inc.

Printed in the United States of America

The paper used in this book complies with the Permanent Paper Standard issued by the National Information Standards Organization (Z39.48—1984).

10 9 8 7 6 5 4 3 2 1

Contents

Figures

Preface

The focus of this book is to take issue with labor productivity control strategies that have proven ineffective or incomplete, and to describe approaches observed to be workable. This involves a look first at basic principles, culled from a combination of historical and modern viewpoints. Techniques used in any control process are discussed next in some detail. Then various overall control functions are examined closely.

The book can be used as a reference source by management and staff personnel within manufacturing and process industries, or by those whose present training is intended to equip them for such work. It is not a rehash of what has been said elsewhere. The reader will find in the chapters that follow a number of differences from other available reference sources. Such exceptions have not been put forth lightly, nor are they derived from casual observations. The logic or experience base is explained in each case.

Various new developments are also described within the book; those of general interest are interspersed with other material. Of more specialized interest to industrial engineers will be the logic charts for computer-aided application of the basic Methods-Time Measurement system (MTM–1), which show how the 4M Data system works. Not previously published, these will be found in the appendix.

Basic functions involved in productivity control for direct labor are usually thought of as having been "buttoned up" long ago. Given impetus through the work of Frederick Taylor and his contemporaries, that area of control has received continual attention. After a hundred years, it would seem that industrial management and staff groups should know how to go about this undertaking, which is so essential to competitive survival. In the process of developing steps along this line, however, we seem not to have fully accounted for changes that have occurred in the attitudes of individuals, in the mores of society, and in technological innovations. Recurring changes have tended to disqualify some of what has been applied in the past.

There have been changes in what is frequently called the "work ethic." The causes for this are debatable, although they undoubtedly have been affected by increased affluence, trends in labor relations, and governmental policies. Response to monetary incentive plans, in which individuals largely determine their own productivity levels, has lessened in recent years. Management's ability to administer such systems effectively has decreased as labor representatives became more adamant in utilizing the perceived grievances of operators to bring about disruptive changes.

Although segments of industry are turning away from such plans, practical alternatives for control have not been clearly defined in the literature. The increase in past years of paced operations or automated equipment seemed to provide an effective basis for control in many areas, but the manufacture of products that lend themselves to paced lines has been dwindling rapidly in American industrial plants: e.g., radios, televisions, other electronic devices, motorcycles and compact automobiles. Although sophisticated automation has been applied to some other kinds of work, operators who can strongly influence the effectiveness with which such equipment is used are always involved.

Various textbook definitions and references still seem geared to wage-incentive thinking. This book covers in detail a number of different control plans, including financial incentives. Three types of nonincentive control systems are described which can properly be considered. The advantages and disadvantages of specific control plans are discussed.

Labor productivity control is typically identified with two categories of work—direct and indirect. Since the latter term tends to exclude staff and management functions, the word "nondirect" has been substituted for it in this book, to emphasize that the control process does not apply just to the hourly work force. The gradual increase in proportions of nondirect to direct personnel during recent years is well known, and it might be expected that this trend would bring with it greater finesse in the application of nondirect labor control functions. Viewed on an overall basis, that has not occurred. There is a lack of clarity and consistency in available literature about how to approach the subject. For example, we are often told that time standards are the basis for control in plant maintenance, even though preventive maintenance—where work measurement standards can be applicable—remains a small part of the total maintenance work requirement at most locations, and is usually intermixed with other assignments.

Too often, the "control process" for nondirect groups seems to be an arbitrary force reduction when the short-term profit picture is not acceptable. There are better ways! This book defines three different approaches, each of which has been applied successfully for productivity control in specific categories of nondirect activity, and which together serve as a basis for control in a broad area of such work. Since the largest nondirect function is usually plant maintenance, particular emphasis is given to procedures for maintenance cost control.

The techniques involved in labor productivity control, as well as design of the control functions themselves, call for engineering training and management understanding. In many cases, there is a need to relearn the fundamentals involved. If industrial engineers—either those now employed or those in training—find in these chapters a challenge to become involved in the improvement of labor control functions, one purpose of this book will have been accomplished. And if managers and supervisors derive from the book an increased awareness of their opportunities to make constructive changes where productivity has been low, a second objective will have been achieved.

Don't expect to agree initially with all the concepts stated here, because some of your past training or experience may have been to the contrary. But please keep an open mind and weigh the evidence carefully.

1
Introduction

PRODUCTIVITY—AN IMPRECISE BUT DESCRIPTIVE AND USEFUL WORD

Although the word "productivity" has a generalized meaning to almost everyone, it is difficult to define this word in a manner that would be useful in evaluating progress toward the real objectives of an industrial organization. Some have tried to do so. For example, the fraction shown below has been used to derive an overall productivity ratio:

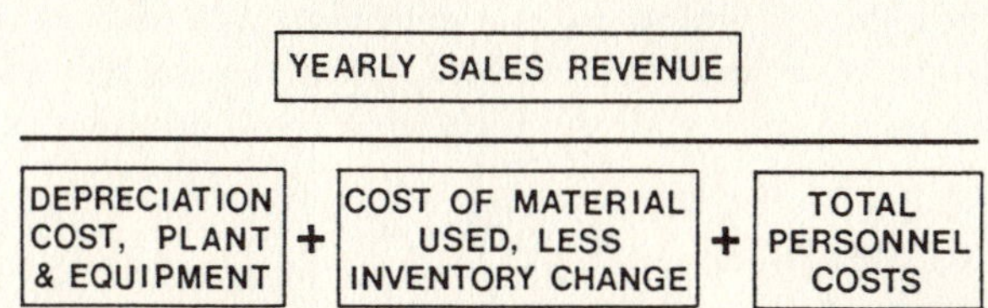

One large company evaluated about thirty of its divisions in this way during a two-year period, on an experimental basis, but gave up the project as not worth the effort involved. Tracking productivity in such a manner did not correspond closely with short-term profit trends.

Within manufacturing divisions of the same company, industrial engineering departments began to use "productivity" as a descriptive label for sectional performance ratios. Generally, such ratios included total standard hours for work accomplished in a specific period as the numerator, and total actual hours of direct labor during the same period as the denominator. Certain allowances were introduced as seemed appropriate at specific plants. In due time, the methods of calculating such

FIGURE 1.
A Productivity Diagram.

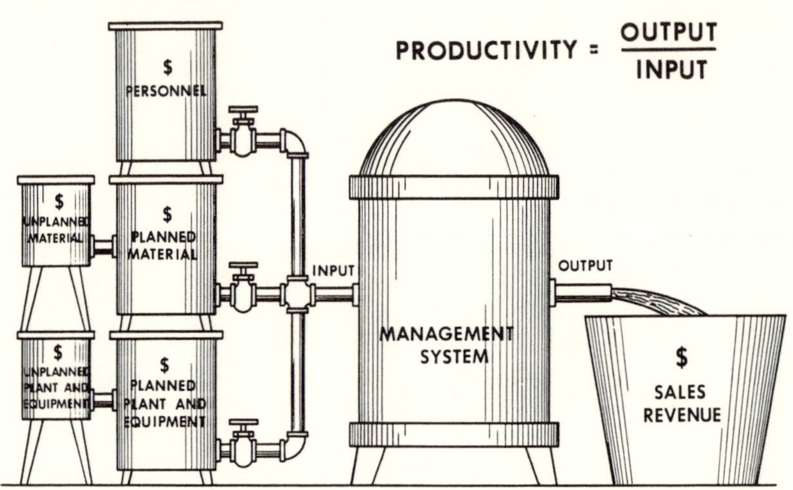

ratios were standardized on a corporate basis, and it was urged that the word "productivity" be dropped from general use as a name for the performance ratio, because of its ambiguous connotations. There was no problem in standardizing the arithmetic involved, but use of the term "productivity ratio" simply would not disappear. So the name stayed, along with a specific corporate definition.

Productivity is clearly a powerful word for use where it seems to fit. However, we need to know what we are talking about when we use it. The sketch in Figure 1 will provide a generalized definition of how the subject of productivity improvement might be viewed. We can also use the sketch as an aid in explaining what this book proposes to cover.

SCOPE OF COVERAGE

To a large extent, the diagram speaks for itself, though not so precisely as the overall productivity ratio noted previously. Others might properly define the ratio somewhat differently for their purpose, while not disagreeing with the attempt to picture what goes on within a typical industrial organization.

Plant and Equipment Costs Affecting Productivity

For purposes of discussion, let us use the terms "planned cost" and "unplanned cost" within the broad general area comprising plant and equipment needs. By planned costs we mean the plant structure, along with tools and equipment, which are determined to be required based on anticipated performance levels. Without demeaning the process of selecting what is required along this line, we can state that the planning process involved can generally be approached in a straightforward, analytical manner. Available techniques are taught in the classroom, spelled out in reference sources, provided as required by equipment sales representatives, or obtained from specialists.

While there are many choices to make, along with potential mistakes, the selection processes involved are for the most part noncontroversial. If lathe machining is required, for example, the analyst may have to decide between expensive numerically controlled equipment or manually operated turret lathes. After identifying the equipment costs, approximate cycle times, setup times, tape programming costs, production quantities, and other factors involved, a competent analyst can be expected to reach sound conclusions. A decision to utilize numerically controlled equipment would require fewer operators but would in itself have no bearing on labor productivity as the term is treated within this book.

Consider, however, what might be called unplanned plant and equipment costs. We will use this term to identify the additional pieces of equipment, or added plant space, that might be necessary if labor productivity is lower than would normally be anticipated. Such a condition could result from poor methods or excessive downtime by operators, lack of competent supervision, inadequate staff planning, ineffective maintenance policies, or various other reasons that will be touched on in chapters to follow. Of course, conditions might also bring about a level of labor productivity greater than expected, in which case the planned space and equipment could support additional sales volume.

This book will not deal with most of the analytical processes required to plan in advance for equipment or plant space. Our coverage of labor productivity will impact directly, however, on what we have termed unplanned plant and equipment costs. When a company or plant establishes a known and dependable level of labor productivity—whatever the ratios or terminology involved—this will have a direct effect on any future costs for equipment or related capital costs.

There is at least one aspect of plant size and equipment analysis which remains shaded in some uncertainty. This is the subject of "learning curves" and their application to equipment planning for a specified output within a given time. A subsequent chapter will explore this subject. Another aspect of capital cost to be touched on later is that of data collection equipment for planning and control. High-cost equipment of this kind may be less effective than simpler approaches.

Material Costs Affecting Productivity

The categories of material required for production processes include raw material, purchased parts, and nondirect supplies used throughout the plant. Maintenance materials and parts are also included. The techniques and procedures for material planning and control are well documented, largely noncontroversial, and will not be dealt with in this book.

The meaning in Figure 1 of both planned and unplanned material is not as clear-cut as was noted above for planned and unplanned equipment costs. Those with plant experience will recognize, however, that the losses associated with lack of needed material, avoidable scrap, waste of nondirect materials, and a portion of the materials used for maintenance repairs may be directly associated with employee or management deficiencies that occur when labor productivity is below a planned level. "Just-in-time" production techniques, an option to reduce inventory costs, may have the potential to affect labor productivity adversely. These points will be emphasized as chapters that follow describe control systems and techniques to be considered.

THE MEANING OF OTHER WORDS IN THE BOOK'S TITLE

Productivity, Control, Labor, New Approaches: all have ambiguous meanings without some explanation. We have defined the first of these words in several ways, noting that certain well-understood functions affecting overall productivity will not be covered. Before looking at other key words within the title, it will help to establish a shorthand way of referring to different types of work. Two acronyms are listed which will serve this purpose:

SC/R Short-cycle, repetitive operations, and
LC/LR Longer-cycle, less repetitive operations.

There could of course be many subdivisions of each category noted. Even though the crossover point between types of work as defined remains indefinite, however, the acronyms will be useful in discussions below and throughout the chapters that follow.

Control. Here is a word to which a more precise definition can be assigned. It is intended to mean three things: (1) Knowing in advance the level of performance that is reasonable to expect in specific operations or job assignments; (2) providing a way to evaluate performance in relation to established goals; and (3) following a systematic approach to work toward improvement when there are deficiencies. Most chapters will enlarge on these three points and discuss practical ways to implement them.

Labor. Go back to Figure 1 and consider what should be included here.

Or go farther back to the typical ratio for calculating overall productivity. We are referring to all employees within the industrial organization: direct operators; nondirect employees; direct supervisors; staff personnel; general supervisors of whatever title, and even the manufacturing or general manager. It is not too far-fetched to say that the performance level of each should be evaluated through application of the productivity control system, provided a practical way to do so can be developed. This book will suggest ways that are applicable in a wide variety of employee categories.

New Approaches. While the general meaning of this term needs no explanation, the scope of what the book attempts to cover that might be termed "new" should be explained. There will be found in chapters to follow a number of new but tested concepts which add to the reservoir of what can be considered for use in specific productivity control applications. But much of what the book covers that can also be classified under the heading of "new" consists of questioning certain concepts previously held by many to be inviolate.

As chapters that follow will emphasize, the policies, techniques, and procedures which have been developed over the years to assist in controlling labor productivity are a complex interweaving of ideas, techniques, and systems. Some are recognizably sound, as will be brought out in describing them. Other traditional ideas are questionable. Most of the latter have been around a long time, have been successfully applied under certain conditions, and may still be widely accepted. But some are of doubtful validity, for reasons that can be noted. We shall attempt to identify certain concepts which are sliding into a category that could be called "folklore." An example may illustrate the point.

It has been almost 100 years since pioneers such as Taylor, Halsey, Gantt, Emerson, and Gilbreth introduced their varied contributions to industrial engineering and management (see Hammond, reference C, 1971). In the next chapter of this book, a set of control principles published by Emerson will be reviewed and compared with a more recent compilation along the same line. We won't find much basic difference between the two sets of principles, but one noticeable difference is an emphasis on the principle of wage incentives in the earlier list. There are still many companies that find some form of wage incentive to be practical as a basis for control, but their number has declined. The basic statement that wage incentives are fundamental in achieving labor productivity control is something that could be labelled folklore. Incentives might be practical in specific cases or they might not. We shall examine the subject in detail later.

THE NEED TO IDENTIFY FOLKLORE IN PRODUCTIVITY CONTROL FUNCTIONS

In any event, it is true that incentive systems of one kind or another were widespread in most manufacturing industries for perhaps a fifty-year period through the 1930s. Many whose contributions within the fields of industrial engineering and management have gained broad acceptance were active during the latter part of that period. As a result, portions of the literature relating to those fields may be applicable within a specific wage incentive system but not necessarily applicable in the same way to other control systems. This book will analyze in detail a number of such examples. There is folklore to be found in various aspects of productivity control. Some of the questions that can be asked are noted below.

Management and Staff Functions

There are questions about how to supervise effectively within incentive or day-work control systems. Is the use of group leaders sound? What are practical operator/supervisor ratios for SC/R and LC/LR activities? There are points that justify attention concerning the duties of industrial engineers, to whom they report, the training or background they require, and their responsibilities to prevent deterioration of the control system. Where centralized staff planning leaves off and supervisory planning begins is significant. How direct supervisors can find the time to plan work assignments and indicate performance targets is a key to productivity in control plans known as measured day work.

Work Measurement and Work Sampling

There are holdover perceptions from wage incentive days that may not be directly applicable in other control plans. The concept of "normal" is one; the allowances that were typically applied to time standards is another. How should a predetermined time system which consists of specific time increments for motion sequences be applied within incentive plans having different task levels, or within measured day work? Has stopwatch time study been outmoded? How can the cost of acceptable work measurement be minimized? How much can a predetermined time system be condensed before it becomes unacceptable? Have computer-based techniques taken over the functions of standard data formulas or "pick-off sheets?" Do random tours that provide numerous sampling observations in a short period satisfy the need for randomness in work sampling? Can performance rating be applied during work sampling? Can work sampling replace work measurement as a basis for control?

Methods Analysis

Are there better ways of seeking out the best method than were available in the past? Whose job is it to specify and improve manual methods for LC/LR operations? Are methods improvements which operators develop a cause for revising time standards?

Incentives or Day work

Can wage incentive systems be managed effectively on a continuing basis? Are group wage incentives practical? How can deteriorated wage incentive applications be revitalized? How can they be changed to alternate control plans? Is there just one way to apply measured day work? Is short-interval scheduling (SIS) a practical concept?

Nondirect Work

Are time standards necessary for control in nondirect departments? How should industrial engineers relate to nondirect control? Can wage incentives be applied in plant maintenance? Can work measurement standards be used as a basis for maintenance cost control?

Performance Reporting

Can the performance level of a section where LC/LR work is predominant be reported without errors caused by job segments not completed or done previously? Should learning curves be considered in reporting performance?

HOW TO ARRIVE AT DEPENDABLE ANSWERS

Any of the points noted above, and many others like them, could serve as topics for debate. It has often been stated that the control phase of industrial engineering is an art, not a science, which implies that there could be various answers to the questions noted, depending on the debater's point of view. I would disagree. There is as much need for the scientific approach in labor productivity control as in medicine, for example. It's just that in neither of these fields have we yet acquired full knowledge about all of the subject matter involved.

How, then, can we know what course of action has the best chance for success where a control system is to be installed or modified? This book does not pretend to answer questions along this line infallibly. It does attempt to present evidence which will suggest logical points to consider. Some of the book's contents will take issue with what has been done or proposed in the past.

Charting a Path in the Face of Conflicting Opinions

It will be recognized that recommended concepts can at times be slanted by those seeking to make a point to their advantage. Recommendations can be incomplete, poorly tested, or not defined as to the scope of application. In chapter 14 of this book, for example, a recent application is described which has not yet been widely tested, but that point is clearly noted. The particular application is included because it seems to point the way toward an unusual combination of simplicity, low cost, and effectiveness of control. (When covering that section, consider how you might find ways to improve still further on the procedures noted.)

Long-term experiences and results, whether positive or negative, can be more informative than short-term results. That should be a key point in evaluating what the following chapters cover. The information that they contain was culled primarily from my observations and experiences in well over 100 plants within a dozen major corporations. Both manufacturing and processing functions were involved. In all cases, there was intimate contact with industrial engineers, staff managers, direct and nondirect supervisors, manufacturing managers, and top general management. The functions involved included consulting, management audits, observations to learn, project development, training, and management. Such contacts have afforded an unusual opportunity to see and understand what has worked well or poorly over an extended period.

Some of the companies and plants are coded and described in the appendix according to size, type of activity, and other points that may lend credibility to the control aspects attributed to them. They are not named, as that would seem inappropriate. If there are sections in chapters to follow where the listings of plant and/or company code references seem overlong, please remember this is done to emphasize that the information given is not just my opinion or material from reference sources, but what has been observed and analyzed in detail.

The Lack of Well-founded Plant Industrial Engineering History

Within one company listed in the appendix, the number of technicians and engineers employed by industrial engineering departments ranged between roughly 850 and 400 for over sixty years of the company's existence. The control plans that had been applied included four kinds of wage incentives and several versions of advanced measured day work. Data collection techniques covered the whole gamut of what was available. Computer applications proliferated in production and material control areas and extended to progressive IE applications. Plant profit situations were acceptable at times and not at other times, at least in part due to the effectiveness or failure of labor control applications. The historical background involved here, if carefully analyzed and described, would have been "dream material" for dozens of theses by graduate-level IE or business administration specialists.

Yet there were essentially no records of labor productivity control or management history except in the minds of those who came into and at some point left the company. There are never adequate clerical facilities in cost-conscious organizations to maintain data considered to be of historical value only. Perhaps a few dozen articles were published over the years by staff or management personnel in the company referred to, describing interesting applications that had worked well at the time. But rarely is there ever published a technical article or book analyzing the reasons why an essential component of a control system has not functioned as intended.

I hope this book will help to correct such imbalance. Of course, the book will primarily strive to cover what can be depended on in the future, as indicated by my observations and by selected reference sources.

AN ILLUSTRATION OF HOW TO USE THIS BOOK

Let us now "jump the gun" a few chapters in order to illustrate what the material that follows is intended to accomplish. While the reasoning involved here won't be covered until later, we will describe a situation—call it a "fable"—that may help show the need for sorting facts from folklore in areas of industrial engineering and management.

Assume that company X has for many years applied a specific group incentive system at plants A and B, which are in the same city. Let's say that about 20 percent of the standard data used at each plant is common to both, since similar operations are involved, and has been properly maintained. Assume that time standards and related data were previously established through applications of direct time study on LC/LR work and the Methods-Time Measurement system of predetermined times on SC/R operations. Assume also that much of the specialized standard time data in plant A was neglected over the years as methods were gradually changed. This has led to a condition in which groups at plant A are now earning an average bonus of 50 percent (roughly 25 percent above the expected level), although work sampling has recently shown that most groups are limiting their actual work effort to about the level of "normal" in order to avoid getting management upset about the loose standards.

The IE manager, a new man at plant A, has reviewed the sampling study with his manufacturing manager. Management now insists on prompt improvement, suggesting a change to measured day work and the use of MTM as the primary basis for new standard data. The IE manager gives this some thought. Having either read this book or learned the necessary background in other ways, he advises his superior as follows:

"MTM would have to be adjusted to a considerably higher task level as a basis for measured day work time standards. And our performance rating guidelines for direct time study would require changing also. This would call for new standard data at plant A on the 20 percent of data already in sound shape. How would these revisions be explained to labor representatives from the two plants, without major arguments? Could we be sure that plant A employees would respond to new task levels without the wage inducements they have become familiar with?

"The realities of sound labor relations policies mean that you don't cut back the long-term level of earnings without serious problems, particularly if those involved are asked to produce more (roughly 125:100). And you realize that negotiated wage rates for measured day work would have to exceed the base rates in our present incentive system.

"I suggest specialized training for our IE personnel; then use a computer-aided version of MTM to establish new time standards in advance on all new work, while gradually developing reliable standard data. In a couple of years we should have the problem licked without having to alter the incentive plan that still works OK at plant B."

After mulling over these points a few days, and after glancing through chapters of this book which he was asked to read, the boss replied: "You will have too many problems doing that! Neither the operators nor their group leaders will respond like you hope they will. And with our group reporting system you won't know how individual operators are performing in relation to standards. You won't be able to identify problem areas."

In due time, the IE manager updated his proposal somewhat: "Then let's consider changing from our old group system to individual incentives in plant A, shifting some of our dependable group leaders to direct supervisors. We could use a form of on-the-job planning and data collection that gives the supervisors a chance to spot weak points as they occur. We would gradually work toward the wage and output levels of plant B." This fable could be continued, of course, but it has gone far enough to provide illustrations of generally accepted folklore which would have brought the IE manager, his crew, and the entire management team a lot of trouble if the facts had not been recognized.

That is what this book is all about!

2
Concepts and Organization for Labor Productivity Control

Perhaps this chapter dealing with organization should have come at the end of the book, following evidence that shows the need for specific control functions. On the other hand, it would be more understandable to discuss the control details after outlining a general picture of how the personnel involved might properly fit into an industrial organization.

THE CONCEPTS INVOLVED

To do this, we will attempt to list the general principles involved in a labor control program which will accomplish what management has a right to expect. If possible, the control principles we seek should be applicable not only to direct manufacturing, where past emphasis has more often been placed, but to nondirect activities as well. After defining such principles, it should then be possible to generalize about the organization involved.

We will first look at two previous attempts to list broad management principles. The first was taken from a book published long ago by one of the pioneers in this area. The second list to be screened is one issued in recent years by a large corporation, as an aid in management and industrial engineering training. We will attempt to compare the two, analyze their differences, and propose a revised list that will shed light on organizational requirements.

An Older List of Principles

One of those who long ago recognized the need for defining the fundamentals of what we are now referring to as labor productivity

FIGURE 2.
Two Sets of Principles for Labor Productivity Control.

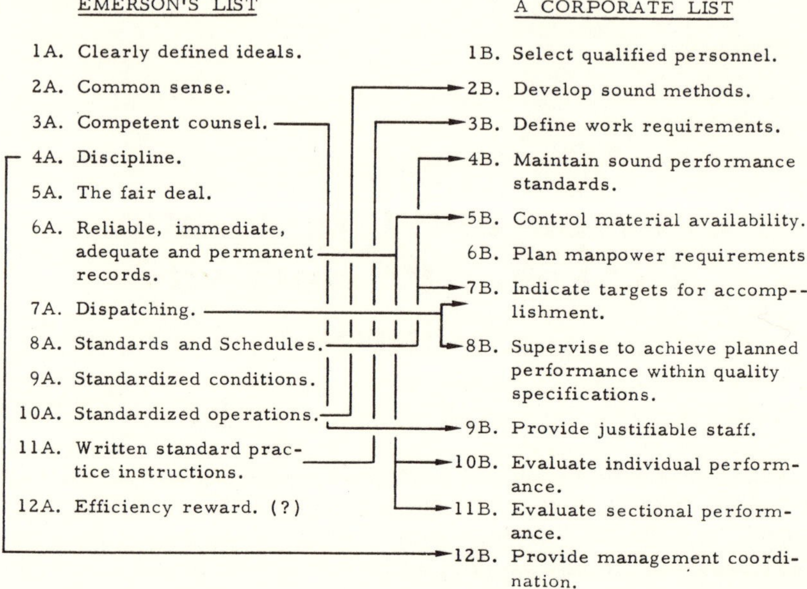
EMERSON'S LIST
A CORPORATE LIST
1A. Clearly defined ideals.
2A. Common sense.
3A. Competent counsel.
4A. Discipline.
5A. The fair deal.
6A. Reliable, immediate, adequate and permanent records.
7A. Dispatching.
8A. Standards and Schedules.
9A. Standardized conditions.
10A. Standardized operations.
11A. Written standard practice instructions.
12A. Efficiency reward. (?)
1B. Select qualified personnel.
2B. Develop sound methods.
3B. Define work requirements.
4B. Maintain sound performance standards.
5B. Control material availability.
6B. Plan manpower requirements.
7B. Indicate targets for accomp--lishment.
8B. Supervise to achieve planned performance within quality specifications.
9B. Provide justifiable staff.
10B. Evaluate individual performance.
11B. Evaluate sectional performance.
12B. Provide management coordination.

control was Harrington Emerson. By 1899, this ex-professor had gained some reputation in management circles, enough to establish a consulting firm bearing his name. Emerson did not elicit the attention which came to Frederick Taylor during about the same period. There can still be found in major libraries, however, a book authored by Emerson in 1911 titled *The Twelve Principles of Efficiency*.

The word "efficiency" is more precise in its meaning than "productivity" but was overworked in previous years and seems to be avoided today as much as possible. Several decades of management improprieties, some of which will be referred to in a following chapter concerning wage incentive systems, made the phrase "efficiency experts" become almost an epithet. Perhaps Emerson's book, which was widely read in its day, helped to crystallize this phrase in the public's mind. But a careful look at the contents of this book would show that the twelve principles can help avoid mismanagement. They are on the left side of Figure 2.

A Newer Set of Management Principles

A more recent compilation of productivity control fundamentals, having the same objective as those proposed by Emerson, was put together in recent years within appendix-listed company K. They are shown on the right side of Figure 2. By coincidence, the number listed was the same as proposed by Emerson.

Similarities

The lines that are drawn connect what appear to be similar listings, even though the wording is different. The reader will note that there are four sets involving somewhat similar meanings: 3A/9B, 4A/12B,10A/2B, and 11A/3B. Looking at item 8A in Figure 2—standards and schedules—we see that it is connected to 4B, which takes care of "standards." And it is also connected to 7B, which says about the same thing as "schedules."

Item 7A lists the term "dispatching," which can be taken to mean knowing when one job finishes and having the next job ready to assign at or before that point. It has not been uncommon in the past to utilize a dispatcher who does just that. In chapters 13 and 14, emphasis will be placed on direct supervisors handling this function, not just to eliminate the need for a dispatcher but because such contacts between supervisor and operator are a fundamental step in the management process. For now, please accept the fact that items 7B and 8B would accomplish the same objective as 7A.

Referring next to item 6A, we see emphasis on the need for records but no indication as to what they should include. In Emerson's book, however, he would seem to agree with the three items to which 6A is connected (5B, 10B, 11B), all of which involve record-keeping. (Luckily, we have computers nowadays so that the subject of records is not so distasteful as it once was.)

Differences

While there is considerable agreement between the older and more recent attempts to define basic concepts, differences between them are worth noting:

1A. Clearly Defined Ideals. Emerson had a valid point here. The corporate list in Figure 2 assumed that sociological points regarding the objectives of management were already well understood. But this principle is one which should be part of any basic list.

2A. Common Sense. None could argue against this point, and in later chapters we will refer to a number of instances where common sense seems to have been disregarded in distinguishing facts from folklore. To me, however, listing this as a management principle would seem redundant, since it would always be implied.

5A. The Fair Deal. Emerson's list was published at a period of time when management/labor relationships were often marked by what would today be considered unfair wage plans, unfair work rules, and unfair management attitudes. The growth of labor unions, bringing with them what might at times be considered unfair labor demands, has been intensified by such practices. A more recent reduction in the percentage of U.S. workers represented by labor unions tends to indicate that unfair management practices are perceived as being less prevalent. Although modern management hardly needs a reminder that fairness is essential in labor relations, this principle should be part of the overall list.

9A. Standardized Conditions. The intended reference here is to equipment maintenance, adequate lighting, ventilation and heating, safe operating practices, etc. The corporate list omitted specific reference to working conditions, possibly because attention to such details had long been standard practice within the organization. But the principle should not be omitted.

12A. Efficiency Reward. This means some kind of wage incentive plan, which was considered fundamental in Emerson's time if efficiency was to be expected. Chapter 12 will point out significant long-term disadvantages in wage incentive applications, and chapter 13 will discuss a practical alternative. While there should always be efficiency rewards in terms of management recognition, experience indicates that a wage incentive plan is not a fundamental requirement. Such plans should not be ruled out, since many companies have shown that incentives can be successful under carefully controlled conditions. A question mark has been added after this point about which Emerson felt so strongly. The reader is urged to draw conclusions after covering chapters that follow.

1B. Select Qualified Personnel. This prerequisite to productivity clearly justifies being listed as fundamental.

6B. Plan Manpower Requirements. Unless there is an approximate match between the actual man-hours of operators on hand and the standard man-hours of work available to be done, one of two results can be expected: either performance levels will be low when the manpower count is high; or there must be a choice between overtime or delayed production when too few operators are available. Possibly Emerson meant to cover this with his broad reference to "records." In any case, advance manpower planning is a key item.

A Combined List of Basic Principles

A manager or staff person who gives careful thought to the fundamentals noted thus far might vary the wording somewhat. But the revised list shown in Figure 3 will serve as a reasonable outline of principles for labor productivity control. The organization should make provision for functions that can implement these objectives.

FIGURE 3.
Resultant Principles for Labor Productivity Control.

1. Develop CLEAR AND FAIR IDEALS.
2. Select QUALIFIED PERSONNEL.
3. Provide JUSTIFIABLE STAFF.
4. STANDARDIZE WORKING CONDITIONS.
5. DEFINE WORK REQUIREMENTS.
6. CONTROL MATERIAL availability.
7. Maintain SOUND PERFORMANCE STANDARDS.
8. PLAN MANPOWER REQUIREMENTS.
9. CONSIDER whether WAGE INCENTIVES are justified.
10. Develop METHODS IMPROVEMENTS.
11. INDICATE TARGETS for accomplishment.
12. SUPERVISE TO ACHIEVE PRODUCTIVITY AND QUALITY OBJECTIVES.
13. EVALUATE INDIVIDUAL PERFORMANCE.
14. EVALUATE SECTIONAL PERFORMANCE.
15. Provide MANAGEMENT COORDINATION.

A Word to Remember

With nondirect personnel outnumbering direct operators in some manufacturing organizations today, the word "justifiable" in the third listing of Figure 3 is particularly significant. There are two aspects to consider: (1) Chapter 15 will discuss how the control principles can apply on an overall basis, not just within the line organization; and (2) some functions that might normally be performed by staff or service groups can, under certain conditions, be handled effectively and at lower cost by operators or supervisors. A few examples are noted below to illustrate the latter point:

- It is fairly common for properly trained operators in some plants to be assigned lubrication or preventive maintenance work on their equipment.
- One plant listed in the appendix (number 104) has a long history of quality control by operators and their supervisors, without separate inspectors being involved.
- Chapter 15 will discuss how maintenance estimates made by maintenance supervisors can serve as a basis for control through planning and scheduling.

EMPHASIS ON PRODUCTIVITY CONTROL IN MULTIPLANT COMPANIES

There are many variables which combine to affect corporate organizational formats and functions. Three examples are noted below to illustrate how different companies have approached the need for guiding those at plant levels toward effective labor control applications.

When Plant Functions are Dissimilar

Although plant management responsibilities within one large company noted in the appendix are decentralized, there have been included within the corporate organization relatively small groups which correspond to the principle staff functions likely to be required in manufacturing plants for cost control: industrial engineering, production and material control, quality control, and manufacturing engineering. Responsibilities of the corporate staff involve development, training, and management consulting. Formerly guided by a manufacturing vice president, these functions were more recently given impetus through the director of a corporate productivity and quality center.

When Plant Functions are Similar

Consider company E, for example, which has under its corporate control a number of processing plants. About half of the work force in each plant consists of operating personnel and the other half largely of maintenance employees. The number of operators required and how they perform work is largely controlled by the processes themselves, but the effectiveness of large maintenance groups is not easy to control or evaluate. There can be wide variations in maintenance labor productivity. From a corporate standpoint, this company emphasized three objectives related to maintenance control: (1) Keeping abreast of applicable control systems and techniques; (2) training those within plants to understand and apply them; and (3) following up at intervals to know that sound practices are in effect. The focus for implementation of these objectives was through a corporate manager, reporting at a level enabling him to deal with plant managers on an equal basis. There was within this manager's direct control a small staff of specialists, and all within the group made frequent plant contacts.

Consider next company M, within which there were various manufacturing plants performing operations closely related although on different products. The corporate organization included an industrial engineering staff having objectives much like the three noted above. In addition, this group developed and maintained standard data elements which would be applicable through computer systems to a large percentage of the operations at each plant. This was made available to all locations. After demonstrating what could be accomplished through proven results, corporate staff personnel were in some cases funded by plant budgets to handle preliminary data applications.

LABOR CONTROL PROBLEMS DUE TO EMPHASIS ON SHORT-TERM PROFITS

Division and plant managers within decentralized organizations must operate within certain corporate guidelines, but to a large extent they determine their own line and staff functions. Such managers are quite likely to "live or die" according to what is reflected by their yearly profit-and-loss statements. If asked, any would agree fully with the concept of managing their business for long-term gain through careful planning. Some are able to do this because their short-term profit picture is not restrictive.

Others are forced to look for quick ways to reduce costs from time to time by curtailing budgets where possible. The easy way to do this may seem to be an across-the-board reduction in nondirect personnel. This is too frequently the route taken. Three results are almost inevitable when such approaches are allowed to recur:

1. Nondirect managers grow adept at overstaffing during normal years so as not to be hurt badly during the lean years.
2. Productivity control projects within nondirect groups, including control functions of which the direct supervisors are a part, become ineffective from lack of cooperation.
3. Reduced manpower within plant industrial engineering groups tends to mean reduced emphasis on standards maintenance and methods improvement analysis. Neglect in either of these areas guarantees problems in future years.

These three negative effects provide corporate management with reasons to consider how such deterioration can be avoided. There will be further discussion along this line in chapter 15.

EFFECTS ON PRODUCTIVITY CONTROL OF LABOR UNIONS IN MULTIPLANT COMPANIES

At the outset of the few paragraphs under this heading, I would point out that observations over the years have shown many examples where profit pressures on plant managers would have tended to bring about unfair labor relations actions had there not been either an existing labor union to deal with or the threat of one coming into the picture. With that having been said, comments are in order concerning ways in which plants have dealt with, or failed to deal with, the pressures exerted by labor representatives in situations affecting productivity control.

Where Wage Incentives Existed

Company K was forced to deal with three major unions in plants applying wage incentive systems. Chapter 12 will explore the problems involved. There were more problems in group wage incentive systems than where individual incentives were applied, for reasons that will be discussed. To summarize what appeared to be the primary difficulty, periodic (often frequent) changes in manufacturing management caused occasional unsound concessions to union demands. It became almost impossible to correct such changes later.

With one or two exceptions, the two dozen plants in company K where wage incentive control plans existed previously are no longer part of that company. They have either been sold, or the work involved has been transferred elsewhere. This is not to say that deterioration in the incentive framework was the sole cause of such actions, but it was the most obvious cause for high labor costs that made such change necessary. Developments in the steel industry show a similar pattern of wage incentive deterioration, high labor costs, and plant closings.

This does not always have to be the case. In plant 104, which was one of various facilities within a large company, detailed discussions with union representatives helped bring about complete overhaul of a collapsed incentive plan. The result was new vigor in the productivity picture. It is perhaps fair to say, however, that a company having numerous union-related plant incentive systems would have more difficulty reviving any one of them than would be the case where problems are somewhat isolated.

Where Measured Day Work Existed

Practically all of the manufacturing plants in company K now utilize the measured day work system as a basis for labor productivity control. Most have remained union-free despite the usual plant elections from time to time. Corporate management, remembering past experiences, strongly encourages labor relations practices that will act to keep this situation from changing. The result is that some plant managers are hesitant to apply some of the control principles of Figure 3. For example, they might choose not to report the performance levels of individual operators, preferring instead to evaluate only sectional performance ratios. Without the aid of systematic data relating to operators' performance in relation to standards, direct supervisors lack a tool they need to know where problems exist. Sectional performance ratios within such plants tend to reflect this weakness in productivity control.

There are significant exceptions to this practice within that company and at other locations I have observed. For example, the plant listed as number 69 has a thirty-year record of applying measured daywork with management and staff finesse. Time standards have been demonstrably sound, and sectional performance ratios have averaged 100 percent or above. Supervisors know each operator's performance level. Industrial relations policies at this plant are topnotch, and repeated employee elections there have ruled out labor union affiliations. A large number of similar examples could be cited. The conclusion to be drawn is that the possibility of labor union involvement, or the need for discussing with existing labor representatives the steps to be taken, should not hinder sound applications of the control principles in Figure 3.

PLANT ORGANIZATIONAL CONCEPTS FOR LABOR PRODUCTIVITY CONTROL

The Manager's Key Role

If there is to be any effective form of productivity control, some staff costs will be involved. For the manufacturing manager or equivalent officer to be supportive of such costs, he or she must be a believer in the results that can be achieved. If the manager's background is in industrial engineering, as may frequently be the case, the initial support should come easily. If the past background does not include exposure to control systems in the past, a certain amount of salesmanship may be required. In all cases, once the control system is underway, frequently updating the manager about progress that has been made is essential. From past experience, it will be realized that mistakes can be made in either the design or implementation of control systems, and regular, convincing information should be provided about what is planned and what has been accomplished.

In turn, the manager would be expected to give more than occasional lip service in making approved control plans function effectively. There will be too many stumbling blocks if this is not the case. And it is the responsibility of the staff manager involved in productivity control to function as sales representative along the management chain, on a continuing basis.

Direct Supervisors

It has been observed that direct supervisors must take an active part in the implementation of a control plan, whether it be incentive or measured daywork. Before a system of any kind is started, the responsibilities of supervisors in this regard should be detailed carefully and approved at a suitable management level. Chapters that follow will suggest how staff personnel can properly interact with direct supervisors in carrying out specific functions. But it is the supervisor who should make work assignments, be aware of progress in relation to standards, and continually search for detracting conditions in order to eliminate them as soon as possible.

This calls for a span of control which is not so broad as to leave little time for necessary duties. The number of operators which one individual can properly supervise directly will of course vary according to conditions such as the following: type of work, length of operational sequences, floor area to be covered, staff assistance provided for scheduling and material control, how performance records are transmitted, frequency and type of detracting conditions that occur, or the details made available concerning work requirements. For manufacturing, one large company has specified an operator/supervisor ratio ranging from about fifteen to forty. The lower number would apply to some LC/LR operations, and the higher to some SC/R work on paced lines.

In large maintenance organizations, direct supervision can at times be a joint function, shared by craft and area supervisors. This calls for clear-cut agreement as to the functions of each. Chapter 15 will provide more background along this line. The recommendations in companies E, F, and M were for twelve to fifteen men per craft supervisor.

The Question of Group Leaders or Assistant Supervisors

During a wartime period in the plant listed as number 107—a large aircraft manufacturing facility—group leaders helped fill the vacuum caused by a lack of experienced direct supervisors. There were few problems of worker motivation and less need for refining some of the control principles listed in Figure 3. Here, group leaders served a useful purpose.

Within group incentive control plans that previously existed in the plants of company K, group leaders were an essential part of the system. As chapter 12 will discuss, however, they tended to act in some ways as a barrier between workers and management. Having been selected because they were skilled employees with some organizational ability, they helped guide intricate manufacturing processes to create quality products. As members of existing labor unions, however, they helped resist the maintenance of time standards. Gradual methods changes which are not recognized and accounted for by standard data revisions will in time destroy the effectiveness of any control plan.

When that company changed from incentives to a more dependable basis for control, the need for management effectiveness was emphasized, and use of group leaders was discontinued. The long-standing term of "foreman" became that of direct supervisor. There were no assistant supervisors, as this was thought to establish another link in the chain of command that tended to erect barriers between operators and their management representatives. In appendix-listed plant 49—a large facility—the division of operations within areas was such that assistant supervisors were first considered justified. In due time, after an ineffective plant start-up period, there was a change to eliminate this extra step in management's communication with operators. The change helped bring about needed improvement.

The Supervisor as Manager

Policies set by management need to be communicated to operators without distortion. Similarly, it should be possible for operators to discuss their problems with a management representative directly, without arbitrary barriers. When productivity problems exist, the steps required to find what they are and correct them should be taken with close adherence to procedures that have been established. Whatever the system of control, there is little assurance that these conditions will apply unless a management representative is in direct contact with operators, and with a minimum of management steps thereafter. Chapters that follow will enlarge on the responsibilities of direct supervisors within specific control plans.

STAFF FUNCTIONS FOR LABOR PRODUCTIVITY CONTROL

We have been referring to industrial engineering as the staff function charged with labor control responsibilities. The department involved may be assigned other staff duties including manufacturing engineering, centralized production scheduling, or material control—functions which this book has listed but will not attempt to cover. How staff functions of productivity control are grouped together and named is quite varied within industry and not inherently significant. In discussing functions considered necessary for labor productivity control, we will avoid trying to say just how they should be fitted into a specific department.

But some name must be used in referring to the staff group with which the subject matter of this book is primarily involved. With that in mind, let us examine the phrase "industrial engineering." That term was applied years ago within industry, before universities began to use it in defining a broad course of study. This broader use, now widespread, has preempted application of the name within industry to define clearly a specific segment of industrial engineering activity.

The corporate staff manager in one large company succeeded in having published a paper titled "Abolish Industrial Engineering!" This was a tongue-in-cheek way of saying that the term no longer has a clear meaning when used within industry. But this paper did not suggest a better name and apparently had no effect, even within the manager's own organization. The name "industrial engineering" has in many companies survived to designate the staff section with responsibilities related to labor productivity control. And "industrial engineer" is a commonly applied job title for the more senior duties involved.

Within a company or plant, those concerned quickly become aware of what a staff group is supposed to do, regardless of what it is called. But for this book to be understood clearly, it would not be appropriate to continue using this broad term that has so many different interpretations. In due time, someone will derive an appropriate name for the phase of industrial engineering with which we are concerned, just as the coined word "ergonomics" jumped to the forefront as a better name for what had previously been covered by the broader field of "methods engineering." Since we need a name now, however, let us list a few possibilities along with brief comments about them:

M&S Group, for Methods and Standards. This term has been used frequently but is too restrictive for our purpose. It implies deriving standards, based on sound methods, but leaves out more important functions, such as doing something constructive with the standards rather than just listing them (as is too frequently the case).

Production Methods and Measurements. This also is a term that has been used, but it has the same disadvantage as noted above.

Management Consulting Group. A generalized description of how the group should function, but this would seem too highbrow for most applications.

MAP Group, for Methods and Productivity. This is easy to say, and the letters spell an applicable word, but it sounds a bit frivolous.

MPA Group, Methods and Productivity Awareness. The last two letters and the words they signify imply deriving time standards but emphasize the more significant aspect of providing management at all levels with an awareness of what has happened and how to improve. We will go with MPA for the balance of this book. The meaning that we want to associate with this term is noted below.

MPA Definition

Staff personnel responsible for methods and productivity awareness within an industrial organization. The various functions involved will be dealt with in chapters to follow. May be a separate department in large plants; more likely to be associated with certain other staff personnel within a specific staff department. The name of the larger department could be Industrial Engineering, or it could be any other suitable term.

MPA ORGANIZATION

Line of Reporting within the Organization

Not everyone is likely to be on the MPA engineer's side during presentations regarding proposed changes in methods, duties, budgets, nondirect manpower assignments, time standards, etc. Sound evidence is required to get most proposals accepted, and a certain amount of judicious sales effort is often necessary. Several in this function have been heard to suggest that their department head should report at a higher level within the organization so that the productivity control process would become more effective. Some changes of the kind noted above may be possible only after the plant manager's approval; so a point could be raised as to where the MPA manager should report for overall effectiveness.

Except in smaller organizations where the plant manager may "run the whole show," there is usually in the picture the equivalent of a manufacturing or operations manager. This is where most of the manufacturing (or operations) staff groups normally report, including the MPA manager. It is the logical organizational pattern, since most day-to-day labor productivity control functions relate to activities that are within the manufacturing manager's area of responsibility. But what about engineering, drafting, accounting, order service, and other nondirect functions unlikely to report through the manufacturing manager? Are they to be exempt from the control analysis techniques which later chapters will show are practical when applied to such work?

There are several approaches to consider here without shifting the plant MPA function away from where it can work smoothly. One approach is a temporary transfer of personnel when work sampling or other studies are called for within nondirect departments such as those listed. The transfer could properly be initiated by the plant manager, and the MPA analyst should channel his recommendations through that manager, after thoroughly reviewing them with department heads involved. Another approach would be to call for assistance from the corporate staff, assuming there might be consulting services of that nature available. A third possibility is to call in outside consultants, although this would tend to be demeaning if there are within the MPA department senior personnel capable of making the necessary analyses.

As an example, appendix-listed plant 57 shifted one MPA analyst for several months to make studies within a large engineering and drafting department. Through specialized work sampling, a form of standard data was developed which was applied to evaluate billing charges by outside design firms that were utilized at times to supplement what could be handled by the plant department. The analysis also led to an improved planning/scheduling method for the in-plant group.

Separation of Control Functions from Various Other Staff Functions

There are tendencies to attempt some combination of MPA duties with those of certain other staff functions, particularly if both are in the same staff department. I urge caution here. Being qualified to handle control functions tends to require a somewhat different temperament and background from proficiency in, say, manufacturing or production engineering. Analysis duties of the MPA engineer often require full-time attention for an extended period, and interruptions would be a handicap. There are other reasons also, as might be indicated by the following example.

One company typically used MPA engineers for labor control and manufacturing engineers for tool and equipment development. Inevitably there is some methods analysis overlap in a separation of duties this way. Since many of those within what we have now termed the MPA group could normally handle ME duties if so assigned, it is understandable that some plants within the company combined the two functions. In the half-dozen plants where this was tried for a period of time, labor productivity gradually dropped because the maintenance of standards and follow-up of detracting conditions slacked off. Once the problem had been identified, this explanation came from some of those involved: ME work always involved a certain amount of "firefighting"—helping supervisors find how to correct equipment or tooling problems. While direct supervisors should take time to do most of this themselves, they tend to pass the problems along to any staff person who is willing and able to help. So the MPA/ME combination became loaded with ME functions, and MPA duties were neglected.

A less obvious but perhaps more significant reason for neglect in the above example lies in the fact that the result of ME duties are more immediately apparent, whereas the results of MPA activities may not be visible until the overall picture shows improvement. At any rate, a change back to the usual two-way approach brought improved operator performance without requiring added staff personnel. Yes, there is always some methods analysis overlap in doing this, but the importance of generating methods improvement suggests there is no real disadvantage here.

MPA Job Classifications

Abilities that should be represented within a well-rounded MPA engineering group are:

- Experience in plant methods technology.
- Training in techniques for time standards development.
- Ability to work with and influence others.

- Ability to analyze complex problems or conditions.
- Experience in standard time data development.
- Managerial potential.

- Training in business administration fundamentals.
- Knowledge of computer programming and applications.
- Experience in developing nondirect control techniques.
- Training in advanced technical IE areas.

Abilities at the top of this list can be found in selected persons with several years of plant experience and general education, assuming that training in specialized techniques has been made available to them. To develop abilities toward the end of this short list usually requires university-trained personnel. The several abilities listed between the two extremes could be achieved in time by either group.

It is clear that a mix of job classifications can properly be included within a department having responsibilities for labor productivity control. There can be a certain amount of specialization, particularly in large MPA sections. However, industrial engineering graduates or their equivalent must realize that it is only through being exposed adequately to methods and standards analysis that they can develop the background required for overall excellence.

Avoiding Problems from Rapid MPA Turnover

MPA experience is inherently the type of background needed by managers at all levels. It is not unusual to see so rapid a turnover of personnel within the MPA group that significant control functions are neglected while new personnel are being trained. There are perhaps three ways to minimize such problems, all of which are recommended:

1. Apply sound job evaluation thinking to establish MPA wage levels. The experience, educational background, and training needed to perform such work effectively should not be overlooked.

2. Provide paths for advancement within more difficult MPA fields, so as not to lose those who want to pursue a career in that area. Some of the functions to plan for are computer technology related to MPA or industrial engineering needs; analysis of nondirect functions to develop practical methods and control programs; the capability to handle budget analysis in a sound manner; operations research assignments; or consulting duties in response to temporary assignments by management.
3. Rule out shifting from MPA to other plant functions until after a reasonable time interval. A two-year period prior to any transfer has been one approach observed.

How MPA Engineers are Assigned

There are too many organizational variables to permit being specific here, but typical approaches for MPA assignment are as follows: (1) according to departments serviced; (2) according to the functions performed, with specific scheduling; or (3) a combination of departments serviced and functions performed. If the first or third approaches are followed, it would be good practice to vary departmental assignments at appropriate intervals, to provide a more rounded experience. If the second approach is taken, there should be a gradual upgrading of functions assigned to an individual, depending on his/her qualifications. In all cases, provision is required for MPA training in techniques such as those which following chapters will describe. Large MPA groups can afford to utilize a training specialist. In some other cases, the MPA manager should be expected to handle training needs.

One function that must not be slighted is the periodic auditing of time standards and standard data. The type of work involved, along with the general history of methods changes, will serve to indicate the needed frequency of standards audits. It is important that management be convinced of the need for budgeting to provide for such work. An aid in doing so is to report a running account of estimated yearly savings from all changes in time standards, both up and down. Figure 4 illustrates how this might be done.

Interaction between MPA Engineers and Direct Supervisors

The MPA engineer is expected to work closely with direct supervisors in identifying and correcting problems, yet the MPA duties also include evaluation of labor productivity within supervisors' sections. The periodic sectional performance reports go not only to supervisors themselves but up the line as well. The same principle applies, however, to profit-and-loss statements that are prepared for the plant general manager.

FIGURE 4.
Cost Improvement Summary.

Date	No. of Revisions	Total Changes in Standard Hours					
		This Week		Year to Date			
		UP	DOWN	UP	DOWN	TOTAL	GOAL

They go to his or her corporate superiors, or perhaps to the board of directors in a one-plant organization. Direct supervisors should use MPA assistance to find out where and how to improve.

Some of the MPA's basic data is partially subjective, such as performance rating in direct time study, or how predetermined times are applied for methods/time analysis. It should be the prerogative of supervisors to approve complete time studies whenever practical, or to question standards established in other ways when there seems to be cause to do so. If the MPA engineer takes enough time to answer such questions fully when they arise, there will be fewer of them as time goes on.

Within any control plan, the range of duties and responsibilities of both direct supervisors and MPA engineers should be outlined clearly. While MPA functions provide service in spotting problems and helping to correct them, the initial follow-up of detracting conditions is likely to be the responsibility of supervisors. There can be some give-and-take in this area, but MPA engineers are not errand boys for either direct or general supervisors. If the overall cost of staff services is to be minimized, this point should be made clear to all concerned.

Cost Improvement Records

In many plants within one large company, MPA engineers are expected to initiate methods improvements that produce at least three times their yearly salary. Cost reduction goals are also indicated for other groups. Most of the plants in the company maintain careful records of first-year savings from all methods revisions. In some cases, there is an agreed-to splitting of specific project savings between those primarily involved in the development and implementation stages. For example, the MPA engineer and the supervisor who worked together on a project might split a $20,000 cost improvement when credits are assigned.

Carrying this approach too far can have a negative effect on cooperation between those who must work closely together. It would seem preferable to keep two sets of books in such cases, one record for each direct or nondirect department and separate records for the MPA group or other staff groups. There would be an overlap, but reasonable objectives could still be assigned.

3
Work Measurement Considerations

Work measurement is a first step in labor productivity control. The process generally involves establishing time standards for required operations. There are many different potential uses for standards. Some of these uses can be served with very approximate data, which tends to obscure the need for more precise work measurement in effective productivity control.

This chapter will first discuss the uses of time standards and the relative precision required for each. Next, we will outline various ways in which standards can be developed, indicating the precision levels expected from proper applications of several techniques. Finally, we will attempt to identify some of the folklore associated with performance rating, the concept of "normal," and general allowances that are typically applied.

The point should first be made that any time standard must be viewed in relation to the type of control plan that exists. For example, an operational time value of .20 hours per part within a specific incentive system might have the same validity as .16 hours per part for the same operation in some other type of incentive plan or in a measured daywork control application. We will discuss this seeming anomaly in more detail later. It should also be noted that the precision level of standards for manually controlled operations can be evaluated only on a subjective basis. There are systematic ways to approach such evaluations, however, and it is possible to distinguish between standards applications which are consistent or inconsistent in the level of performance represented, or which do not correspond with the target level for standards in a specific control plan.

STANDARDS APPLICATIONS REQUIRING WORK MEASUREMENT PRECISION

The usual objective of MPA analysts, when precise standards are necessary, is to use sufficient care in both the work measurement process and in later maintenance of the data to stay within plus-or-minus 5 percent of the correct time values. Considering the subjective nature of the processes involved, and considering the possibility of methods changes, this level of precision is often an elusive goal. But it is a worthwhile objective for conditions such as those that follow.

Assembly Line Balancing

With the net output of a group of operators dependent on each individual's being able to work at the pace established for the entire group, there must be a consistent performance level derived for the work increments involved. And since a primary objective of paced operations is to assure efficient performance, the incremental standards must not only be consistent but must also define the targeted performance level.

Evaluating the Performance of Individuals in Relation to Standards

Such an evaluation might be on a weekly, daily, or short-interval basis. A later chapter will discuss what can be gained through scheduling job completion targets for individuals and following a practical routine to identify reasons for variance so that problems can be corrected. In such cases, the basis for effective control will disappear if operational time standards are not consistent and close to the defined target level. A good supervisor will of course stress the importance of achieving targeted performance levels on an average basis, since job conditions or individual standards will inevitably vary from true consistency. But both the operators and their supervisors must be convinced that time standards are generally dependable if there is to be a continuing basis for control with sound labor relations.

Basis for Pay in Wage Incentive Systems

There can properly be a difference in the task level represented by incentive time values, depending on the specific system involved. But there is certainly a need for consistency in setting standards at the given task level. The application of any wage incentive plan implies an expectation that operators will be motivated by the fairness of time standards to work at a methods/pace level that will produce bonus earnings.

If standards are perceived to be on the high side of the specified task level, operators will not respond as anticipated, and the incentive system will not be effective. If there is marked inconsistency in time values, the tight values will be spotted and complained about through supervisors, groups leaders, or union representatives. The result can be an average loosening of standards that acts either to increase earnings unduly or to lower productivity through controlled work effort.

Evaluating the Performance Level of a Supervisor's Section

If this is the primary basis for labor productivity control, without systematically determining the true reasons for failure to meet the work targets, there will not likely be adequate control even with sound time values. However, this is and should be a much-used supplementary aid in productivity control. Unless standards are consistently set at a sound level, there will properly be complaints by supervisors about the values that are too tight. As noted above, when individual operators are the source of such complaints, a gradual loosening of the values may occur and lead to a lack of confidence in the system by all concerned.

STANDARDS APPLICATIONS WHERE PRECISION IS NOT CRITICAL

The heading above is not intended to imply that time standards used for applications listed below can be less precise without some penalty being involved. But it seems fairly clear that a number of the ways in which standards are often utilized can continue, despite inconsistent or inaccurate time values, without management's recognizing that there is a problem.

That fact, in itself, is one of the problems. Some members of the management team within a plant may be more familiar with applications noted below than with the detailed labor control applications that were first listed. And when it seems that the uses of time standards to which they have been exposed are apparently functioning as intended, they may be less inclined to support the functions required to keep time standards consistent and reliable for all uses. There will be comments under headings that follow to explain how time standards that are not reliable can still be utilized for the purposes listed. This does not mean that we are condoning sloppy work.

Production Scheduling

This heading covers both the preliminary scheduling of completion dates for accepted orders and the periodic (often daily) listing of jobs released to specific sections of the shop. In both cases, there are likely to be enough such listings for inconsistent time values to be averaged out, and any deviations between published standards and past performance in relation to standards can be factored into the arithmetic (usually computerized) which is involved. Also, the daily listing of jobs scheduled for specific sections normally includes more than could actually be done, to allow for variations which will always occur. Time standards comprise the basic data used for these necessary functions.

Evaluation of Potential Methods Changes

Whether the proposed new method involves expensive equipment, a simple fixture, or a manual methods change, comparisons between existing and estimated time values are usually required. Too often, equipment funds are justified based on time values that are incorrect. Good practice would involve the auditing of standards that might be questionable. Carrying this a step further, it was the practice in appendix plant 27 to require predetermined time analysis of the manual work content where new equipment was being considered, along with similar analysis of the operations required with proposed equipment changes. Not only did this guard against unjustified expenditures, but it provided a way to spot-check the validity of existing standard times.

Machine Loading

This becomes significant where bottleneck or very expensive equipment is involved. Although inconsistent standards may average out, and a correction can be made to consider the overall performance level in relation to standards, the machine loading function becomes less useful when time standards are not dependable on an individual basis.

Plant or Equipment Capacity Studies

The same comments apply here as noted for machine loading.

Manpower Planning

One of the productivity principles noted in Figure 3 involves looking ahead at the predicted work load in order to assure that work requirements will be in a reasonable balance with available manpower. So long as the scope of such planning is fairly broad, valid records of past performance levels in relation to time standards are perhaps more significant than the accuracy or consistency of standards.

Standard Cost Accounting

Most of the plants listed in the appendix develop standard product costs, utilizing such data both in the accounting process and as a guide for pricing. While the accounting system will function undeterred by a lack of time value consistency or accuracy, some of the decisions based on standard costs will be made incorrectly if the basic data are unsound.

Flexible Budget Administration

As will be discussed in chapter 15, appropriate study may serve to establish formulas indicating a viable relation between specific nondirect budget costs and the predicted standard hours for direct work. The flexible budgets that result in this way can function with inconsistent time values, but there will be more credibility and acceptance if the standards are known to be dependable.

Improvement Curve Applications

There will be some discussion in chapter 9 of "learning curves," which are more correctly referred to as improvement curves. They can have significant applications for load planning. In defense-related industries particularly, they may serve as a basis for pricing at different production levels. The later chapter will point out how time standards are typically brought into the picture when improvement curves are being applied.

WORK MEASUREMENT TECHNIQUES THAT CAN PRODUCE SOUND STANDARDS

The above listing of significant uses for time standards focused on direct manufacturing applications. There are also potential needs for work measurement in some form within various nondirect or nonmanufacturing sections, as will be discussed in chapter 15. The paragraphs that follow will refer to ways in which time standards or estimates can be developed, together with the relative accuracy expected.

There are various aspects within the work measurement process that must be considered, regardless of the technique used. The principal steps involved are:

- Determining and defining the standard method.
- Evaluating the time required when using that method.
- Adjustment of the measured time to conform with the task level established for a specific control plan.
- Application of required general allowances.

Direct Time Study

The timing function is a fairly routine task that can be done with precision after some training and experience. This tends to obscure the fact that considerable experience is required for methods analysis, where wide discrepancies can occur later as operators or their supervisors find ways to refine and improve upon the manual methods or machine cycle-times involved. Training is also essential for sound results in the performance rating function that is a necessary part of time study. The cost of time study can be reduced greatly through computerized work-up of the data following direct input from a microprocessor that is also a timing device (to be described in chapter 4). Some major plants rely entirely on direct time study for standards development because of the direct evidence it brings to those within a section that operations can be performed in specified time intervals.

Predetermined Time Analysis, Using Basic Systems

There are several predetermined time systems which include a sufficient number of time increments, along with definite rules of application, so that net times for either individual or simultaneous motions can be derived with some chance of resulting accuracy. Most of these techniques are proprietary. In only one case—that of the basic Methods-Time Measurement system, or MTM–1—have the procedural rules and time data been made readily available. For a specific, two-handed motion pattern, each of the basic systems will produce a different net time value. The question then becomes whether this is because of inherent inconsistencies or because the systems were intended to represent different performance levels. The latter would be an acceptable explanation, since a multiplying factor could be used for conversion to depict an intended level of performance. Claims made by the promoters of these systems concerning their consistency or inherent performance level, until verified by thorough testing, should remain in the category of what we are calling folklore. Further information will be found in chapter 5.

Unlike direct time study, a sound predetermined time system is capable of sorting through the various methods choices so as to define a near-optimum method along with the standard time involved. A predetermined time system that produces consistent results representing a known performance level can be applied systematically to develop standard time data or formulas, whereas numerous direct time studies would likely be necessary to measure all of the elements involved in such data. This feature extends the length of operation cycle times for which it is practical to utilize basic predetermined times. A development in recent years to make the use of predetermined times feasible has been the introduction of computer-aided analysis techniques. Chapters 5 and 6 will describe one such system, which also provides for improved consistency of analysis.

Standard Time Data

Manufacturing feeder sections usually have equipment groups such as punch presses, shears, power brakes, or turret lathes for which standard data tables can be developed to cover the required operations on a wide variety of parts. In such cases, parts handling methods are a key variable. Similarly, there are often families of parts involving operations that can be cataloged by standard data to cover pertinent variables. Inputs to develop standard data can be drawn from direct time study or predetermined times, with the latter having an advantage as noted above. The data are typically arranged either in tabular form, for easy selection, or as formulas. A mathematical technique known as regression analysis, applied with available computer programs, is used under certain conditions to simplify formula development. With appropriate formulas, computer recognition of time standards can in some cases be automated as part of the order processing system.

Another arrangement of standard data, when computer-aided predetermined time analysis is used, consists of coding elements likely to be of future use and storing them within the computer system. To develop specific time standards, elements for possible use are first reviewed on the screen of a computer terminal. Those selected can then be combined in appropriate format, with alterations as may be required. For SC/R assembly operations, where other forms of standard data are often difficult to derive, this approach has proved to be a practical one. When operations become lengthy, conventional forms of standard data construction are used.

There are two primary advantages in establishing and maintaining standard data: reduced work measurement costs and identification of standard time values before work goes to the floor. In addition, carefully prepared standard data will tend to produce more consistent time values than individual studies.

WORK MEASUREMENT TECHNIQUES FOR APPROXIMATE STANDARDS

There will be some cases where the cost of fully dependable time values, or the delays necessary to obtain them, call for less dependable techniques to be used. In other cases, average values are necessary because work functions are repetitive but work content varies. The techniques noted below may apply when more reliable approaches are not practical.

Condensed Predetermined Time Systems.

To speed up manual applications of basic systems, numerous abbreviated predetermined time systems are available. In general, they combine motion categories, reduce the number of variables, and eliminate the analysis concerning simultaneous motions. For SC/R operations, these systems are obviously inaccurate and inconsistent. For LC/LR work, claims that inaccuracies will "average out" should be viewed with skepticism, as will be further discussed. In general, the use of condensed predetermined time applications need not be considered if computer-aided techniques for applying basic systems are available.

Work Sampling Procedures

When individuals within a group perform a limited variety of functions, the work sampling technique (chapter 8) can be used to find the percentage of time spent on selected functions. If the group size and number of functional repetitions are tabulated, then the man-hours per individual function can be calculated. In groups such as an order service department, where an average time for order processing may be useful for control through scheduling, this can be a practical way to develop needed time values.

Estimates Based on Comparisons

When available standard data or previously developed time standards do not cover a required operation on a job order for which manufacturing information must be prepared, it is common practice to identify closely related operations performed in the past and develop an estimated standard. By using a designated code, such as an asterisk after the time value, the temporary nature of estimated values is made clear. Unless such occurrences are minimized, the control system in effect would be downgraded.

On the other hand, more systematic comparisons with available data on other jobs may be the only justifiable way to develop standard times where there is not sufficient correlation between parts or operations to construct real standard data. To do this properly, precise standards are first collected for a range of operations that have some relation to each other. Descriptions of each operation, along with pertinent drawings or photographs, are then arranged in sequence according to the time values. A slotting capability results, which provides a way to estimate new time standards more closely.

Estimates Based on Past Experience

As chapter 15 will emphasize, productivity control in work such as that within large maintenance departments depends more on advance planning and scheduling than on comparing actual performance with time standards. Not only are true standards or standard data costly to develop and apply for typical maintenance sequences, but in most cases they can be applied only after the work is done and full details are known. There is much to gain, however, through the use of preliminary estimates based on job-site inspection and work-related experience. And so this more approximate way to develop job performance targets should not be ruled out as a valid basis for control in some types of work.

PERFORMANCE LEVEL REPRESENTED BY STANDARD TIMES

As we get into the subject noted here, the reader must realize that we are attempting to deal in a rational way with two general kinds of framework for a labor control system: wage incentive plans, which rely on the attraction of bonus payments to produce acceptable performance; and measured daywork plans, which involve supervisory and management staff functions aimed at securing equivalent results. Unfortunately, most of the terminology that exists within this particular field of industrial engineering evolved during a period in which the application of wage incentives was predominant. And even more regrettably, many of the terms were apparently slanted in a way that was intended to promote incentive thinking and downgrade the idea of daywork applications.

The Fallacy of "Normal"

As an example of a slanted definition, the much-used term of "normal pace," notwithstanding its current definition in IE literature, represents a performance level just barely acceptable in any incentive plan. When an operator's performance level falls below this so-called normal point, it behooves the supervisor or MPA analyst to investigate quickly and find what went wrong. If the word "normal" were used in a way that would be applicable in both incentive and daywork control systems, it would simply replace currently used terms such as "incentive pace," or "high task" standard time. The level of performance represented by those terms is in reality the normal performance in a well-managed incentive system. And, as we shall discuss in chapter 13, it is the approximate target level that is achievable with sound measured daywork controls.

The Concept of 100 Percent Performance in Relation to Standards

Everywhere but within the field of industrial engineering, it would seem, 100 percent means "right on target." But in an incentive system this can mean either a good, bad, or indifferent performance level, depending on the system involved. (Chapter 11 defines various wage plans to illustrate this point.) In measured day work, achieving the 100 percent level means that time standards have been met. The task level represented by 100 percent is a function of how the MPA analysts were trained in standards development for the control plan that is in use.

Negative Thinking within IE Literature Regarding Day Work

In various reference sources dealing with wage incentive systems, we read that day work is to be avoided wherever a basis for incentives can be devised, since the resulting performance level is likely to be in about the 60–70 percent range. (Of course, we cannot know just what that percentage means when 100 percent is variable, but it obviously sounds bad!) Such comments invariably seem to omit the qualifying phrase "within an incentive system" in discussions of day-work performance, but of course that is what should always be stated. Few dayworkers can be expected to perform efficiently when those across the aisle are receiving extra pay for doing so. But that has no bearing on how dayworkers can be expected to perform in a separate, well-managed plant, when their pay is in line with area rates.

A Serious Attempt to Calibrate Wage Incentive Performance Levels

We have already noted that the IE use of "normal" neither means what the word implies in wage incentives nor has a clearly defined application in other control plans. It is a word that should be dropped from use by any company that is not unequivocally devoted to the application of wage incentives. The term was in fact dropped from corporate training material in company K, to avoid confusion in measured day-work terminology. Nevertheless, the term "normal" has a long history within wage incentives, along with related terms mentioned above. To the neophyte, it often seems incomprehensible that there should not

FIGURE 5.
Excerpt from S.A.M. Performance Rating Guide.

		PERCENT EXPECTED ATTAINMENT OF AVERAGE OPERATOR, AT INCENTIVE PACE										
PERCENT	0					100	105	110	115	120	125	130
OF TOTAL	5				100	105	110	115	120	125	130	135
ALLOWANCE	10			100	105	110	115	120	125	130	135	140
FOR	15		100	105	110	115	120	125	130	135	140	145
OPERATION	20	100	105	110	115	120	125	130	135	140	145	150
	25	105	110	115	120	125	130	135	140	145	150	155
	SCENE:											
RATINGS	1	116	121	128	134	140	146	152	158	164	170	176
FOR OPER-	2	94	98	103	108	113	118	122	127	132	137	142
ATION D,	3	68	71	74	78	82	85	89	92	96	99	103
DINK TILE	4	52	54	57	59	62	65	67	70	73	76	78
	5	79	82	86	91	94	99	103	107	111	115	119

be a uniform way to recognize these or other benchmark performance levels in a control system.

A number of years ago, the Society for Advancement of Management (SAM) sponsored the distribution of a collection of training films depicting various performance levels on different kinds of work. These films had been rated by hundreds of qualified analysts in various companies where wage incentives were applied. The results of such ratings had been evaluated in conjunction with data describing the specific incentive plans that provided background for the ratings by each individual. The material that was finally issued went with the approval of leading IE authorities, and hundreds of sets of these rating films have been sold over the years to various companies.

Figure 5, which shows the suggested ratings for one portion of the SAM films, is a good illustration of the wide spread in correct performance ratios for incentive systems, and the reasons for such a spread. First, the percentage is identified which would be applied within the system to define average incentive pace. One of the commonly used plans would call this value 125 percent. Next is identified the general allowance value usually applied within the system for operations such as those in the film. Here, a typical incentive allowance might be 15 percent. The recommended set of answers is in a column below the 125 percent figure on the 15 percent allowance line. Thus, for film sequence 2, the suggested rating for that kind of incentive system is 122 percent.

There are commonly applied incentive plans in which the bonus begins at about 80 percent rather than 100 percent, and 100 percent defines average incentive pace. In such a system, the recommended rating for the same film sequence is 98 percent, assuming that the same general allowance would be applied.

Although the SAM rating films date back many years, they are still perhaps the best available way to check out a specific plant's performance rating technique for wage incentives in relation to what might be considered the national average at the time these films were issued. It should be noted that there is no scale provided with the films that is recommended for anything but wage incentives. For measured day work, MPA analysts must derive their own benchmarks. This has of course been done within many organizations.

The Target Level for Measured Day-work Performance

Unlike the selective numerical scales applied to denote the task level of wage incentive standards, 100 percent in measured day work means what it implies: a target level for operators to accomplish on an average basis. Whether a day-work control plan is applied instead of a wage incentive plan involves many considerations other than average performance levels, as chapters 13 and 14 will discuss. It would be significant, however, to investigate any available evidence concerning how the target level of measured day work relates to average incentive pace as defined above, and whether the target levels can be achieved over a period of time. A brief overview bearing on this point is given in paragraphs that follow. Conclusions presented here are explored more fully in later chapters.

In appendix plant 18, which manufactured major appliances, a change from wage incentives to measured day work was accomplished, after wage negotiations, by maintaining the identical manning and speeds on paced lines, and by factoring other time standards so as to convert average incentive pace to day-work target levels. The performance level on paced lines improved. During the next year, all time values were restudied using computer-aided MTM, adjusted for measured day work as described below.

The Methods-Time Measurement system of predetermined times was originally developed for application as the 100 percent level, after typical allowances, in a wage incentive system where incentive pace was expected to average about 125 percent (see Honeycutt, 1962). Appendix-listed companies K, M, and N have in the past undertaken major studies indicating that MTM–1 time values should be factored by .83 or .84 for measured day work in which SC/R operations were involved. Each of these three companies printed their own MTM data cards at this factored level. Other large companies have made similar revisions in MTM for measured day-work applications. A similar approach was taken with Work Factor (another predetermined time system) when plant 47 shifted from incentive to measured day work.

Appendix plant 83, which had always applied measured day work, was one of some ten plants in five major companies which were studied in detail by research personnel from a major university, to investigate measured day-work effectiveness. Half of the plants applied wage incentives and the other half measured day work. The researchers' conclusions were that the best work effort was seen at plant 83, where the control plan was measured day work. The daily performance ratios at that location were regularly known to be in the 100 percent range.

Other examples could be cited, but without providing conclusive answers. As previously stated, performance rating is a subjective task, and the target levels of performance are not easily defined. The author's conclusions regarding an appropriate level for measured day-work target standards in relation to the performance level represented by average incentive pace in a well-managed incentive system are that the two should be about the same.

PERFORMANCE RATING TECHNIQUES

Now that we have explored some of the facts and folklore concerning performance-level percentages in various control systems, let us examine a few techniques developed over the years for performance rating. We will find a certain amount of folklore here also, perhaps aimed at making the subjective rating process appear more objective than is actually the case. Two requirements for performance rating will be considered. One is the familiar need to evaluate an operator's performance during direct time study. Another requirement is that of determining how a specific predetermined time system should be evaluated for application within a plant.

A trained and experienced MPA analyst is generally able to rate an operator's performance without guidance from a detailed rating system. But adhering to a systematic rating procedure assists those with less experience, and the rating format helps any analyst explain to supervisors or operators the reasons for high or low rating values.

Systems Involving Multiple Factors and Point Rating Scales

One rating technique extensively used in the past attempted to subdivide the factors which affect performance so that each of four factors can be rated in from six to eleven steps. For each selected step, a positive or negative fractional rating value is assigned. After the fractional values are totaled algebraically, the net amount is added to 1.00 to derive a leveling factor. This factor is then used to adjust the observed time up or down to derive a time value representing the performance level of incentive normal. This rating procedure was in time replaced within the company where it was first originated by another point rating technique involving some eight different factors, with point values applied in about the same way. (Both systems were in time discontinued.)

A percentage rating based on incentive normal would not be applicable to define measured day-work performance levels. It may help to focus on what is involved in performance rating, however, to review the twelve factors which are a part of these two systems. They are as follows:

System A: Skill of the operator (M)
Effort applied by the operator (P)
Working conditions that affect operator's performance (−)
Consistency of performance (M)

System B: Ability to use equipment and tools (M)
Certainty of movement (P)
Coordination and rhythm (P)
Ability to replace and retrieve tools and parts properly (M)
Eliminating, combining, or shortening motions (M)
Use of both hands with equal ease (M)
Confining effort to necessary work (M)
Attentiveness (P)

While there is no doubt that each of these descriptive terms deals with an important aspect of performance, it is clear that some of the components in each system interact with each other rather than being identifiable separately. Consider now those factors followed by the letter M. Can we not regroup all of these under the general heading of *methods which are under the operator's control*? Even the first item, skill, seems to fit better under such a heading. An operator's skill often is in hiding during a time study. It is the displayed methods proficiency that really counts.

Consider next the factors followed by the letter P. Together, they are a good description of what is involved in the operator's *work pace*. While a faster pace usually involves more effort, the term "effort" should be avoided because its meaning is not always clear. For example, a foundry operator working at 80 percent of expected pace may exert more effort than a small-parts assembler working at a 110 percent pace level.

Consider next the third item listed. If conditions which reduce effectiveness can be improved, such as inadequate lighting, this should be done before a study is taken. If they are an inherent part of the job, such as sharp edges that hinder grasp, or a difficult positioning requirement, good judgement will avoid downgrading either methods or pace because of such conditions.

A Performance Rating Technique for Any Control Plan

References in the bibliography list various forms of performance rating that can be considered. We will describe here one technique that has been found workable in a number of measured day-work plants where 100 percent was the targeted performance level. The same technique could be used with any other basis for expressing time standards, after appropriate training. This approach consists of observing and evaluating the net results of (a) the operator's working pace; and (b) manual methods controlled by the operator. A summarized description follows:

Primary Methods Details. Time studies should be initiated only after a sound basic method has been specified and the operator is following this method. Accordingly, the performance rating of an operator being studied should not have to include the effect on performance of primary methods aspects such as workplace layout, tools or equipment involved, or unnecessary work increments. Of course, there may be cases where possible improvements in the primary methods are either overlooked by the analyst or could not be made until much later. When changes occur later, a new study is required. Elemental descriptions and layout sketches on a time study can assist in recognition of primary methods changes.

Pace Rating. Items coded with *P* in the previous list describe what to look for in evaluating an operator's pace. Do not confuse pace with effort, as previously noted. The working pace may be high, with methods effectiveness low, or vice versa.

Secondary Methods Rating. This rating is an evaluation of the methods effectiveness where manual methods can be controlled by the operator. The percentage derived may be above or below 100 percent. Conditions that would tend to influence the methods rating are illustrated by items coded with *M* in the preceding list.

The P/SM Rating Percentage. After deriving two rating components, pace and secondary methods, multiply them together to obtain the overall percentage rating.

Rating Specific Elements. Machine-controlled elements are not rated. For manual elements, there may properly be variations in the evaluation of secondary methods. Generally, the pace ratings for manually controlled elements will be uniform over the cycle.

Required Training. For consistent applications of this or any other performance rating technique, films or television sequences of typical plant operations can be utilized to obtain a consensus of MPA and other opinions. If a predetermined time system has been evaluated in relation to the 100 percent benchmark for the plant's control system, a checkout of the ratings can be made in this way. The operational sequences can then be viewed periodically as a basis for training.

An Essential Difference between Wage Incentive Rating and Measured Day-work Rating

Despite differences in the numerical framework of various incentive plans, there is generally identified a low-task performance level called normal, as has been noted. In the arithmetic of most incentive plans, normal equals 100 percent. The rating technique calibrates an observed performance level in relation to normal. After applying general allowances, which may be in excess of factual requirements, operators are encouraged to work above the low-task level in return for bonus payments. In a well-managed incentive system, the expected average performance ratio (high-task level) may be about 25 percent above the designated normal, or perhaps 20 percent in excess of the methods/pace level at which normal was calculated before allowances.

If an operator's observed performance during time study is considerably below the high-task level (as most operators would want to see happen), the observer is able to discuss the rated level in terms of normal. To tell the operator or supervisor that the rating was near 100 percent, or about normal, is clearly a psychological advantage over having to say that the rating was 80 percent of the expected level.

In measured daywork, it is essential that this misuse of the word normal be avoided. It would not be acceptable to say to the operator, "You are working at normal, but our time value will be 20 percent higher." The fact that the plant's pay scale might be on a par with earnings in an incentive plant across town would not salve the blow. The analyst in such a system clearly must develop a rating in relation to the expected performance level. The operator and supervisor would be told that the rating was 80 percent if that level were derived, not a much higher figure which sounds better but is not.

That could be termed a disadvantage in the administration of measured day work. Plants listed in the appendix have generally coped with this by being quite frank with operators from the start of their employment. A typical comment would be: "We pay good wages, are able to select above-average operators, and we must expect good performance to stay in business." If the MPA group does a sound, consistent job of time standards maintenance, the disadvantage referred to may be more than offset by advantages that will be noted in chapters to follow.

Adjusting a Predetermined Time System to Correspond with Intended Task Level

Earlier in this chapter, we indicated how one specific predetermined time system was initially developed to define the low-task point in wage incentives, and how that system was adjusted to measured day-work target levels for SC/R operations. It is strongly suggested that the use of any such system be preceded by a systematic analysis as to how it relates to established performance targets.

In adapting the MTM system to define measured day-work standards for SC/R operations, the approach taken in company K was to utilize five MTM analysts, who had been certified as instructors, to analyze a number of filmed operations for which measurements and other data had been recorded. At least two analysts checked each operation, working separately, after which their studies were screened and correlated. Next, the films were rated by a number of qualified MPA analysts at five plant locations. The film speed was monitored to correspond with the synchronous drive on the original camera, and there were about twenty successive cycles for most of the operations. After averaging the ratings, comparisons were made with the MTM studies. The conclusions arrived at in this way were found to be valid during years of application for SC/R operations. A less rigorous form of checkout could be made by comparing carefully rated direct time studies with predetermined time analyses made concurrently.

WORK MEASUREMENT COST CONSIDERATIONS

The many potential ways in which time standards can be useful, along with labor savings from their applications in a valid control plan, should not obscure the need to minimize the cost of standards development. Wherever the use of standard data is practical, this is generally the approach that should be taken. The question then becomes how best to develop individual time values required to prepare such data.

As chapter 4 will describe in detail, the use of a hand-held microprocessor to make numerical inputs for direct time study, followed by direct input of the stored data for computer processing and printout, can reduce MPA time study costs by about one-third. The costs for predetermined time analysis can be reduced by a much greater ratio through computer aids, as chapter 6 will illustrate.

The wide variations in manual motion complexity within industrial operations do not permit a simple statement as to where predetermined time analysis should stop and direct time study should begin. In general, the break-even point between these two work measurement techniques will be at a considerably longer cycle time for the studies involved in standard data development. This is because of the duplication in measurement usually required when time study is the basis for data construction. Qualified MPA analysts will be proficient in either technique and able to select the one best suited for specific analyses.

THE QUESTION OF ALLOWANCES

Before getting into this subject, it should be pointed out that many industrial operations involve tasks which can be measured but which do not occur as part of every operation cycle. Examples include the movement of parts in tote pans, the periodic changing of drills and cutting tools, or average times for workplace cleanup. Such irregular elements of an operation should be accounted for on a percentage basis, but these are work requirements, not allowances.

Delay Allowances

A competent supervisor or MPA analyst will take steps to minimize the detracting conditions that tend to interfere with full performance. At the same time, a combination of allowances and time records is called for to account for delays that have not been eliminated and which are not caused by the operators affected. The work sampling technique can be applied to measure the average percentages of delay time within a section. With care, such observations can designate the major reasons for delays, along with their respective percentages.

Wage Incentive Delay Allowances. The operator should not be penalized for unavoidable delays. A typical approach is the combination of two ways to avoid such penalties: (1) authorization, after screening, of the claims for delays beyond a specified time interval; and (2) a percentage allowance applied to the time standards covering shorter delays that occur on an average basis. The longer delay intervals are reported and deducted from actual hours in the calculation of incentive bonus earnings.

Measured Day-work Delay Allowances. A somewhat modified approach is needed so that detracting conditions are not camouflaged. By making delay allowances in time standards only for short delays that tend to occur every day, the standards have a more dependable meaning as a basis for assigning a full day's work. Examples are getting job assignments, making data collection inputs, or entering performance records. Such delay allowances might typically be in the 2–3 percent range. When less frequent and perhaps longer delays occur which an operator cannot avoid, the supervisor should investigate reasons and authorize the operator's valid claims. Efficiency records for the operator should reflect such deductions from actual hours. But sectional performance ratios should in most cases be lowered as delaying conditions occur. Most of the measured day-work plants listed in the appendix have taken approaches along these lines.

Personal Allowances

There is no question that personal allowances in some form are necessary, but there is a divided opinion as to whether specified break periods should be established rather than encouraging operators to take their breaks individually. By staggering the break periods in various sections, the obvious disadvantage of overcrowded facilities can be reduced somewhat. But another disadvantage in that approach is that it cannot rule out other personal breaks being taken. In some cases, the nature of production facilities is the deciding point in this regard.

A 5 percent personal allowance, applied to time standards, is typical within manufacturing plants. When working at standard, the 5 percent allowance amounts to twenty-two minutes per eight-hour shift if the total general allowance is 10 percent, or twenty-one minutes if the general allowance totals 15 percent.

Fatigue Allowances

General allowances for personal time, fatigue, and unavoidable delays (commonly referred to as PF&D allowances) have usually been applied to develop time values for wage incentive systems. The personal and delay allowances can be analyzed with some logic, as we have tried to show, and there are logical differences in how delay allowances should be applied. When we come to the subject of fatigue allowances, however, the logic involved becomes very fuzzy.

A certain amount of fatigue comes with a person's normal activity, whether at home, on the golf course, or at work in a factory or an office. A slowdown in working performance is undoubtedly caused by excessive fatigue, but modern equipment has removed many of the work-related causes of undue fatigue. In the gradations of physical activity that now exist, it is customary to assign heavier work to those physically equipped to handle it, and job evaluation techniques usually consider manual effort as a factor in determining job classifications which affect rates of pay.

Direct time study involves observations during a continuing interval and at times when average conditions of fatigue are likely to apply. Performance rating can be expected to evaluate the pace of operators in terms of that which can reasonably be maintained during the typical two-hour work interval, assuming two personal breaks and an extended lunch break during an eight-hour shift (see Mundel, 1960).

Many industrial operations are machine-controlled, with periods during the cycle when there is nothing for the operator to do except to wait. Of course, good MPA practice involves finding useful work increments that can be performed during such waiting intervals, but rarely is it possible to completely balance machine-controlled intervals with manual elements. If there is a 10 percent portion of the machine cycle during which an operator must wait, for example, this is to some extent the equivalent of a fatigue allowance.

A comparable situation exists in operations that are entirely manual in nature. The 4M DATA system for computer-aided application of predetermined times calculates automatically, at the end of each analysis, the percentage of manual work time during which the two hands were fully engaged in useful work. Chapter 6 will explain this further. In seventeen typical SC/R operations used for 4M DATA training, this percentage ranged from 55 percent to 88 percent, averaging 69 percent. Further study would be expected to show that there is some correlation between the "motion assignment index," as this percentage value is called, and the extent of operator fatigue.

There are mixed opinions and practices regarding the application of fatigue allowances to develop valid time standards for industrial operations. Most of the plants and at least two of the major companies listed in the appendix do not apply such allowances for typical measured daywork operations. Most plants where wage incentive systems are in effect will continue to apply fatigue allowances, usually in the 5 percent range, because that has long been standard practice as a step in defining the concept of incentive pace within such plants.

To conclude this discussion of fatigue allowance practices, we must recognize that there are some jobs where modern technology has not yet been applied to permit working without excessive effort. Examples are uninterrupted heavy lifting, or drop forging where heat is unavoidable. Such jobs should be analyzed on an individual basis to assure that fair standards are developed. Whether the applicable factors are termed fatigue or added personal allowances is of no particular significance.

4
A Fresh Look at Direct Time Study

Direct time study techniques were developed long ago, when consistent time standards became necessary within industry. During the period when inept or greedy management practices spawned the resentment of workers, helping to bring about labor's organized resistance toward what was perceived as unfairness, the "time study man" was not held in high esteem. The symbols of his profession—stopwatches affixed to clipboards along with complex forms—became a focus for this resentment.

Recognizing this, one proficient management consultant, whose work as an implementer of incentive systems involved frequent methods/time observations, used nothing but a wristwatch and a small notebook with blank pages as a means of entering time observations. He found that the extra interval required to summarize observations at a desk was more than offset by added cooperation received in the shop. The accuracy of his results did not suffer.

As labor relations policies and practices have continued to improve in recent years, the past resentment toward those whose duties involve making direct time studies has abated. However, this change in attitude suffered somewhat when analysts found that three separate stopwatches, linked together by lever action and mounted prominently on clipboards, could reduce the need for later subtractions in recording elemental times. Fortunately, electronic timers are currently available that replace the three watches and are less obtrusive.

We do not mean to be cynical regarding direct time study applications. On the contrary, as has previously been noted, the function of methods analysis within the time study process is inherently significant in making a control system effective. An effort should be made, however, to do away with objectionable time-study symbols. A computer-aided concept for doing that will be discussed which improves on the three-watch system. We will consider first in this chapter the needed qualifications of an MPA analyst who makes direct time studies. The steps involved will be covered, and the potential advantages and disadvantages of direct time study will be noted.

QUALIFICATIONS NEEDED FOR MAKING DIRECT TIME STUDIES

A knowledge of methods fundamentals is necessary, which requires training and experience. The principles of motion economy can be taught; one way is through learning how to apply basic predetermined times. But knowing how work should be performed where studies are made requires on-the-job observations and a questioning attitude. For example, the observer must not just theorize about the number of passes required to buff a part. Neither can he or she simply refer to tables of feeds and speeds to check those being used on specific shop equipment, since condition of the equipment has some bearing on this. There is much to learn about methods requirements wherever complex operations are performed, and knowing how to ask questions without arousing antagonism is essential.

Time studies will often be used for standard data development. That means the analyst should know how to construct standard data, so that elements are properly selected and identified. A working knowledge of predetermined time applications will mean the analyst can use whichever technique is more practical in specific cases, without wasting time on unnecessary or duplicate time studies.

Training in performance rating is essential before direct time studies are attempted. This is particularly important if the analyst has come from another location where the control plan may have been different. Such training should not be a one-time event, as the concept of working pace tends to drift toward what is viewed from day to day. Many MPA groups require refresher training in performance rating on a yearly basis.

Tact in dealing with operators, labor representatives, or direct supervisors is a requirement that cannot be overemphasized. Being interested in work details, and showing that interest by asking tactful questions, is a good way to start.

Attention to detail is a requirement for time study analysis. Remember that the purpose of a study is not just to derive currently needed standards or standard data. The study will probably be referred to years later in determining whether specific methods details have changed.

Adequate descriptions are necessary concerning the workplace layout, equipment, parts, and the designated elements of an operation.

STEPS INVOLVED

When a study is to be made, the direct supervisor should first be contacted by the analyst. A typical approach would be for the supervisor and analyst to view the operation together. They should either agree that the layout, methods, feeds/speeds, and other factors are acceptable, or the supervisor should make revisions before the study is taken.

Designating Elements within an Operation

If the cycle is relatively short, the analyst will determine in advance how the operation as a whole will be divided into sequential elements. For lengthy operations, an experienced analyst may decide to begin the study as the job starts and denote elements as the job progresses.

One purpose of dividing an operation into specific elements during the timing process is to identify segments that may be required for standard data construction. If gaining control of large parts and moving them toward a fixture is likely to vary according to part size, for example, the analyst will want to separate the time for that element from fixture clamping, subsequent machining, removal from fixture, and part disposal. Any of such components may also be used as building blocks in future data.

Another reason for subdividing an operation is so that a review of times for each element can be made upon completion of the study. If an operator's working pace is being limited intentionally, this can be detected to some extent if there are marked variations in successive elemental times. Extreme variations without reason can be circled and omitted from final averages, if care is used to avoid confusing this with the performance rating step.

A third reason for identifying elements in direct time study is to facilitate the revision of individual standards or standard data when methods change in the future. If new cutting tools permit improved feeds and speeds, for example, a revision of machining elements can be made without affecting other segments of the data. There can be a disadvantage here, depending on precedents or agreements that may have been established with labor representatives. Many changes in methods affect some elements directly but have indirect, hard-to-prove effects on other elements as well. To illustrate that, consider an operation in which four parts are clamped in a holding fixture for spot welding. A design change may eliminate a projecting part that was previously welded in the fixture. Clearly the elemental time for spot welding that part should be deleted.

The analyst may also realize that the workplace layout has been changed slightly to reduce handling on all parts; a simultaneous placement of two parts in the fixture may have been changed to a one-handed placement of one part; and disposal of the assembly may be easier because there is one less clamp to open. The entire job should be restudied. But the major change is in just one element, and other changes are so slight that they might be hard to prove.

The point here is that precedents should not be established for having to prove changes in specific time-study elements rather than restudying an entire operation when this is called for. Unfortunately, such restrictions have come about in the past, particularly in wage incentive systems where strong labor unions were involved.

Timing Successive Cycles

It was indicated previously that stopwatches are not a necessity for direct time study. That is because the preferred approach is to use continuous timing once the study has begun. Subtractions are of course required to calculate elemental times unless more modern techniques are used that automate this step. With continuous timing, all that happens must be accounted for, and it can be demonstrated to questioning individuals that this has been done. Of course, what occurs during a lengthy time study is not always done in a sequential, orderly manner, and some occurrences may not be considered useful work. Terms that have been applied to describe some of the nonroutine occurrences follow.

Foreign Elements. Timed intervals that have no direct relation to the time standard for a job being studied may occur between two regular elements, or they may occur during an element. If an operator stopped work briefly to retrieve a tool someone had borrowed, that would be a foreign element which should be identified as such.

Irregular Elements. The interval during which an operator stopped during a study in order to change a cutting tool would be classified as an irregular element. A necessary function of this kind would be accounted for on a percentage basis after further evaluation.

Elements Performed Out of Order. It would make the observer's job easier if repeated elements in an operation were always performed in the same sequence, but the analyst must be able to handle variations in sequence when they occur.

Elements Omitted by the Operator. If parts generally require deburring before assembly, the analyst may call that step an element of the study being made. When deburring is not required and the element is omitted, there must be a routine way to account for this during the study and as a standard is developed.

FIGURE 6.
Approximate Number of Cycles to be Studied.

WHEN TIME PER CYCLE IS GREATER THAN:	STUDY THIS NUMBER OF JOB CYCLES: Over 10,000 cycles/year	1,000-10,000 cycles/year	Under 1,000 cycles/year
1.0 hours	5	3	2
0.5 hours	8	4	3
0.1 hours	17	9	7
0.05 hours	25	12	10
0.01 hours	55	27	22
0.005 hours	80	40	30
(Under .002)	140	80	60

Elements Missed by the Observer. This can happen, of course. It is not sound practice to make a guess as to when the missed reading should have occurred. Doing so would affect the validity of elemental times that are used for standard data or for review of the operator's consistency.

Number of Cycles to be Timed

It is necessary to study enough cycles of an operation for valid performance rating of the elements and to reveal conditions of difficulty normally present in the work. Other factors that bear on length of the study include the estimated cycle time for an operation and the estimated repetition of that operation during a period such as one year. Whether the study is for standard data development or for individual job standards must also be considered. Good judgement is necessary to keep the cost of work measurement within practical bounds as well as to keep accuracy within acceptable limits. Various reference sources suggest the minimum number of cycles to study. These guidelines are quite arbitrary. The MPA group should develop its own policy along this line. Figure 6 illustrates how one specific location has done so.

The Time Study Format

Unless specialized techniques are used, such as the computerized listing of time data which will be described later, a record format will be required for manual entries. The format should be developed after considering the type of work involved and the performance rating technique used. Typically, one side of a record form is reserved for sketches and general descriptive data. The other side is for continuous observations of element ending times, with spaces adjacent to each entry for later subtractions to show the elemental times. For simplicity of arithmetic, a decimal-hour timing device is generally preferred. Time readings are to the fourth decimal, but only the digits required for elemental subtractions need be entered. Typically, the time entries are in pencil and later subtractions in ink, for contrast. Design of the record format should include the following:

Identification. Provide spaces for the study number, operation involved, drawing data, department, date, equipment, parts or material, etc.

Sketch Space. Leave enough room to picture the workplace layout, with needed dimensions.

Time Entry Spaces. If most operations within the plant are SC/R, there will likely be more repeated times for an element than there are elements. In such cases, the element numbers and descriptions, time readings, and decimal-hour subtractions can go in columns extending across the narrow width of the form, with repetitions along the wider portion. Where LC/LR operations predominate, consider using the length of the form for element entries, in which case there will be fewer spaces for repetitive entries.

Starting, Finish, and Overall Times. Such entries are needed with continuous timing, as evidence that nothing was omitted.

Foreign Element Descriptions. Leave spaces for start/stop times, along with a short description of each occurrence.

Element Summary Times. For each element, provide spaces to show total time, number of observations, and average time.

Performance Rating and Allowances. In line with element summary times, provide needed spaces to calculate and enter performance rating by element, percent allowance, and standard element times, with spaces for totals.

Remarks. Spaces are needed to enter substantiating remarks as justified for evidence if the study is questioned later, or for reference to determine whether methods have changed.

Division of Time Standards, as Required. The later uses of standard times may differ for "setup" (once per order) and "each piece" (to be multiplied by order quantity).

COMPUTERIZING THE CLERICAL FUNCTIONS IN TIME STUDY

Experienced analysts know that about as much of their time is required to make subtractions, develop averages, and complete other entries as is needed for on-the-floor observations. The three-watch system previously referred to, or electronic devices that do the same thing, permits the analyst to enter elemental times directly while the next element

FIGURE 7.
Portable Microprocessor Used for Direct Time Study.

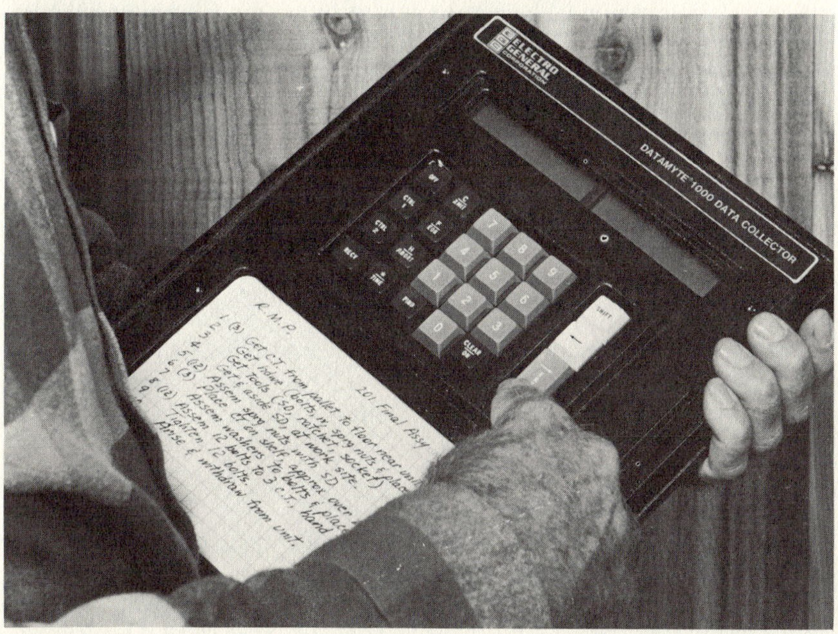

occurs, but the operator's performance cannot be observed as this is done, and much remains to be summarized later.

Figure 7 shows a portable microprocessor that records and stores internally, when an "enter" button is pressed, the elapsed time in minutes plus other data selected from a keyboard. The stored data can later be transmitted directly into a computer system, where a program will interact with the data just as would be done if the input had been through the computer terminal. This device has been used for direct time study because it can assist in handling the tedious arithmetic and clerical details involved.

Other units of this type are also available commercially. This particular unit has been applied within one company for direct time study, predetermined time analysis, and multicategory work sampling. The steps involved in its use for time study will be described here. MPA engineers can develop programs that fit their own needs, perhaps enlarging or improving on the steps listed.

A notepad is affixed to the lower portion of the device pictured. With the unit held in one arm, element numbers and descriptions are written sequentially, along with the usual heading data and layout diagram. A brief description of any foreign elements that occur must also be noted on the pad. Before a study begins, the study number is entered on the keyboard, preceded by a double asterisk which indicates that a new study is beginning. As the "Enter" button is actuated, the study number is recorded internally, and a continuous record begins. An element number is depressed on the keyboard at any time during progress of that element. When one element ends and the next begins, the Enter button is actuated, which records and stores three things electronically: a sequence number, the element number, and the continuous clock time in decimal-minutes. For regular elements, no further entries are required, and the analyst can devote more attention to job progress than when times must be recorded manually.

Handling Nonstandard Occurrences

A time record system must be capable of dealing with any of the variations from a sequential routine which were listed previously. To do this, it is necessary only for the analyst to depress selected keys in order to provide needed instructions which the program can recognize. For one specific program, applied with the microprocessor in Figure 7, the following steps were taken:

Foreign Element Recognized by Analyst and Entered by Number on the Data Sheet. Depress "F," followed by the number assigned, and enter when the foreign element has ended. Time data will be listed in the printout under "noncyclic" elements. Later, if the analyst decides a foreign element should be an "irregular element," this can be done manually at the end of the computer printout.

Element Performed Out of Sequence by Operator, but OK to Use in Study to Derive the Average Value for that Element. Depress "C," following the appropriate element number, and enter when the element has ended. The computer program will then place and summarize the time data correctly.

End of Element A (Same as Start of Element B) Missed by Analyst, but End of B (Start of C) Entered Correctly. Omission of the entry for A/B will trigger the deletion of total time for A + B, which will be listed as an error. (This is what the analyst would do with manual entries.)

Element Repeated by Operator. The analyst is called upon to decide how this should be handled, just as would have to be done if all of the entries were manual. Before the repeated element ends, the analyst should enter the element number followed by one of three codes, as follows:

- CC1 - Use the second of the two elements in the computer summary, with the first considered a noncyclic deletion.
- CC2 - Use the first and delete the second as noncyclic.
- CC3 - Classify both as noncyclic, since neither is a true picture of the element time involved.

Wrong Key Punched but Not Entered. Depress the CLEAR button, as with an electronic calculator.

Element Number Entered Too Soon, or a Code-plus-time Must be Deleted for Some Other Reason. Enter "H" immediately following the mistaken entry. (This will have no bearing on the timing in progress after the preceding entry.)

Wrong Element Number Entered at End of Element. Here the analyst must change the element number without revising the previously recorded clock time. Enter HXX, where XX = correct element number.

Wrong Element Number Entered but Not Recognized before Next Entry. The Next Element Number Correctly Entered. The computer program will correct this automatically by recognizing the unauthorized lack of sequence in numbers.

Performance Rating, at End of Study. A selected code is entered following the last element entry. The code used was **H. This signified that the time recorded along with the preceding element was the conclusion of the study. Next, enter XXHHYYY, where XX is the highest numbered element in sequence with a performance rating of YYY. Follow by similar entries as required to account for all elemental ratings. Example: Assume there were nine elements, with the first seven rated at 90 percent, the eighth (a process interval) rated at 100 percent, and the ninth element rated at 105 percent. Entries would then be **H, 7HH90, 8HH100, 9HH105.

Miscellaneous Data Revisions. If there is an occasional need to make revisions not covered by above instructions, or in situations where inputs of the codes listed were not made correctly, changes can be made during an editing step, using the computer terminal.

Processing the Study

Data stored electronically within the portable unit are transmitted to the computer system in accordance with instructions provided. Proper responses to questions asked by the computer program during processing of a study will make it possible to combine the data with previous or future inputs for the same operation.

Illustrated in Figure 8 is the preliminary listing of raw data for a short study after it has been transmitted from the microprocessor to the computer system. Reference numbers in the left column begin at one hundred and continue to the right in steps of ten. Most of the assigned codes previously discussed are illustrated by this set of data. An editing process can come as the next step, if required. The times listed should not be edited, only the action codes if mistakes are seen.

There were seven cycles of five elements each in this short study. Figure 9 illustrates how the third and fourth cycles would be printed.

FIGURE 8.
Input of Time Study Data from Microprocessor.

100	**1009,00000	1,00015	2,00031	3,00043
140	4,00057	5,00077	1,00092	F1,00108
180	2,00130	3,00143	4,00156	5,00172
220	1,00192	2,00210	3,00221	4,00237
260	F2,00281	1C,00298	2,00314	3,00328
300	4,00344	5,00365	F3,00382	1,00395
340	2,00411	3,00426	4,00439	5,00455
380	1,00472	2,00491	3,00502	4,00516
420	5,00535	1,00551	2,00572	3,00587
460	4,00611	5,00629	**H,00638	5HH95,00654

FIGURE 9.
Computer Printout of Cycles 3 and 4 from Data in Figure 8.

```
CYCLE 3

      1      2      3      4
     20     18     11     16
    192    210    221    237

CYCLE 4

     1C      2      3      4      5
     17     16     14     16     21
    298    314    328    344    365
    281    298
```

FIGURE 10.
Listing of Noncyclic Elements.

```
        F1     F2     F3
        16     44     17
       108    281    382
        92    237    365

TOTAL TIME DUE TO NONCYCLIC ELEMENTS: 0.77
NUMBER OF ELEMENTS IN ERROR:          0
TOTAL TIME DELETED DUE TO ERRORS:     0
```

Other cycles would appear the same way, in sequence. Figure 10 shows the listing of noncyclic elements for the entire study.

The computerized summary is shown by Figure 11. Note that the standard deviation for each element is listed. The calculation required for this is something that is considered too complex for manual time study procedures, but it was thought to have a more definite meaning than the usual scanning of repeated elemental time values. The latter step can still be done easily, however, since times for each element of

FIGURE 11.
Computer Listing of Time Study Summary.

ELEM	OBS	TIME	AVE	STD DEV	RATE	STND MIN.	STND HRS.
1	7	1.13	0.16	0.02	95	0.1534	0.00256
2	7	1.28	0.18	0.02	95	0.1737	0.00290
3	7	0.91	0.13	0.02	95	0.1235	0.00206
4	7	1.10	0.16	0.04	95	0.1493	0.00249
5	6	1.10	0.18	0.02	95	0.1742	0.00290
TIME USED		5.52	0.81			0.7740	0.01290
DURATION		6.29					

the seven cycles would be listed uniformly in a vertical column, spaced as in Figure 9. Note also that the noncyclic total (0.77 minutes) added to the time used (5.52 minutes) equals the study duration time of 6.29 minutes. In other words, nothing has been omitted from the computerized data. A conversion from minutes to hours appears in the last column, to conform with standard practice within the company.

This sample study has been kept short in order to simplify the illustration. It is intended to show a general approach that can be taken in developing the computer program. It is not intended to define specific codes to use, a specific format of printout, or a specific microprocessor to be applied.

Reasons for Considering Use of This Technique

It should be obvious that a great deal of arithmetical drudgery can be saved through a technique of this kind. Those who have used this particular system for combining inputs to a portable microprocessor with computer analysis of the data agree that at least one-third of the usual MPA time involved in making a direct time study can be saved. And there is less distraction from observing the methods and pace of work being done.

The long-standing antipathy of some workers toward stopwatch time study is another reason for taking this approach. Although it would be realized that time is being recorded, no timing device is visible, and the written list of elemental descriptions would appear logical to an operator who is shown the notepad after a study is completed. Computer applications have become commonplace to everyone, and the air of mystery about what a computer might do with the analyst's push-button entries at the job site need not be a frightening thing to operators unless the analyst fails to pave the way through explanations at the start.

There is a disadvantage in that sketches and descriptive details are separate from the computer listing that comes later. If this is disturbing to some, it would be possible to design the program so that an office clerk could type into the computer system all details except the sketch. With specific models of the unit pictured by Figure 7, wording can be entered into the microprocessor on the shop floor, but this would tend to complicate an otherwise simple routine. By merely stapling the note sheets to a computer printout, adequate permanent records are possible.

The required program involves considerable detail but does not involve complex logic. MPA engineers could prepare specifications for development of the computer program, or perhaps handle the programming function completely.

POTENTIAL ADVANTAGES FROM USING DIRECT TIME STUDY

Direct time study or predetermined time analysis? These are the two possibilities to be considered for reliable time standards covering industrial operations. Each technique has certain advantages, as noted below for direct time study.

Believability

Barring low extremes in performance rating, which can be avoided if the analyst insists on having a competent operator perform the work, a direct time study provides evidence that an operation can be performed in the elapsed time represented by the standard. It is unlikely that a predetermined time analysis would serve as equivalent evidence to operators or union representatives.

Less Chance of Omitting Problem Conditions

If a number of successive operation cycles are studied, the analyst can hardly escape noting the detracting conditions or irregular elements that may be caused by parts, tools, or equipment. Examples are parts sticking in press dies, poor fits during assembly, or burrs that must be removed before a step in the operation can be performed. Of course, each occurrence of this kind brings with it the need to question whether the problem involved can be eliminated. But some cannot, and direct time study will be more likely to make needed allowance for such conditions than would be the case with predetermined time applications.

Operator/Supervisor/MPA Coordination

The forced interaction between these three individuals helps bring about a mutual understanding of what is expected in work performance.

The training thus provided to all concerned is more positive and more prompt in some ways than is likely to occur when predetermined times are applied after a workplace review by the analyst alone. A direct time study shows that at least one operator knows the method identified as standard. With predetermined time analysis, there is an obligation for training if the recorded method is complex in nature.

POTENTIAL DISADVANTAGES WITH DIRECT TIME STUDY

History of Negative Reactions

The appearance of concentrating on how fast the operator works rather than on operational methods, although not a true picture of the time study process, leads some operators into an adversarial position. Operator subterfuge is a common result, making it difficult in some cases for the analyst to evaluate methods and pace correctly.

Tendency to Neglect Methods Refinement

It was previously noted that the relative simplicity involved in the timing process tends to obscure the need for the analyst to have experience and training in methods analysis. To the extent that this may cause the assignment of less qualified analysts for time study duties, methods effectiveness will not be given its deserved emphasis.

Another influence has a similar effect. When any analyst approaches a job in progress to make a study, time constraints often preclude experimenting with alternate method patterns. An operator who has become accustomed to one method may be reluctant to change when the reason for doing so seems marginal or unclear. Thus it is unlikely that even the most qualified analyst will consistently produce time studies representing the manual methods effectiveness which could be simulated by predetermined time analysis. This opens the door to a loosening of time values when operators later develop the shortcuts that may have been overlooked during a study.

Masking Recognition of Methods Changes

The MPA analyst making a direct time study will describe how each element was performed, and added details will be shown in a layout sketch. But the few words that can be written in concise spaces of the time study format are by no means comparable to the precise methods description embodied in a detailed predetermined time analysis. Not only might the analyst experience difficulty in knowing whether a methods change has occurred, after years have passed, but there would be added difficulty in proving the point to others.

Cost Considerations

As previously indicated, sweeping claims about the relative costs of direct time study and predetermined time analysis will not hold up. This is because of variations in the complexity of industrial operations, variations in techniques used for work measurement by either system, and some of the hidden costs noted in the previous listing of advantages and disadvantages. In general, the analysis cost with direct time study will exceed that with computer-aided predetermined time applications for many SC/R operations. For LC/LR operations, the reverse will often be true. A chapter to follow will provide time comparisons between specific predetermined time analysis techniques. Using this, MPA analysts with direct time study experience will have a better means of selecting the most cost-effective approach.

Potential Errors in Performance Rating

Not all analysts become consistently effective in rating an operator's performance, even after a training period. Variations from true ratings are more likely to occur at low performance levels, where overrating is common, and at superior performance levels, where underrating is typical.

Job Performance Required before Time Study

It is difficult to prepare reliable standard data for many assembly operations. Because of this, job performance must often come before standards are set when direct time study is the only analysis technique available. In designing paced assembly work stations, this would be a particular disadvantage. With predetermined time analysis, close approximations of each work increment could be derived before the line is manned.

5
Methods and Standards Analysis with Predetermined Motion Times

The need has long been recognized for a way to design manual work sequences, without trial and error on the shop floor, to achieve a practical and superior method. Using direct time study, Frederick Taylor attempted to establish a series of elemental times for a specific category of work. Frank Gilbreth carried the idea further by cataloging basic motions. By spelling his name backwards, he coined the term "therbligs" to designate subdivisions involved. Gilbreth used films, which included a chronometer for timing, to develop simultaneous motion patterns as an aid in the analysis of manual motion combinations.

PRACTICAL APPLICATIONS

The first practical collection of motion time values, along with procedural rules for applying them in methods analysis, was developed about 1930 by A. B. Segur (see Hammond, reference C, 1971). Made available only through his firm's consulting services, Segur's "Motion-Time Analysis" system stressed what was called an "Avoidable Loss" concept. This involved a tabular record, maintained during the process of analysis, which was aimed at recording possible improvement if certain job impediments could be removed.

The "Work Factor" system of predetermined motion times, developed by three industrial engineers with the RCA Corporation, was partially described in an article published in 1945 (see Hammond, 1971). Later applied through consulting services, Work Factor came to be used in a number of electronics manufacturing plants. There have been applications on other work as well.

Following a study of sensitive drill press operations, sponsored in 1940 by Westinghouse Electric Corporation, H. B. Maynard, G. J. Stegemerten, and J. L. Schwab developed a basic predetermined time system that became known as "Methods-Time Measurement," or MTM (see Hammond, 1971). A 1948 book authored by these men described the procedures involved. Unlike MTA or Work Factor, details for the application of MTM were made available to industry, as well as to other consulting firms. Karger and Bayha (1987) provide a thorough description of MTM procedures.

The MTM Association for Standards and Research, located at Ann Arbor, Michigan, for a number of years after 1951 produced through research at the University of Michigan various publications exploring aspects of motion/time fundamentals. Certain refinements in the subdivisions of MTM data resulted from this work. An international MTM Directorate was established in 1957. Offices of the MTM Association—a not-for-profit organization directed by industrial and other members—is currently located in Fair Lawn, New Jersey.

SUMMARY OF MTM FUNDAMENTALS

Whether because of this more open release of MTM for use within industry, or because of its demonstrated merit, the MTM system has become much more widely used than other available predetermined time techniques. It is not within the scope of this book to list the detailed procedural rules for applying MTM or other systems noted. To provide a basis for further discussion, however, a summary is given below of general motion content within the MTM system. The significant procedures involved in applying basic MTM are also summarized. To avoid lengthy definitions, we will omit some of the terminology prescribed by the system, and will use substitute wording instead.

Manual Motions Identified

There are five motion categories that account for most of the time content within any MTM analysis, and there are about the same number of less significant motion groups:

Reach. The actual path of hand or fingers is measured in reaching from one location to another. One of five purposes for the Reach motion must be identified to select time increments for the specified distance, since the purpose has an effect on motion time involved. There is also a refinement to provide for time reductions when a Reach is made or ended with the hand in motion. More than a hundred Reach times are listed as variables.

Move. Measurement is in terms of the actual distance an object is moved. One of three purposes for the motion must be selected, and there is a two-step calculation to increase Move times according to the object weight involved. The system lists eighty-four Move times, each of which could be adjusted by some twenty correction factors for weight involved.

Grasp and Release. The MTM data card lists average times for some ten forms of Grasp. These include a Regrasp value. Consecutive Regrasp motions can serve to increase the Grasp values as conditions justify. Although what is grasped will eventually be released, a separate time increment is applied for the releasing action.

Position. The MTM data lists average values to cover the task of positioning an object, once it has been moved near the point where that action is required. The original MTM values for Position include a spread of eighteen values, along with procedural rules that apply. Research at the University of Michigan served to develop a more systematic way to derive any of forty-five position values that presumably cover the same scope of motions. This "supplementary" MTM data is listed separately on the current data card.

Body, Leg, and Foot Motions. There are sixteen listed categories, three of which can be extended according to specified motion descriptions.

Turn. Defined as a rotation of the forearm, there are thirty-three time increments to be selected according to degrees turned and resistance encountered.

Apply Pressure. This incremental application of force without resulting movement involves two principal categories.

Other Motion Groups. There are subdivided time listings for less significant motions, including Disengage, Eye Motions, and Crank.

Combined or Assisting Motions

Combined motions are those which one body member makes while a separately defined motion is made by the same body member. Examples are Regrasp during Move, Turn during Reach or Move, or Reach during a body motion. Assisting motions are those which one part of the body makes to aid in progress of a primary motion being made at the same time. Examples are shoulder rotation to assist an arm motion, or leaning forward while moving an object farther than the arm's extension. As one would expect, combined motions are simply assigned the time of the longer one. It has been observed that minor assisting motions are generally ignored by most analysts. Those having a significant effect can be handled in line with procedural rules of the system.

Simultaneous Motions

These are motions by two body members, usually the two hands and arms, in which each is performing a separate function. Reference to a simultaneous motion chart is a key step in the procedures for MTM application. For any two motions, this chart indicates whether simultaneous action should be expected of typical operators for either of two conditions involving practice opportunity.

The chart indicates that certain motions involving a higher level of control cannot be performed simultaneously by typical operators. An example would be a Reach by each hand to parts jumbled in a hopper. In such cases, however, the application rules may permit reducing the difficulty level for one of the two motions so that the hand involved—say the right hand—reaches *toward* the intended Grasp location during the controlled Reach by the left hand. But a short controlled Reach by the right hand must then precede the Grasp by that hand.

To illustrate the importance of applying correctly the procedural rules for simultaneous motions, let us consider a simple example. Assume that there is a tray of pegs and a tray of washers directly in front of an operator, with a pegboard located eighteen inches farther to the front, as if on an assembly conveyor line. The operation is to assemble pegs into holes of the board and washers over the pegs. The Reach and Grasp concepts and time values would have to consider points such as:

- the relative difficulty of grasping a jumbled part;
- part size, which affects Grasp difficulty;
- whether the two hands can reach, move or grasp simultaneously; and
- average distance of trays to the point of assembly.

During assembly, there are similar questions which MTM procedures must be able to deal with:

- positioning clearance between pegs and holes of the board;
- positioning clearance between pegs and washers;
- whether the pegs are round, square, triangular, etc.;
- whether the peg ends are rounded or sharp-edged;
- whether two Positions, or one Position and a jumbled Grasp, can be performed simultaneously; and
- how far the pegs are inserted into the board during Position.

Consider first a work pattern that operators would typically apply on their own initiative: equal and opposite hand motions, with a washer

FIGURE 12.
Graphic MTM-1 Analysis of Typical Method.

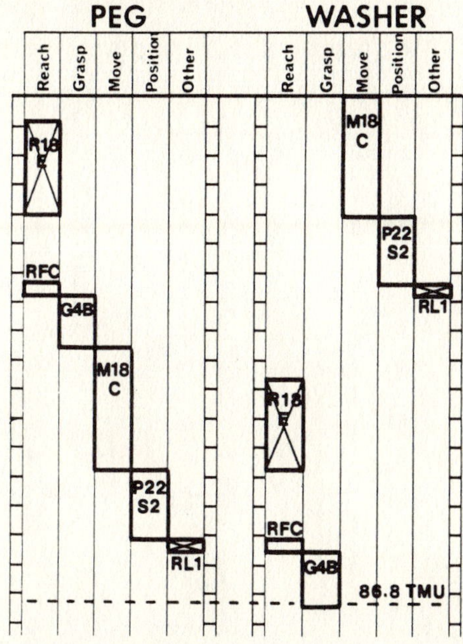

placed by one hand over a peg that has been assembled by the other hand. For a typical selection of variables from the above lists, a standard time for one cycle of.000868 hours or 3.12 seconds, before allowances, could be derived with basic MTM. A graphic picture of the correct analysis is shown by Figure 12. The unmarked blocks represent times for controlled motions, and the blocks with crossed lines represent the less precise motions of reaching or moving toward a location. The blank spaces between consecutive blocks are incremental waiting intervals required to conform with the MTM simultaneous motion chart. Film analysis would be expected to show that such intervals are fairly realistic, which has been confirmed repeatedly for operations of this kind.

Improving the Method

If the analyst gave some attention to the method, without changing the workplace layout or parts involved, the method pictured by Figure 13 could be developed. With two parts in each hand, the operator positions a peg with the right hand, then a washer over a previous peg with the left hand. After a Regrasp motion with each hand, this is repeated. Then there are Reaches by both hands to Grasp a peg and

FIGURE 13.
Graphic MTM-1 Analysis of Improved Manual Method.

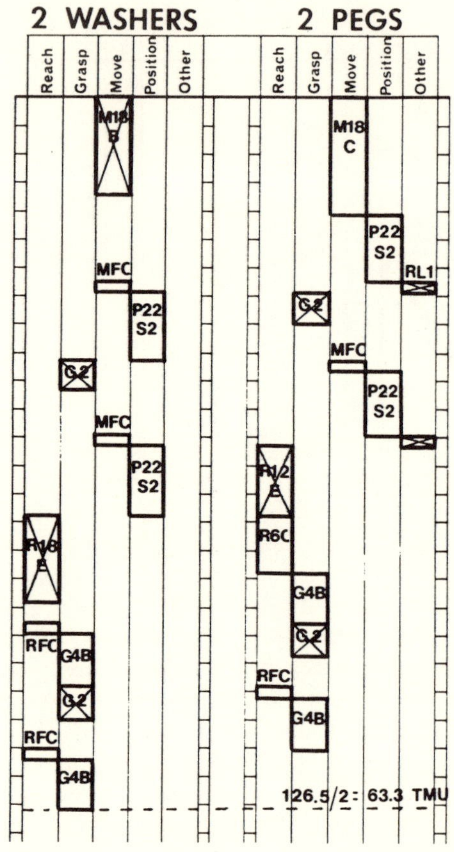

washer. Next, a Regrasp plus another Grasp by each hand. This analysis shows.000633 hours or 2.28 seconds per individual cycle, which is 27 percent less than in Figure 12. If this were a real and repetitive job, the potential saving would certainly be worth the time for operator training.

If the same predetermined time analysis technique were applied to evaluate other possibilities, the analyst could properly consider the automated feeding of parts down inclined slides, since the equipment cost for simple mechanisms to do this would not be excessive. With minor changes in peg or board design to provide greater positioning clearance, with simple grasping of each part from the open end of slides, and with distances shortened by locating the slides over the belt conveyor, a cycle time of.000305 hours or 1.10 seconds could be derived, which is only 35

FIGURE 14.
Graphic MTM-1 Analysis After Design and Equipment Change.

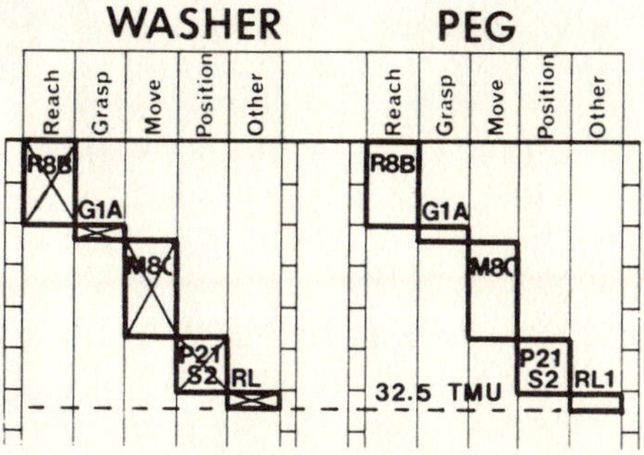

percent of the labor cost for the first method. Figure 14 shows the graphic MTM analysis.

Continuing to speculate regarding this simple task, which does in fact compare realistically with many SC/R operations, the next step to consider would be a fully automated or robotics function. Here we are talking about a sizeable equipment cost. Should this be justified by basing the labor saving on the time value derived in Figure 12, which could well have been the original situation that was observed during a direct time study? Of course not! The comparison should be with data derived in Figure 13, or with a method about like that of Figure 14, involving a much less expensive mechanism. Such comparisons would require applications of a basic predetermined time system.

Conclusions to be Drawn

It is clear that the basic system used should be of tested consistency in deriving time values where many different motion variables are frequently involved. As previously noted, several large companies have made extensive surveys to compare correct MTM analyses of filmed operations with actual times, after the filmed performances had been levelled through extensive performance rating. Within company K listed in the appendix, this was done not only to adjust the inherent performance level of MTM to the target level of performance in a specific control plan, but was also done for the purpose of checking the consistency of standards derived with MTM. For SC/R operations, consistency was observed to be satisfactory with MTM but unsatisfactory with other basic predetermined time systems that were in use within two of the company's plants. Remember that these studies were made by applying the basic, detailed system, referred to currently as MTM–1.

Another conclusion that stands out is that even short studies with

MTM–1 can be complex. This is evident from the graphic analysis in Figure 13, for example, and mistakes made on the usual MTM–1 analysis format are much harder to spot than if they were in chart form like the preceding illustrations. There is a way to minimize such errors, however, as we shall soon discuss.

Assembly operations such as those on paced conveyor lines seem to cry out for analysis with MTM–1 or its equivalent. The short work increments needed for line balancing can properly be analyzed in advance with such a system. But the cost of manually applied MTM–1 is significant, even on short operations. And for much longer jobs the analysis cost becomes prohibitive in comparison with the cost of direct time study.

THE PROLIFERATION OF CONDENSED PREDETERMINED TIME SYSTEMS

Recognizing both the advantages of predetermined time analysis and the cost of applications in basic form, consulting firms and some companies have developed a number of condensed or "second level" systems. Usually said to be "based on MTM," they differ somewhat in their degree of condensation. Many have the following characteristics:

Combination of Motion Categories and Reduction of Variables

Typically, Reach and Grasp are combined into one module given the term Get, or its equivalent. Move and Position are combined into a module called Place, or its equivalent. With MTM–1, over a thousand different time increments could be derived for each of these combinations. With a condensed system known as MTM–2, there are only fifteen possible variables for Get, and the same for Place. In one of the more highly condensed techniques, MTM–3, the condensation goes to the extent of combining Get and Place into Handle, which has a total of only four time variables. Although MTM–1 has relatively few body motions to contend with, the condensed systems reduce these variables also. There are only two within either MTM–2 or MTM–3.

A condensed predetermined time system called MODAPT contains twenty-one commonly used values, five for Reach and Move, six for Get and Place, and ten for specified auxiliary motions. The original version of another condensed system, MOST, utilizes just five interval definitions, the first two of which are applied to substitute for the hundreds of MTM–1 motion times within categories of Reach, Move, Position and Grasp.

Obvious Errors Involved

Condensed predetermined time systems depend on the analyst to decide whether the prescribed motion aggregates can or cannot be performed simultaneously. It is evident that the inflexible combinations referred to above rule out application of the simultaneous motion chart on which MTM–1 depends. As noted, the condensed predetermined time techniques are generally said to be based on MTM–1. A review of the various systems suggest conclusions that may be summarized as follows:

It is misleading to say that any of these systems are based on MTM. How the larger blocks of time were derived is of no consequence. What matters is whether they can be selected to define motions that are part of a given operation, and whether systematic adjustments are possible to account for simultaneous motions. Clearly, these conditions will not be met in a specific set of motions except by accident. There will be very large positive errors and very large negative errors, along with errors of lesser magnitude.

To say that such errors will come close to averaging out when jobs are a minute or so in length (as is typically claimed) would seem to imply greater faith than is justified regarding the mix of motions within industrial operations. To list just one example, a ten-minute operation to assemble electronic components on a printed circuit board consists primarily of many repetitions of the same few motions. A work sampling analyst can rely on the randomness of observations to claim that the results of a sampling study, made without bias, will fall within a specified error percentage. But there is no assurance of randomness in the mix of motions within operations for which time standards are required.

The chance of wide error swings in deriving time standards through application of a condensed system of predetermined motion times suggests strongly that there should be a careful check before any such technique is widely applied. This can be done through comparisons with either direct time studies or MTM–1 by a qualified analyst. In any case, there now is less reason for using the condensed systems, as will be discussed below.

DEVELOPMENT OF COMPUTER-AIDED MTM–1

In chapter 3, a number of potential uses of time standards were listed. It was emphasized, however, that effective labor productivity control can come only if standards are consistently set to represent performance levels which are appropriate for the control plan in effect. The question then arises as to how basic systems such as MTM–1 can compete with direct time study other than where very short operations are involved.

As computer technology and versatility increased in the 1960s, it became apparent that here might be a way to reduce the cost of MTM–1 applications without losing its inherent accuracy and consistency. The MTM Association was working in this direction through its research group. By about 1970, some developments of computerized predetermined times by other groups had occurred. One computer program had been offered for sale, but without any identification of the system it applied. The Work Factor Company had announced a computer-aided system involving as a first step the input of X, Y, and Z coordinates for significant points in the workplace layout. Distances between various points were calculated from this and used thereafter as a basis for Reach or Move distance in the study.

In the early 1970s, I developed, within the Westinghouse Electric Corporation, what was found to be sound logic for automated handling of the slow and tedious part of MTM–1 applications, leaving the analyst free to concentrate on the methods thinking. Get and Place notations were utilized, as in many of the condensed systems, but with provision for automated recognition of MTM–1 motion components involved. A definitive check-out of this logic was made with numerous filmed operations for which MTM–1 analyses had previously been prepared. When these operations were analyzed with Micro-Matic Methods and Measurement Data (4M DATA), as the new system was called, results were in effect identical with previous MTM–1 studies. A computer program was then developed within the company, utilizing the logic steps. Extensive applications were soon made by Westinghouse plants, and a paper titled "The 4M DATA System" was published in 1974 by *Industrial Engineering*.

Later, the computer program was acquired by the MTM Association. Since then, applications of 4M DATA have been made in hundreds of plants through sale of the program by the Association.

In order to further simplify the input of 4M notations for computer processing, I developed in 1982 a way to use the microprocessor pictured in Figure 7 for this purpose. The program involved made possible a less structured input of method details, at the job site, which had not previously been possible. A paper describing how this technique functioned was published by *Industrial Engineering* in August, 1982.

Neither the logic diagrams for the initial 4M DATA system, nor that for the processing of inputs through the microprocessor, have been published formerly. Details for both will be described in chapter 6 and in the appendix, along with a summary of how the computer system is used. Careful review of these logic diagrams by those who have been trained to apply MTM–1 will provide clear evidence that 4M DATA does follow MTM–1 rules of application. And a review of how the system is applied will serve to illustrate the ease with which this can be done.

In addition to MTM–1 precision, along with computer-aided speed of application, there are other features which the 4M program makes possible, such as:

Improvement Indices. There is an automatic calculation for each study of four ratios which indicates the extent to which both hands are being utilized effectively within the analysis. They give clues as to where further improvements can be made.

Applications of Specialized Data. Coded data aggregates, derived either from MTM or direct time study, can be stored within the original 4M program and applied through input of the codes.

Manual Functions Performed During Process Intervals. Process times can be entered, along with concurrent entry of a set of motion codes. The 4M program will list both but will apply the time for the longer of the two.

Automated Retrieval of Previously Analyzed Elements.

Adjustment of MTM–1 to Fit Control Plan. Once the factor has been indicated for adjustment of MTM–1 to define standards for a specific control plan, the manual times (excluding process times) are adjusted accordingly.

Alternate Codes for Motion Aggregates. For ultimate application speed, where some accuracy can be sacrificed, it is possible to make inputs of shortened Get and Place notations which do not evaluate certain workplace details that are normally considered. Not only does this involve less mental effort than the application of MTM–2 data, for example, but the computer program will analyze the two-handed interactions in line with MTM–1 rules. However, those who have used 4M DATA state that the input of precise Get and Place notations (defined in the next chapter) requires little added time and is generally unnecessary for ease of application.

Allowance Calculations. Indicated allowances are applied automatically at the end of a study.

POTENTIAL ADVANTAGES OF PREDETERMINED TIME APPLICATIONS

At this point, let us assume that there are ways of applying MTM–1 without involving excessive analytical time. (The next chapter will reinforce this assumption.) Advantages are as follows:

- Time standards on hand before the job starts.
- Improved methods analysis capabilities. (True only if the basic system is applied with care.)
- More precise methods definitions for recognition of future changes. (Only if the basic system is applied will any but major changes be clearly flagged.)

- Potential relief from confrontational problems brought by time study. (Unless labor representatives and supervisors are given clear evidence that the system is reliable, this potential advantage may not be realized.)
- A consistent performance level represented by standards. (Only if the basic system is applied carefully, after adequate training.)
- Correct performance level built into time standards. (Only if the system has previously been adjusted to fit the control plan involved, and the basic system is applied carefully.)
- Reduced cost to develop methods/time analyses. (Depends on cycle length, whether 4M DATA techniques are applied, whether the applications are for standard data, and other factors.)
- Reduced cost to develop and maintain standard data. (The automatic retrieval of data elements may not be a viable answer in many cases, as will be explored in a chapter to follow. When specific elements are revised, automatic standard data corrections may be possible in advanced applications, as will be discussed later.)
- Improved basis for balancing operator work assignments on paced lines. (Only if the basic system is applied.)
- Easier preparation of operation methods charts for SC/R jobs. (Significant only if applicable 4M DATA techniques are utilized.

POTENTIAL DISADVANTAGES

There are many ways that predetermined time analyses can prove unrealistic, costly, and unacceptable, as noted by qualifications in the above listing of potential advantages. The best approach for methods/ time analysis in LC/LR operations is usually a combination of computer-aided techniques, including both predetermined times and direct time study.

6
Computer-aided Application of Basic MTM

The purpose of this chapter is to show how MTM–1 can be applied easier and faster, so that there will be little reason to consider the condensed versions of predetermined times that lack precision and consistency.

At the beginning of chapter 3, four potential uses of time standards were listed that require work measurement precision. Later in this book, we will discuss several different plans for labor productivity control in which these applications of time standards are involved. Any of the control plans would be doomed to mediocrity, if not complete failure, unless time standards were reasonably consistent and in line with the target level defined by the specific control plan.

One question that might properly be asked is: "Why concentrate on MTM–1 in discussing computerized predetermined time analysis?" A partial answer is the previously noted fact that this system has become much more widely used than any of the others, and procedural details are readily available. There is general agreement among its users that MTM–1 provides consistent results, and the way that one company tested this has been described. Another part of the answer is the availability of 4M DATA, the tested system that uses computer technology to minimize the clerical effort and cost of MTM–1 applications. The program, which can be purchased from the MTM Association, is applicable in various computer environments.

To be convinced that 4M DATA is a fast, practical way to apply MTM–1 requires an understanding of how the system functions. It is beyond the scope of this book to provide complete reference material about it, but several illustrations follow that can help explain the general approach involved. It has been the policy of the MTM Association to solicit, through periodic group meetings with 4M users, various ideas for adapting the system to fit specific needs. There has been some rearrangement of the data input format, for example, without change in notations or program logic. The illustrations that follow in this chapter, as well as logic diagrams in the appendix section, are based on how the system was initially developed. The 4M program provides for storage and retrieval of selected elements. There has been considerable emphasis by 4M users on data retrieval techniques as a basis for standard data application. Our coverage of this subject will be in a following chapter concerning the broader aspects of standard data development.

THE 4M DATA TIME VALUES

Figure 15 lists motion times stored within the 4M program. They do not have to be referred to in applying the system, but it is of interest to know that all are basic MTM–1 time values. There will be some strangeness here to MTM–1 analysts, which the following explanations should clear up:

- Entries under headings for Get and Place (G11, G42, P132, etc,) are the 4M motion aggregates to be described shortly.
- All times are in "micro-units" (MU), defined as one-tenth of the TMU values within MTM–1, or.000001 hour. This means that the decimal entries required to list MTM–1 time increments can be omitted with 4M DATA.
- The alphabetical entries that follow each comma under headings for Get and Place are not part of the computer programming requirements. They are simply a shorthand way to identify Grasp and Position times which they follow, without requiring use of specific MTM–1 codes that are in many cases quite lengthy. Figure 17 will serve to explain this point further. Thus, 4M DATA training does not require knowing MTM–1 notations.
- The formula listed for "Added Time with Weight" is an alternate way to calculate the same values that are listed on the MTM–1 data card.
- Release values, which involve only a finger motion of less than one inch, are included within the Get aggregates, although they occur later. A review of numerous filmed SC/R operations showed that only one-half as many Releases were additive in the analyses (not overlapped by other motions) as there were Grasp values which were additive. Thus, half of the MTM–1 Release time has been included with all Get aggregates involving Grasp. A subsequent analysis with 4M DATA of the same films showed that errors in this approach were negligible in all cases.
- The Position time values are those for "supplementary data" on the MTM–1 data card, not the earlier values.

FIGURE 15.
Motion Times, 4M DATA.

G01	G0 G02		G03		P01	P0 P02	P03
RA	RB	RC	RE	DIST.	MA	MB	MC
20	20	20	20	F	20	20	20
25	25	36	24	1	25	29	34
40	40	59	38	2	36	46	52
53	53	73	53	3	49	57	67
61	64	84	68	4	61	69	80
65	78	97	74	5	73	80	92
70	86	101	80	6	81	89	103
74	93	108	87	7	89	97	111
79	101	115	93	8	97	106	118
83	108	122	99	9	105	115	127
87	115	129	105	10	113	122	135
92	122	136	112	11	121	128	144
96	129	142	118	12	129	134	152
101	137	149	124	13	137	140	161
105	144	156	130	14	144	146	169
110	151	163	136	15	152	152	178
114	158	170	142	16	160	158	187
119	165	177	149	17	168	164	196
123	172	184	155	18	176	170	204
127	179	191	161	19	184	176	213
131	186	198	167	20	192	182	221
136	194	205	174	21	200	188	230
140	201	212	180	22	208	194	238
145	209	219	186	23	216	200	247
149	215	225	192	24	224	206	255
154	222	232	198	25	232	212	264
158	229	239	204	26	240	218	273
163	237	246	211	27	248	225	282
167	244	253	217	28	255	231	290
171	251	260	223	29	263	237	299
175	258	267	229	30	271	243	307
184	273	281	242	32	286	256	324
192	287	295	254	34	302	268	341
201	302	309	267	36	317	281	358
209	316	323	279	38	333	293	375
218	331	337	292	40	348	306	392

PLACE

P110	MC+ 34,s	P225	MC+205,x
P111	MC+ 66,s	P226	MC+252,x
P112	MC+ 77,s	(P227 P2D	MC+263,x
P113	MC+ 88,s	P228	MC+275,x
P115	MC+ 90,t	P230	MC+202,w
P116	MC+122,t	P231	MC+249,w
P117	MC+133,t	P232	MC+260,w
P118	MC+144,t	P233	MC+272,w
P120	MC+103,u	P235	MC+258,x
(P121 P1	MC+135,u	P236	MC+305,x
P122	MC+146,u	P237	MC+316,x
P123	MC+157,u	P238	MC+328,x
P125	MC+159,v	P310	MC+ 95,w
(P126 P1D	MC+191,v	P311	MC+163,w
P127	MC+202,v	(P312 P3	MC+187,w
P128	MC+213,v	P313	MC+210,w
P130	MC+155,u	P315	MC+151,x
P131	MC+187,u	P316	MC+219,x
P132	MC+198,u	(P317 P3D	MC+243,x
P133	MC+209,u	P318	MC+266,x
P135	MC+211,v	P320	MC+173,y
P136	MC+243,v	P321	MC+241,y
P137	MC+254,v	P322	MC+265,y
P138	MC+265,v	P323	MC+288,y
P210	MC+ 72,u	P325	MC+229,z
P211	MC+119,u	P326	MC+297,z
P212	MC+130,u	P327	MC+321,z
P213	MC+142,u	P328	MC+344,z
P215	MC+128,v	P330	MC+229,y
P216	MC+175,v	P331	MC+297,y
P217	MC+186,v	P332	MC+321,y
P218	MC+198,v	P333	MC+344,y
P220	MC+149,w	P335	MC+285,z
(P221 P2	MC+196,w	P336	MC+353,z
P222	MC+207,w	P337	MC+377,z
P223	MC+219,w	P338	MC+400,z

WEIGHT ADDER = 5 + 3.5w + .011wT
(w=wt./hand >2.5#; T=mu, no wt.)

GET

G11	RA+ 30,a
(G12 G1	RB+ 30,a
G13	RC+ 45,c
G2	56,b
G3	RA+ 56,z
G41	RC+ 83,d
(G42 G4	RC+101,d
G43	RC+139,d

BODY MOTIONS

FM		85
FMP		191
LM	06	71
LM	08	95
LM	10	119
LM	12	143
SSC1		170
SSC2		341
B		290
S		290
KOK		290
AB		319
AS		319
AKOK		319
KBK		694
AKBK		767
SIT		347
STD		434
TBC1		186
TBC2		372
WP	#p	150p
WPO	#p	170p

EF = 73
ETxx=9.5/inch,
16" from eye
(max. 200 mu)

PRESS
APA-106
APB-162
AF-34
DM-42
RLF-30

DISENGAGE
D1E- 40,h
D2E- 75,j
D3E-229,x
D1D- 57,h
D2D-118,k
D3D-347,x

TURN		
T1S-28	T1M- 44	T1L- 84
T2S-41	T2M- 65	T2L-123
T3S-54	T3M- 85	T3L-162
T4S-68	T4M-106	T4L-204
T5S-81	T5M-127	T5L-243
T6S-94	T6M-148	T6L-282

THE 4M DATA NOTATIONS

Get or Place

Over 90 percent of the notations required for analysis will be for Get or Place motion aggregates. Consider first the Place notation, as defined in Figure 16. In most cases, three digits following the letter *P* will be used to define the Position involved. The next two digits indicate the distance of Move. The last digits shown for this notation in Figure 16 are omitted for an object weighing 2.5 pounds or less. If over that amount, the effective weight per hand is entered. A Place notation of P123/08/20 indicates a Move of eight inches, with Position involving clearance, degree of symmetry, and secondary engage as indicated by the diagram, and with weight per hand of twenty pounds.

The computer program will select the Move purpose, or "Case," when the Place involves a Position. For Move notions without a Position, only two digits are needed after the letter *P*, with the first being zero and the second indicating the Move purpose.

The Get notation requires an entry of only two digits plus the Reach distance. The first digit indicates the kind of Grasp involved. The second digit is a modifier, as defined by Figure 16.

For those who have not had training in the application of MTM–1, additional background material will be needed before these notations are clear in all respects. With training in 4M DATA fundamentals, and after a few hours of practice, decisions about Get or Place notations can be made quickly after the general method has been determined. Distances can be closely estimated without the need for measurement.

The shortened Get and Place notations of G1, G4, P2, etc., as shown by Figure 15, may be entered when maximum analysis speed is required. The computer program will assign to these notations the average values shown by brackets in Figure 15. Subsequent analysis by the program is the same as if P121 were entered instead of P1, for example, and the resulting error is quite small. This is rarely necessary, however, since the complete notations become obvious when observing the workplace.

Other Notations

For the small percentage of 4M DATA analysis components that are not comprised of Get or Place (Body Motions, Turn, Apply Pressure, etc.), the applicable notations are shown within Figure 15.

HOW THE PROGRAM HANDLES SIMULTANEOUS MOTIONS

Figure 17 pictures the simultaneous motion rules that have been incorporated within the 4M program. This chart includes MTM–1 supple-

FIGURE 16.
Get and Place Notations Used in 4M DATA.

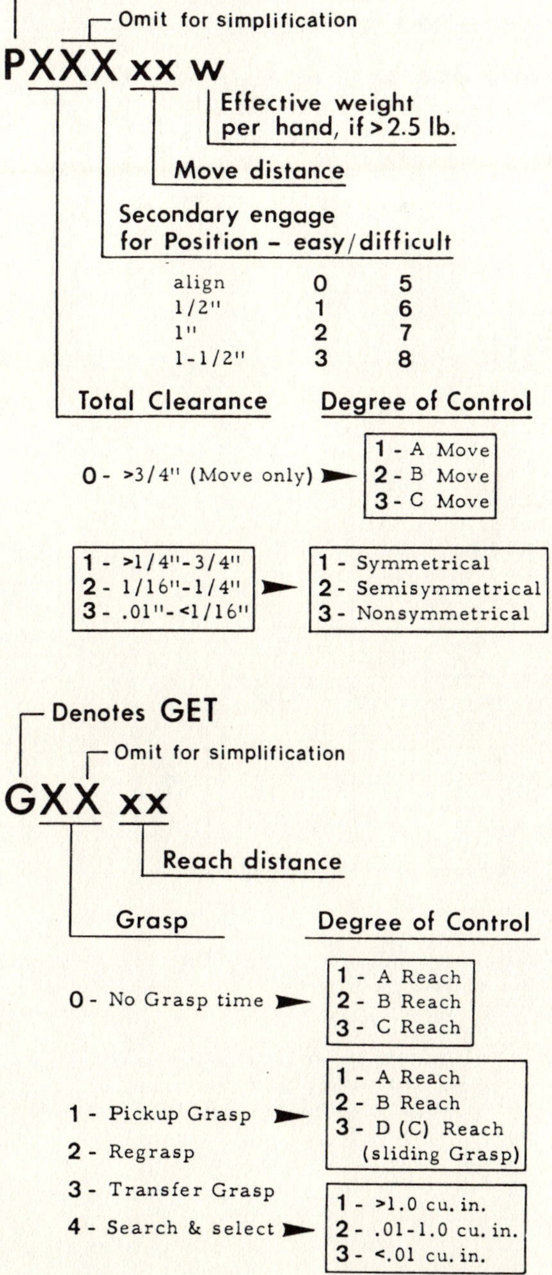
Denotes PLACE
Omit for simplification
PXXX xx w
Effective weight per hand, if >2.5 lb.
Move distance
Secondary engage for Position – easy/difficult
align 0 5
1/2" 1 6
1" 2 7
1-1/2" 3 8
Total Clearance
Degree of Control
0 - >3/4" (Move only)
1 - A Move
2 - B Move
3 - C Move
1 - >1/4"-3/4"
2 - 1/16"-1/4"
3 - .01"-<1/16"
1 - Symmetrical
2 - Semisymmetrical
3 - Nonsymmetrical
Denotes GET
Omit for simplification
GXX xx
Reach distance
Grasp
Degree of Control
0 - No Grasp time
1 - A Reach
2 - B Reach
3 - C Reach
1 - Pickup Grasp
2 - Regrasp
3 - Transfer Grasp
4 - Search & select
1 - A Reach
2 - B Reach
3 - D (C) Reach (sliding Grasp)
1 - >1.0 cu. in.
2 - .01-1.0 cu. in.
3 - <.01 cu. in.

FIGURE 17.
Simultaneous Motion Rules Applied by 4M DATA Program.

RA		RB		RC		RE		MA		MB		MC		a	
RA	4	RB	3	RC	1	RE	4	MA	4	MB	3	MC	1	a	4
RB	4	RC	3	RE	4	MA	4	MB	4	MC	3	a	4	b	4
RC	4	RE	4	MA	3	MB	4	MC	4	a	4	b	4	c	4
RE	4	MA	4	MB	3	MC	4	a	4	b	4	c	1	d	4
MA	4	MB	3	MC	1	a	4	b	4	c	3	d	0	h	4
MB	4	MC	3	a	4	b	4	c	4	d	1	h	2	j	0
MC	4	a	4	b	4	c	4	d	4	h	4	j	0	k	0
a	4	b	4	c	1	d	4	h	4	j	4	k	0	s	4
b	4	c	3	d	0	h	4	j	4	k	2	s	0	t	4
c	4	d	1	h	2	j	4	k	4	s	2	t	0	u	4
d	4	h	4	j	0	k	4	s	4	t	2	u	0	v	0
h	4	j	4	k	0	s	4	t	4	u	2	v	0	w	4
j	4	k	2	s	0	t	4	u	4	v	0	w	0	x	0
k	4	s	2	t	0	u	4	v	2	w	2	x	0	y	0
s	4	t	2	u	0	v	2	w	4	x	0	y	0	z	0
t	4	u	2	v	0	w	4	x	2	y	0	z	0		
u	4	v	0	w	0	x	2	y	2	z	0				
v	2	w	2	x	0	y	2	z	0						
w	4	x	0	y	0	z	0								
x	2	y	0	z	0										
y	2	z	0												
z	0														

t-z		s		k		j		h		d		c		b	
														b	4
												c	1	c	4
										d	0	d	1	d	4
								h	4	h	0	h	0	h	4
						j	4	j	4	j	0	j	0	j	0
				k	4	k	4	k	4	k	0	k	0	k	0
		s	1	s	0	s	0	s	0	s	0	s	0	s	4
t-z	0	t	0	t	0	t	0	t	0	t	0	t	0	t	4
		u	0	u	0	u	0	u	0	u	0	u	0	u	4
		v	0	v	0	v	0	v	0	v	0	v	0	v	0
		w	0	w	0	w	0	w	0	w	0	w	0	w	4
		x	0	x	0	x	0	x	0	x	0	x	0	x	0
		y	0	y	0	y	0	y	0	y	0	y	0	y	0
		z	0	z	0	z	0	z	0	z	0	z	0	z	0

Practice		MINIMUM FOR SIMO
Yes	No	
1	3	Within normal vision
2	4	Outside normal vision

STEPS:
Find number N_1 in matrix.
Find N_2 for motions X,Y.
If $N_1 \leq N_2$, X can be simo with Y.

Consider following to be simo with other motions listed on same line: Turn, AP, ET, EF. List Body Motions separately.

FIGURE 18.
4M DATA Analysis for Short Element.

ELEM NO	LINE NO	LEFT HAND MOTIONS LITERALS	NOTATION	DIST	WT	LEAD H	RIGHT HAND MOTIONS NOTATION	DIST	WT.	LITERALS	PROCESS (TMU)	FREQUENCY DEC.	DIR CODE
3	X	ASSEMBLE 2 PARTS TO HUB, 1 PART TO PREV. ASSY.											E
	1	BEARING IN HUB	P131	14			G42	8		RETAINER			B
	2	FITTING	G42	12			P121	8		RETAINER			B
	3						G11	12		PREVIOUS ASSY			B
	4	FITTING IN HUB	P216	10			P01	10		ASSY. TO LH			
	5						P02T	20		ASSY. ASIDE			

mentary Position data, whereas the simo chart on the MTM data card covers older Position data. However, the chart of Figure 17 corresponds with basic MTM theory as specified by MTM Research Report 105. Alphabetical listings on the chart correspond with similar references opposite the time values in Figure 15. They can be used for manual analysis, without having to learn or apply the lengthy MTM–1 notations for specific Positions or other motions. 4M manual analyses are made graphically, as in Figures 12–14, although times and motion identifications would be penciled within the blocks of the previous illustrations. Of course, the normal use of 4M avoids any need for manual analysis of this kind. (It might be noted, however, that the MTM analyst at appendix plant 22 began using this graphic technique until his computer facilities became available, and he found it to be easier than the usual way in which MTM–1 is applied.)

Application of the rules governing simultaneous motions is made by the 4M program. The complex logic patterns involved are summarized at the conclusion of this chapter and illustrated in detail within the appendix section.

The Listing of Motion Aggregates

There are optional ways to prepare a 4M DATA analysis. One way is to record the notations on a printed format, for later input by a keypunch operator. Figure 18 illustrates the body of a concise format that provides for element headings followed by line data. 4M users will be familiar with an alternate format, somewhat more detailed, that is applied where the intention is to code elements for possible storage and later retrieval. The program logic for data analysis is the same in each case. Several heading entries are not shown in the illustration. Most of these involve literal data, typically required to identify any study. There are a few entries within the heading that are necessary for computer action. These include:

- The MTM adjustment factor (100 percent for low-task incentives involving SC/R operations, less than 100 percent for similar operations in some other control plans referred to within chapter 3, etc.)
- YES or NO for "practice opportunity," which conforms with MTM–1.
- Allowance value, to be applied at end of study.

The element will continue until the analyst enters another code *E* in the last column of the format shown, along with a literal heading for the next element.

How the Program Analyzes a "Set" of Motions

When two notations are entered on the same line of the input format, the analyst has signified that the motions involved can be performed simultaneously if so authorized by the rules pictured in Figure 17. In many cases, the motion aggregates listed on several adjacent lines can be performed in their listed sequence for each hand, without any conflict in relation to motions of the other hand except as may be caused from restrictions imposed by the simo rules. In such cases, a bracket code (letter *B*) is entered in the last column of the format for each line within the motion set. Without such a code, the program will not intermix the motions on one line with those on an adjacent line.

In Figure 18, the first three lines are bracketed as one motion set. The set of motions on line 4 can be simultaneous with each other if the simo rules permit. Line 5 is a separate action that must come after prior motions have been completed. There would be a major difference in standard time for the element if the motion sets had not been identified. It can be seen from this illustration that the 4M DATA analyst has complete control regarding the method he or she intends to portray.

Figure 19 pictures a manually developed MTM–1 analysis for this same element. There are twenty notations on thirteen lines, compared with eight notations in the 4M analysis, on five lines. Those familiar with MTM–1 applications will realize that considerable mental and clerical effort was required to develop what is shown by Figure 19. To develop the 4M input of Figure 18 required knowledge of what the operation involved, but all of the notations could be entered quickly and without reference to any procedural data.

The Computer Printout

Figure 20 shows the analysis printout of this simple element. The total time is the same as in Figure 19. Subtotals are listed for each set of motions. Note the value of 73 percent calculated as the "Motion As-

FIGURE 19.
MTM-1 Analysis of Data in Figure 18.

LEFT-HAND MOTIONS		TMU	RIGHT-HAND MOTIONS	
Bearing toward hub	M9B	11.5	R8C	To retainer
		9.1	G4B	Retainer
Bearing to hub	M5C	9.2	M8B	Retainer toward hub
Bearing in hub	P21NS2	18.7		
	RL1	2.0	MfC	Retainer to hub
Toward fitting	R12E	13.5	P21SS2	Retainer in hub
To fitting	RfC	2.0	RL1	
Fitting	G4B	9.6	R12A	To prev. assy. in fixt.
		2.0	G1A	Hub
Fitting to hub	M10C	13.5	M10A	Toward other hand
Fitting in hub	P22SE	11.9		
During Position	G2	5.6		
		18.2	M20B	Assembly aside (toss)
	TOTAL	126.8		

FIGURE 20.
4M DATA Printout of Input from Figure 18.

```
                         PRACTICE OPPORTUNITY                 ALLOWANCE  .08
              LH MOTIONS  RH OR BODY MOTIONS        FREQ. LH      RH TOTAL
                                   PROCESS TIME OR DATA INSERT
001 ASSEMBLE 2 PARTS TO HUB, 1 PART TO PREV. ASSY.

   01 BRG. IN HUB     P131-14   G42 - 8  RETAINER                            B
   02 FITTING         G42 -12   P121- 8  RETAINER                            B
   03                           G11 -12  PREVIOUS ASSY.   633     603     776B
   04 FITTING IN HUB P216-10    P01 -10  ASSY TO LH       310     113     310
   05                           P02T-20  ASSY ASIDE               182     182
                                                  ST                     1268
TOTAL     1268 MU STANDARD TIME    .08220 MIN.  RMB 61%
STANDARD TIME .00137 HOURS           MAI 73%    GRA 12%    PROC  0%
CYCLES PER HOUR    729.9                        POS 26%
```

signment Index." This quantifies the forced waiting time involved by the two hands, either because the analyst found no action for one hand to perform (as on line 5), or because of simo chart restrictions due to the types of motions involved. The other percentage values show that grasping time was a minor part of the job (12 percent), but attention should be given the workplace design in at least two ways: attempt to

FIGURE 21.
Input of Short Element to Computer, from Microprocessor.

```
*3    C42,8     F121,8     C11,12    FF131,14    CC42,12
*     F01,10    FF216,10   *         F02H,20
```

reduce the motion distances, because Reaches and Moves were 61 percent of the total; and question the Position components (26 percent), to make this function easier if possible.

ALTERNATE WAYS TO DEVELOP A 4M DATA ANALYSIS

A portable microprocessor, such as that pictured in Figure 7, can be used for direct input of 4M notations on the shop floor. Heading data and element descriptions are listed on the pad attached to the unit. Information required by the computer program to make a 4M analysis is then keyed into the unit. Figure 21 shows inputs made with microprocessor for the same element covered in Figure 18.

When data from the portable microprocessor is transferred to the computer system, a short, "front-end" program adjusts the data so it can be handled by the regular 4M program. Significant points are as follows:

- Available keys on the microprocessor are substituted to designate Get, Place, and other 4M prefixes for the right or left hands. A review of what is shown by Figures 21 and 18 will make this clear.
- The preliminary program will revise and rearrange data to develop the correct format. Without literal data, the computer will supply any of thirty "action words" derived from the notations (Get, Place, Reach, Move, Walk, Turn, etc.).
- Asterisks are used with numbers to identify element separations. By themselves, the asterisks separate motion sets.
- Motion aggregates within a set may be entered in any order, if in sequence for the hand involved. Instead of the entry shown in Figure 21 for the motion set of Figure 18, an alternate entry could have been C42,8 FF131,14 F121,8 CC42,12 C11,12. This frees the analyst from unnecessary regimentation as the data input is made.

The front-end program for microprocessor entries is not part of the MTM Association's 4M DATA program. From the logic diagram in the appendix, however, an MPA group could develop the needed interacting program to fit their own needs and electronic equipment.

Two ways have been illustrated for making 4M DATA analyses. A third possibility is to input the data directly into a computer terminal. This has been accomplished in several different ways, while still using

FIGURE 22.
Analysis Times Using Different Ways to Apply MTM-1.

	Manually Applied MTM-1 (minutes)	4M DATA, Terminal Input (minutes)	4M DATA, Batch Processing (minutes)	4M DATA, Microprocessor Input (minutes)
1. Visualize general method	3	3	3	3
2. Record data or notes at job	4	2	2	1
3. Develop detailed analysis	20	4	2	- -
4. MPA time, computer entry	- -	0.2	- -	0.2
5. Keypunch requirements	- -	- -	yes	- -
ESTIMATED TOTALS	24	9.2	7	4.2

essentially the same format as for the written input. An easier approach would be to apply the front-end logic referred to for use with the portable microprocessor. Developing the analysis by keying directly into a terminal has few advantages, however, since it must be done in the office and requires more of the analyst's time. But it does facilitate getting results promptly.

TIME REQUIRED BY THE ANALYST FOR 4M DATA APPLICATIONS

Just as the analysis time for manually applied MTM–1 varies greatly according to the type of work involved, so does that for 4M DATA. The preceding chapters have stressed that methods improvement and precision of results are the most significant aspects of predetermined time applications, but the analytical costs must not be overlooked. Now that different 4M analysis techniques have been illustrated or discussed, it may be helpful to estimate the time for analyzing the short element described by Figures 18–21. The collective estimates of several qualified analysts are shown in Figure 22.

Those who are promoting a specific predetermined time technique tend to understate the total analytical times in making comparisons such as those shown above. With the fastest technique, whether with microprocessor input or something else, step 1 is still a requirement if results are to be anything more than a wild guess. The differences in MPA costs for four different ways of applying MTM–1 to analyze SC/R operations are shown as estimates in this illustration.

FIGURE 23.
Typical Motion Patterns in One Line of 4M DATA Analysis.

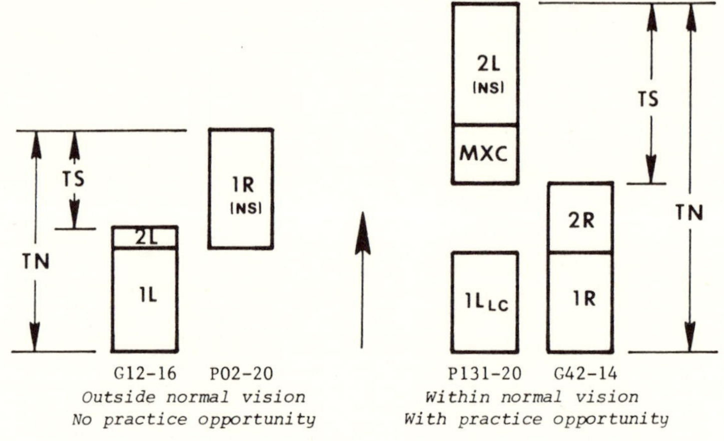

THE COMPUTER PROGRAM FOR 4M DATA ANALYSIS

Logic diagrams in the appendix will be of interest to those who want conclusive evidence that the 4M program does apply MTM–1 correctly. At this point, a summary is given of the functions involved in the analysis process. There are five logic segments within the program, as follows:

1. *Establishing a Direction for the Analysis to Take.* As previously noted, each line of the input is considered a set of motions that are independent of previous or subsequent motions, unless a code is applied to show that adjacent lines are a continuing set. In the first analysis step, the program looks at beginning motions in the set, after interpreting the motion aggregates recorded by 4M notations. If there are notations on the first line for just one hand, the time content for that line is readily apparent. If there are notations for both hands, the beginning motions serve to indicate a choice between steps 2 and 3 for subsequent analysis within the program.

2. *Beginning Motions not Subject to Revision.* If there is no possibility of Reaches or Moves being reduced to a lower Case, the analysis is simplified. The notations on one line can refer to as many as four motions (two for each hand), or as few as one motion for only one hand. With step 1 having ruled out the latter situation, there are still some thirty-four possible configurations of motions for the first line, depending on how the simultaneous motion chart (embodied within the program) may restrict interaction between the two hands. The left side of Figure 23 pictures graphically just one of the motion patterns that may be identified. The rules say that motion 1L cannot be simultaneous with 1R, but 2L and 1R can be performed simultaneously. Logic illustrated in the

appendix will determine that this situation exists. The program will then identify and store for later use the following information:

- Motion times, each hand (TL, TR). These times are needed for calculation of the improvement indices. In the example at the left of Figure 23, TL = 1L + 2L, and TR = 1R.
- Next motion to be considered for simultaneous action with a motion by the other hand (NS), if a continuation of the motion set has been indicated by the bracket code. In the example, a portion of 1R extends beyond 2L. Thus, NS = motion 1R.
- Motion time available for interaction with a motion by the other hand, if the set continues (TS). In the example, TS = 1R − 2L. If TS is less than 30 MU, the program will not look for a motion interaction by the other hand, even if the set continues. This rule was built into the program to avoid differing from approaches normally taken by competent MTM–1 analysts.
- Net time (TN), if no continuation of the motion set. For the example at the left, TN = 1L + 1R.

3. *When the First Motion in Notations for Either or Both Hands Involves Case C or Case D Reaches or Moves*. This is a frequent occurrence, since both jumbled Grasp motions and Position motions are preceded by closely controlled (Case C or D) motions. As indicated previously, the MTM–1 procedures permit reducing one of the controlled motions to a lower level of control, if this would lead to simultaneous action. There must always be a short, controlled motion after this is done and before the Grasp or Position. In the example on the right of Figure 23, motion 1L has been reduced to a lower Case during the full extent of the shorter controlled motion, 1R. Since the lower Case motion ($1L_{LC}$) cannot be simo with 2R, any remaining distance must be allocated to the controlled Reach or Move, MXC (Move, Case C, distance X). The complex logic required to handle the wide variety of motion interactions in this category is illustrated in the appendix.

The following data will be recognized by the program for the example shown at the right side of Figure 23: TL = $1L_{LC}$ + MXC + 2L, TR = 1R + 2R, NS = 2L, and TS = MXC + 2L. A question might be raised concerning the listing for NS, since the motion MXC is also to be considered for simo interaction by the right hand if the motion set were bracketed to continue. However, it can be observed that the MTM–1 simo chart is always just as restrictive of the jumbled Grasp or Position as for the preceding Reach or Move. Thus, only motion 2L in this example requires a simo check if the motion set shows a succeeding entry for the right hand.

4. *More than One Line Bracketed as a Continuing Set of Motions*. When there is no obstacle or other condition to interfere with successive mo-

tions by the two hands, code B is applied to show that consecutive lines of 4M motion aggregates should be handled as a continuing motion set. (Code C may be entered to differentiate between two adjacent motion sets.) The program logic to accomplish this becomes very complex, as shown in the appendix, just as the manual analysis with MTM–1 becomes even more tedious and slow. It is where motion aggregates of this kind are encountered that the 4M DATA system provides maximum improvement over the manual approach, both in analytical speed and accuracy.

5. *Process Time Analysis.* It was previously noted that the 4M program permits the entry of motions that could be performed during a process interval, along with the previously measured process time. The program lists the process time, compares this with manual time, enters manual time that can be done during the process interval, and lists any remaining manual time as an adder following the process.

FOR REFERENCE BY THOSE WITH PRIOR MTM–1 TRAINING

In developing 4M DATA, there were two primary objectives: (1) simplicity and ease of application; and (2) precision on a par with that of MTM–1. It was possible to achieve both of these objectives. Those who have had MTM training will recognize from previous illustrations a few condensations and revisions in 4M DATA, as compared with corresponding MTM training material. So that it will be clear that these differences are not significant, an attempt has been made to list below all of the reasons for discrepancies that could occur between 4M DATA analyses and correctly developed manual MTM–1 analyses of the same motion patterns:

- Release increments are applied by 4M on an average basis, as previously noted.
- Weight values are applicable with 4M to the nearest pound (above 2.5 pounds), rather than in steps specified on the MTM data card.
- Distance values with 4M are applicable to the nearest inch, including values above thirty inches when they occur.
- 4M uses the supplementary MTM–1 Position values, which are easier to apply and cover more variations. MTM research data supports these as being interchangeable with the original Position data.
- Position clearance is redefined in terms of total clearance. In effect, this does not differ from MTM–1.
- 4M DATA provides for reference to "difficult" positioning by the automatic application of separate Regrasp time values, as required with the supplementary Position data.

- Volumetric definitions are given for "Search and Select" Grasp categories. Obtained by multiplying the three separate dimensions on the MTM data card, this makes applications more consistent without introducing real differences.
- For simplicity, the illustrated 4M time values do not include the rarely used G1C family of Grasps, but 4M procedures provide alternate ways to achieve the same numerical result when such motions are encountered.
- Again for simplicity, 4M provides a rule of thumb for converting Reach or Move times to "in motion" times, very close to MTM–1 times.
- 4M simo-chart rules for two R-C motions performed together comply with recommendations in MTM research report 105, which differ slightly from the MTM–1 data card.
- For simplicity, 4M notations for Turn identify 30° increments, and Sidestep distances other than the usual twelve inches are not included.

7
Developing and Applying Standard Time Data

Definition

Standard time data consists of a composite arrangement of times derived through work measurement, which can be used to develop standard times for a specified category of operations. The data base involved may have been collected through any combination of direct time study, predetermined time analysis, or specialized work sampling techniques. Synthesis of the data elements into usable form may have been through logical arrangement by the analyst, through mathematical analysis, or through identification of elements for later selection. The end product may be in the form of tabular information, formulas, or coded elements. While the data so derived may be applied in various ways, expedient methods of application are easy-to-use "pick-off sheets," computerized derivations from data inputs, or computerized selection of coded elements.

Objectives

The primary objectives that make the use of standard data imperative, wherever its development is practical, are to reduce work measurement costs and provide a way to denote time standards before the work is started. Other objectives are noted below.

- The accumulation of related data elements tends to level out possible inaccuracies, and time standards derived from the completed data become more consistent.
- To apply standard data correctly requires that the analyst first identify the method or method parameters involved (distances, weights, equipment

used, speeds/feeds, etc.). This can and should result in either a listing by the analyst of methods specifications or an automated listing by the computer system.

- If standard data development is properly done, the synthesis procedure will include a precise record of how the separate elements were combined to make up the data package. When methods change over time, how such changes affect the data compilation will then be clear, and time standards can be revised. This possible advantage can revert to a serious disadvantage if data maintenance is not given careful attention. Further discussion of this point will come later.

Standard data applications are made to cover operations for which time values have not previously been derived. When such operations repeat later, the same manufacturing information would be used unless there have been reasons for change.

Requirements for Skill, Ingenuity, and Common Sense

The analyst who looks around at what others have done or are doing to develop and apply standard data will find a somewhat confusing array of techniques, both for initial work measurement, for the synthesis of standard data, and for applications of the data. A senior MPA analyst should have the ability to select and apply different techniques along these lines, depending on variables such as type of work, volume of standards to be established from each data category, and the availability of computer programming assistance. Ingenuity is needed to avoid unnecessary complications in utilizing the end product. And the analyst should have enough common sense to realize that the most technically advanced way to do the job is not always the best way.

TECHNIQUES FOR STANDARD DATA DEVELOPMENT AND APPLICATION

Basic Predetermined Times

MTM–1 and other basic predetermined time systems are in themselves a form of standard data. When the cost of using these systems is reduced through computer-aided applications, as described in the previous chapter, they become a viable way to develop standards for SC/R operations. Consider the time comparisons in Figure 22. After a short review to understand details involved (required for any form of data application), the MPA analysis time with portable microprocessor was estimated to be less than two minutes. If this five-second job were six times as long, for example, as might be expected on some assembly lines, a number of short elements would still be required for line balancing. The ten or fifteen minutes of analysis with 4M DATA, estimated for data input after the initial review period, would be competitive in cost with other ways in which standard data might be applied.

The question arises next as to what maximum length of operation could be analyzed economically through direct application of 4M DATA, in comparison with other forms of standard data application. There are too many variables here to answer this question conclusively. A later illustration will show how punch press operations of about the same length as the element in Figure 22 can have standards set from a simple pick-off sheet in less time than through direct 4M analysis. A reasonable answer to the above question might be something like this: Wherever standard data can be arranged in easily understood and easily applied form, the application time will generally be less than that required for direct analysis with predetermined times.

But the standard data itself can often be developed economically through predetermined time analysis. It was previously noted that applying direct time study to evaluate elemental times needed for standard data often involves delays in waiting for specific operations to occur. Considerable repetition of work measurement may also be required with direct time study, in order to obtain the time values for specific elements. When predetermined time systems are used to develop standard data, these problems need not occur.

In considering operations with different time spans, there is some point at which direct time study becomes less expensive to apply than predetermined times, even when fast-acting computer-aided techniques are used. In standard data development, this break-even point can properly be extended, because of repetition required with direct time study to cover all of the needed elements.

Macro Applications of Predetermined Times

The version of 4M DATA in which average values of Get and Place are applied was referred to in the preceding chapter. This technique has a built-in learning adder of 5 percent, because of the assumption that it would be used on longer cycles where some of the finer motion details might be ignored. (If necessary, this adder could be negated by an entry in the heading data.) Figure 24 shows average and maximum errors that occurred when the Macro notations were substituted for 4M Micro notations in seventeen filmed operations. The graph tends to indicate that the maximum plus-or-minus error with Macro 4M would be about 3 percent for half-minute cycle times. That makes this version of 4M DATA attractive for longer-cycle analyses in standard data development. The reasons for this small amount of error are as follows:

FIGURE 24.
Observed Deviations from MTM-1 with Applications of Macro 4M DATA.

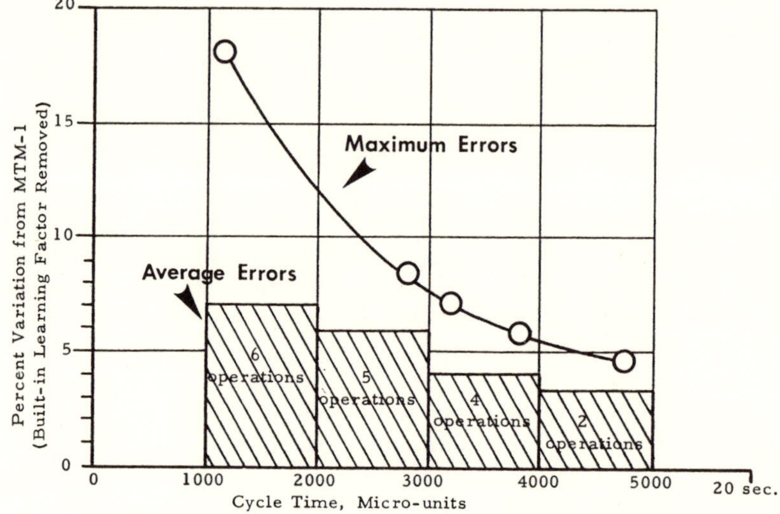

- Although Get and Place notations combine a Reach or Move distance with the Grasp or Position, the distances do not have to be averaged even though just eight average Grasp and Position times are used. Distances can be estimated by the analyst at a glance and entered easily as part of the Macro notations. Thus there can be hundreds of different notations.
- The 4M computer program derives simultaneous motion interactions with Macro notations in the same way as for Micro notations. It is not left up to the analyst to decide how complex motion patterns should be handled.

Other condensed predetermined time systems, such as those listed in chapter 5, do not have these features. Claims that such systems will result in low error percentages on longer operation cycles should be tested by qualified analysts, in ways similar to that illustrated by Figure 24.

Coded Data Aggregates Applied with Computer Assistance

It is possible to introduce into the original 4M DATA computer program any number of coded blocks of time, so long as the codes are distinctive. In general, such data blocks would be developed as 4M elements, but that is not required. The codes should be such that the letters involved remind the analyst of their meaning. Typical mnemonic codes, developed at appendix-listed plant 86, are as follows:

GBH-X Walk average required distance to Get Bolt Hardware (X sets).

GPP-X Walk average required distance to Get Parts from Pallet (X parts).

ACB-X Assemble X number of ⅜ Carriage Bolts and nuts, hand-tight.

Times comprising data blocks like the above examples were relatively simple to derive. They applied to just one product line at a specific plant. Much more extensive analysis was involved by one company in developing a broad assortment of coded motion aggregates that could be applied in a number of plants within the company. The mnemonic codes were such that analysts could in most cases recall them through association with the work elements involved. A computer program was used to assist in their application. There were about two hundred coded data groups. The scope of their application is indicated by the following list of general categories which were covered:

Hoist elements	Miscellaneous assembly elements
Gaging elements	Welding
Clamping elements	Machine tool elements
Threaded fasteners	Position parts

Computer-aided Retrieval of Elements Derived Previously

In a computerized system such as 4M DATA, elements that have been derived as part of the analysis for a specific operation can be coded and stored for possible use in the future to derive methods and standards for related operations. This is somewhat like the computer-aided application of coded data aggregates just described. One difference is that the codes may be longer, to accommodate more of the variables that will assist in later recall of needed data. Another difference is that the elements are generally viewed before actual use in a specific analysis. This can be done on the screen of a computer terminal, at which time there may be a process of selection or revision.

Soon after one large plant with SC/R operations (appendix plant 18) began to use the 4M DATA system, there was a restudy of line balancing elements on three assembly lines. Each line involved roughly a hundred work stations. All of the elements for the first line were derived through a straightforward application of the 4M analysis process. Even though different products were assembled on the second and third lines, some elements to be studied were similar to those analyzed previously. About 20 percent less MPA time was required for the second line and 30 percent less for the third line, largely because of shortcuts made by using the data retrieval process.

The most effective aid in identifying previous elements so they can be reused is a careful application of subject codes, following a study of how such codes should be tailored to fit the conditions in a specific plant. There must be choices between definitive components such as department involved, product subdivisions, equipment utilized, and various other conditions that combine to indicate approximately what an element portrays. Whether this technique for standard data application can compete with other techniques described herein, or which may evolve through the ingenuity of MPA analysts, is something that only those with intimate knowledge of work done within a specific plant can determine.

Manual Derivations of Standard Data Formulas

One of the ways in which standard time data can be applied is through a formula that covers detailed steps involved. The content of such formulas may frequently consist of a series of fairly obvious steps, with each step involving variables to account for product differences. In other cases, the formula content may be intricate and complex, requiring advanced mathematical analysis to derive. Let us consider first an example in which the formula arrangement is obvious but variations are numerous.

This example is from plant 67 listed in the appendix. The formula covered standards for ring-type current transformers of a general design. Sufficient methods details were given in an orderly manner, so that any future changes could be identified. Once a method revision had been spotted, the analyst could determine how a segment of the formula, or the data tables referred to by the formula, should be revised to reflect the change. The standard data formula for "Multi-layer Transformers of Standard Type" is illustrated below:

Each-piece time = .5520 + .2117(L–1) + .0379L
(in std. hrs.)
+ data from table I
+ data from table II
+ F (data from table IIIa)
+ G (data from table IIIb)
+ data from table IVa + data from table V
+ data from table VI + .005N + .004T

The definitions for L,F,G,N,T, and the variations shown within data tables involve such part variables as number of layers of windings, number of turns of wire, insulation layers, etc. It is not the intention here to completely define the formula but simply to indicate the way that it was developed and listed.

This method of expressing standard data formulas for LC/LR operations dates back many years. As computer applications came into the picture, formulas of this type within appendix plant 62 and others were programmed, so that the arithmetic and reference to data tables was done by the computer. The saving in time to develop standards was modest but significant. Realizing that getting programs changed in the future could be a roadblock in correcting for revised methods, the MPA analysts were trained to handle their own programming details.

Developing Easy-to-Use Pick-off Sheets

The much-used technique of arranging data components on a printed format, for manual derivations, can often be an economical approach. That is more apt to be the case if care is used to make the data components clear and easy to apply. Figure 25 may serve as an example. This one format shows how to derive standard times for punch press operations on small parts that are fed by hands or tongs. Developed at appendix plant 18 during some two weeks of analysis with graphically applied 4M DATA increments, this format lists at the top left a way to identify the applicable methods. Formulas covering some twenty-six possible methods are at the lower left. After determining a specific method and formula, it is necessary only to add the designated time increments from charts on the right half of the format.

Somewhat simpler pick-off sheets were also developed to cover press methods involving automated feeds and larger parts that were hand-fed. With practice in using these three data sheets, the time values for most punch press operations could be developed at lower MPA cost than with more sophisticated techniques.

Specialized Computer Programs

Obtaining accurate standards for metal-cutting operations requires input from drawings concerning dimensional data plus feeds and speeds based on type of metal, type of cutting tools, and other factors. Handling elements must also be included. To simplify the arithmetical computations involved, computer programs have been developed that accept as input a standard array of data components and produce as output the needed methods details plus time standards. For example, the input data for one such computer action included the following: material code, finish code, depth of cut, length of cut, tool material code, and number of locations for similar cuts. The computer output included RPM, feed and number of rough and finish cuts, cutting time per location, total

FIGURE 25.
Example of Standard Data in a Pick-off Format.

PUNCH PRESS STANDARD DATA

Small parts
Hand fed

1. SELECT METHOD.

LOAD

1. One hand, same that gets part, alternate left and right.
2. One hand, same that gets part, left or right-hand only.
3. One hand, after transfer of part from hand that gets.
4. Tongs in one hand, after transfer of part from hand.
5. Both hands, one part, after get by one hand.
6. Both hands, one part, after get by both hands.

ACTUATE

A. Foot-pedal, die fully guarded, no sweep arm.
B. Foot=pedal and sweep arm.
C. Two hand buttons (hold for half stroke).

UNLOAD

1. Automatic
2. Knock out as next part inserted.
3. One hand (hand that does not load).
4. One hand (hand that loads).
5. Tongs in one hand.
6. Both hands.

2. OBTAIN FORMULA.

Method	Formula
1A1:	I1 + L + W1 + X2
1B1:	I2 + L + W2 + X2
1C1:	S1 + I3 + L + X1
2A3:, 2A5:	S2 or (X2 + W1) + I1 + L + W1
2B3:, 2B5:	S2 or (X2 + W2) + I2 + L + W2
2C1:	S2 + I2 + L + W3 + X1
2C3:, 2C5:	S2 + I2 + L + W3 + X1
3A1:	I1 + L + W1 + X2
3B1:	I2 + L + W2 + X2
4A1:	I1 + L + W1 + X2
4A5:	I1 + L + W1 + X2 + U1
4B1:	I2 + L + W2 + X2
4B5:	T2 + I2 + L + W2 + X2 + U2
4C1:	S1 + T2 + I2 + L + X1 + 105 (Part in hand to actuate); or S2 + T2 + I2 + L + W3 + X1 (Actuate before get part)
4C5:	(S2 or U3) + T2 + I2 + L + W3 + X1
5B1:	(S2 or X2) + I2 + L + W2
5B4:	I2 + L + W2 + X2 + U2
5C1:	S2 + I2 + L + W3 + X1
5C4:	(S2 or U2) + I2 + L + W3 + X1
6B1:	(S2 or X2) + I2 + L + W2
6B6:	S2 + I2 + L + W2 + X2 + U2
6C1:	S2 + I2 + L + W3 + X1
6C6:	S2 + I2 + L + W3 + X1 + U3

Add for handling and irregular elements.

3. DERIVE TIME 4. Add allowance and setup time.

SECURE (S)

			Reach or Move Distance 6"	10"	14"	18"	24"	30"
S1	Jumbled parts	> 1 cu.in.	165	191	213	235	268	302
		< 1 cu.in.	180	206	228	250	283	317
	Stacked sheets		197	223	245	267	300	334
S2	Jumbled parts	> 1 cu.in.	220	273	322	371	445	519
		< 1 cu.in.	235	288	337	386	460	534
	Stacked sheets		271	323	367	411	477	545

Weight factor: 3#=8; 4#=19; 6#=30; 8#=43
Other:

TRANSFER: T1 (to hand)=47; T2 (to tongs)=53
Add for tongs alignment closer than ½": 76

INSERT (I)

I1	Foot trip, no sweep arm	112
I2	2-button trip, get part after trip	146
	Foot trip, sweep arm, med. press	146
	Foot trip, sweep arm, small press	126
I3	2-button trip, hold part to trip	207

Weight factor: 3#=8; 4#=19; 6#=30; 8#=43
Other:

LOCATE (L)

Move to stop: L=0
Very easy, L=40 (back & side gages, hand control; small part over pin, hand control)
Easy, L=110 (same as above except tongs used; or position in tapered nest, hand control)
Intermediate, L=165 (into tapered nest with tongs; or over pin with less than 1/8" clearance; or double position & backstop)
Difficult, L=205 (double position, with each classified as #3)
Very difficult, L=265 (double pos, both dif.)
Add to tap part, 47; to tap & check, 136
Other:

WITHDRAW

W1	Foot trip, no sweep arm	105
W2	Foot trip, sweep arm, med. press	132
	Foot trip, sweep arm, light press	116
W3	Press tripped by hand buttons	142

Add for 5" recoil: hand=32, tongs=68
Other:

PRESS TRIP AND ACTION (X)

	SPM	X1	X2
Bliss 19½, 19C	150	92	182
Niagara A2¼	130	100	199
Bliss 20C	125	103	205
Niagara A3, Bliss 21S	100	120	238
Verson 7	50	203	405
Bliss 21B, 21½	45	221	441
Bliss 23, Cleveland 40G	42	235	468
Bliss 28	40	245	488
Cleveland 105-90	38	256	510
Cleveland 8K-800	25	375	748
Minster SS-175-60-42	18	499	996

Other:

UNLOAD (U)

Unload distance	6"	10"	14"	18"	24"	30"
U1: Foot, no sweep	232	262	291	325	376	432
U2: Foot & sweep arm	270	288	318	347	395	474
U3: 2-button trip	303	321	351	380	428	507

Weight factor: 3#=8; 4#=19; 6#=30; 8#=43.
Add for tong alignment closer than ½": 106
Add for stack and align edges: 180
Other:

Add for normal parts handling: 10 mu per cu. inch of overall part volume: 10 x (   )
Add for irregular elements (list):

TOTAL MICRO-UNITS PER PART:

cutting time, setup time, and run time. Some programs of this nature are commercially available. Others may be developed by MPA analysts for specific applications.

A specialized computer program applied by the John Deere Company to derive standards for wage incentives has been described by Robert Trunnell, Jr. The steps in developing this system began with the use of MTM to define basic data elements. When combined with applicable Position or Disengage times, also from MTM–1, various tabulations of specialized MTM–1 time values, termed "Universal Data" were obtained. Going further, still more specialized sets of "Operational Data" were developed that could be used to define specific elements. Complementing this information for manual activity were mechanical details for specific machines. Both sets of data were computerized, with one computer program being developed for each type of Operational Data. For example, one program was developed for Gate Shear Standard Data. To apply this program, eleven numerical inputs were required for categories as follows:

Part number	Sheet length	Pieces per cut part
Operation number	Sheet width	Machine number
Reason for change	Part length	Trim method
Thickness	Part width	

The computer output listed all steps involved for the operator to perform the shear operation, with a time value for each step and total standard time for the order quantity.

Computer Derivations of Standard Data Formulas

Formulas used to apply standard data can be developed routinely when it is clear how segments of the data fit together to comprise individual time values. There are other cases in which available time measurements do not indicate clearly how a standard time formula should be developed. A possible solution in such cases is to utilize the mathematical technique of multiple regression analysis, along with a computer program to simplify the task. Programs for applying this technique are readily available. The illustration in Figure 26 is taken from IBM Technical Report 22.783. It shows a partial listing of twenty-four sets of observations concerning three types of duties performed by inspectors. The formula that was derived could be used to determine the man-hours required to perform specific inspection functions.

Another example of regression analysis application can be found in the above reference to formula development within the John Deere Company. Operational data consisted of time measurements in tabular form. Regression analysis was used to develop formulas so that each table of this information could be applied by the computer with a minimum of input.

FIGURE 26.
Formula Derived by Multiple Regression Analysis.

Observation No.	Inspection Hours per Production Shift	No. of First-piece Inspections per Shift	Total Production Statistically Sampled per Shift (/100)	Total Production 100% Inspected per Shift
	(X_1)	(X_2)	(X_3)	(X_4)
1	14.9	40	48.0	82
2	13.2	12	13.2	23
3	5.4	4	11.3	30
-	-	-	-	-
23	7.8	4	10.8	33
24	5.3	2	12.3	32

Formula: $X_1 = 4.6895 + .06361X_2 + .11493X_3 + .02790X_4$

Automated Selection and Application of Standards

At appendix-listed plant 36, the products manufactured were similar in general concept but with many differences in size, electrical characteristics, and included features. The MPA group at this plant developed standard data formulas which were then programmed for computer application. The manufacturing information for a specific product triggered the computerized calculation of time standards for each operation involved. There were some exceptions for unusual deviations in product design, requiring manual derivation of standards in such cases.

At plant 73, the operations in one department involved the shearing of metal strips and stacking of the strips to develop cores for large power transformers. The custom designs required size variations and major differences in stacking times. Standard time data for these operations were computerized, and applications of the data were triggered by the respective engineering design reference numbers.

MAINTAINING STANDARD DATA AND STANDARDS

Those who develop standard time data are concerned with getting what is required to serve the plant's current needs, and properly so. In most cases there is some urgency to complete the task. Preparations for integrating future methods changes into the data framework can easily be slighted in order to reach current objectives faster. But methods changes will always occur as time passes. There should be enforced discipline in the way that standard data tables, pick-off sheets, or formulas are prepared. The paths for data synthesis should be clear-cut when later changes must be accounted for.

The Disadvantage of Computer-applied Standard Data

Advantages that can result from computerized data applications have been noted in this chapter. It should be realized, however, that a complex computer program, which may be required to achieve this advantage, will stand as a roadblock in the path of future revisions. That is particularly true if required programming must be done by a staff group not associated with the MPA activity. There may be a long waiting line filled with other departmental needs that must be serviced. When a data application program is known to function smoothly, disrupting this to make minor changes does not come across as a high priority project. If the computer programs are developed by MPA analysts themselves, this disadvantage may be lessened.

Automated Correction Techniques

A computer system in which programs act to assign specific elements of data to form larger blocks that function as standards can also be programmed to upgrade the larger data blocks automatically when there are changes of any kind within a specific element. This has long been recognized as a valid objective, and there are continuing applications of this principle within industry. The 4M DATA system has been adapted by the MTM Association, through the cooperative action of 4M users, to handle "mass updating" of element blocks when component elements must be revised. Other computer systems are commercially available that are reputed to accomplish the same objective. Even if added time is required in data applications, because of the need to screen coded elements and make necessary changes, the ability to update previous time standards helps in justifying such an approach.

Need for Periodic Standards Auditing

There is no sure way to monitor all methods changes as they occur. The revisions that are required after equipment or layout improvements can generally be spotted by MPA analysts involved. But many significant changes are initiated by operators, supervisors, design engineers, manufacturing engineers, and others within the organization. Those changes that act to make an operation more difficult to perform will be reported promptly if there is a control system in effect that compares actual performance with time standards. The changes that make jobs easier will frequently remain hidden. In many labor control applications, resistance from labor representatives makes it difficult to revise standards to account for previous methods changes unless that action is taken soon after a change has been made.

Questions may arise as to whether time standards should be revised when operators originate methods changes. Despite such questions, the policy should always be to restudy a job when methods are improved for any reason. A control plan cannot be maintained on a continuing basis unless such a policy is enforced. There can be a tolerance in the amount of change required before making a revision. A tolerance range of plus-or-minus 5 percent from previous time values could properly be considered. Suggestion award plans can be implemented to avoid unfairness and encourage improvement.

Over a period of time, a gradual loosening of standard data and time values will occur unless a procedure is set up for standards auditing. This can be done in various ways, ranging from sampling to a complete review. A low-key continuing function is better than an intensive, short-term approach. For example, analysts could be asked to audit a specific number of operational standards each month, selecting at random those which have not been checked during the past three years.

For time values established by direct time study, the original study can be viewed for completeness, and methods in effect can be compared with those noted on the study. Further checking might be considered unnecessary unless there are discrepancies. Where predetermined times are the basis for standards, a brief observation of the operation cycle would serve to point out whether methods variations have occurred. When standard data applications are involved, the steps for effective auditing must be developed to fit specific needs. Occasional cross-checks between direct time study results and predetermined time analyses are worthwhile, both to evaluate performance rating and to test the effectiveness with which predetermined time systems have been applied.

As previously noted, the cost of an auditing function is not something that a cost-conscious manager will tend to accept readily without convincing evidence that the activity is worthwhile. Regular reporting, as suggested by Figure 4, can help provide such evidence.

8
The Work Sampling Technique and Its Uses

The work sampling concept utilizes brief and randomly spaced observations of selected functions to determine activity percentages. This can be done with a calculable level of statistical precision, depending on (a) the number of samples taken, and (b) the percentage occurrence of a specific activity, usually the one considered most significant. This chapter will not dwell at length on the statistical theory involved, but will discuss how the technique is used, its advantages and disadvantages, and how multicategory work sampling can be applied with a portable microprocessor and computer summarization.

Obtaining a measure of equipment delay times through random sampling was described in a 1934 publication in England by L. H. C. Tippett. A similar approach for measuring delays was given the name "ratio delay" by R. L. Morrow, in 1941, and that phrase soon became widely used (see Brisley, reference C, 1971). In a *Factory Magazine* article published by C. L. Brisley in 1952, the term "work sampling" was applied in describing a somewhat broader use of the sampling technique. This more descriptive name soon became infused within industrial engineering literature, and applications of work sampling have expanded.

WORK SAMPLING FUNDAMENTALS

The Need for Random Observations

For the results of a work sampling study to be as valid as would be indicated by statistical concepts, the observations must be made at random times during the working period. An understandable reason for

FIGURE 27.
Typical Productivity Variations During a Working Shift.

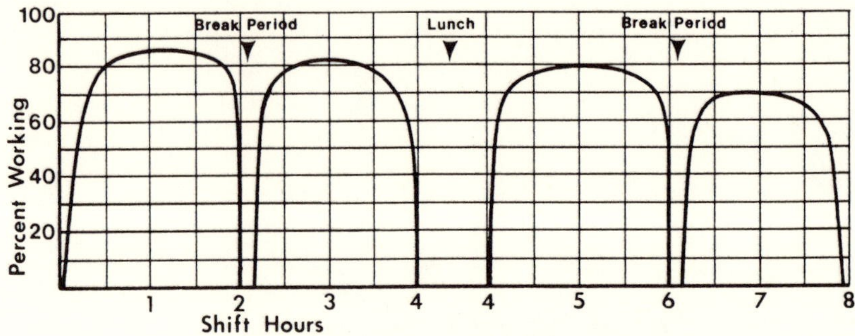

this lies in the fact that the work habits of operators tend to follow a pattern of variance that repeats itself from day to day. Typically, during the first ten to thirty minutes after the start of a work shift, a number of operators may be involved in such activities as waiting for assignment, looking for material, getting instructions from supervisors, or perhaps talking to an associate about what happened the night before. There are predictable increases and declines in the number performing useful work at intervals during the shift.

In a plant where improvement is needed, a charting of the percentages of operators at work might look something like that in Figure 27. If it were possible to survey the plant at very frequent intervals, say every two minutes, a close approximation to the true average percentages of operators working and not working could be derived, provided a representative number of days were covered during such a study. But that kind of sampling review would be impractical. Not only would considerably more time be required to make any one tour, but such frequent observations would upset any group of workers.

If the tours to make sampling observations require a half-hour to complete, for example, it is equally obvious that the time to begin a tour cannot be simply a matter of convenience for the designated observer. The chart shows about 50 percent at work during the first half-hour, 55 percent at some period in the morning, and about 40 percent during the last half-hour. It does not take statistical theory to indicate that repeated sampling observations to evaluate nonrandom work practices would produce more realistic results if made at randomly selected intervals.

Making the Observations without Bias

Most readers of this book will be familiar with the "normal curve," and with the concept of "standard deviations" with respect to the mean

FIGURE 28.
Relation of the Normal Curve to Percentages Derived from Groups of Random Observations, Made without Bias.

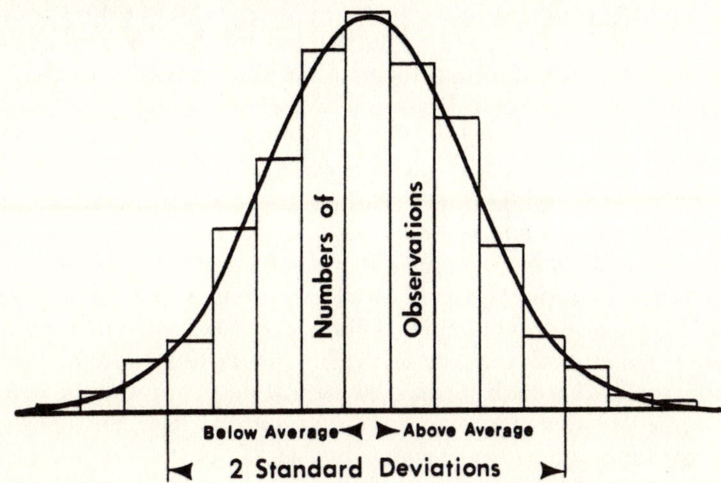

value (center point) of the normal curve. Figure 28 illustrates these statistical fundamentals. In considering the relation of this curve to work sampling, the vertical blocks that approximate its shape may be thought of as ranges of percentages derived for the significant activity in a work sampling study that is made *without bias* of any kind. The greatest number of percentage values derived from groups of random observations would be expected to fall in the center block. Somewhat fewer results would deviate above or below the average, as represented by blocks on each side of the center. And only a very few observation groups (omitting the lunch and break periods) would be expected to result in the high or low extremes of deviation from the average. We will shortly denote an equation derived from statistical concepts which can be applied to make the interpretation of work sampling results fairly routine. But first let us examine more closely the phrase "without bias."

Random Times. Not only is it intuitively apparent that randomly selected observation times are required, but the fundamentals of sampling theory underscore that point. It is not practical, however, to make each observation at a random time. A number of samples are obtained economically by making tours through the designated area. Starting the tours at random intervals is a step toward compliance with the principle of randomness. A certain amount of statistical bias is inevitable with this concept, however, particularly when tours are lengthy and the number of observations is appreciable. Further discussion of this point will come later.

Designated Break Periods. If the sampling objective is to measure a nonworking percentage during periods when operators are supposed to be at work, the possible introduction of lunch periods or authorized break periods into the sampling tour creates an element of bias. Continuation of the sampling process during lunch periods would of course be omitted. The same should apply to authorized breaks, when they occur throughout a section during a tour within that section. But what is to be done if a tour is started, from random selection, just a few minutes before a break or lunch interval? Several MPA groups are known to have rationalized this by stopping the tour when the designated time for a break occurs, and starting it again at the same location immediately after the designated break-ending time.

Adapting the Study to Consider Personnel not Visible During a Tour. This will require some thought, based on a determination of what is practical in specific cases. Recognizing that individuals may at times be away from their usual work location to perform work-related tasks, such as obtaining material or tools, some observers attempt to count the workers observed in a section, compare this count with the number reported to be present, and contact the supervisor to find whether absences have been authorized. This complicates and slows down the sampling study. Others would define the study to cover only those workers visible within an area, realizing that this leaves uncovered an indefinite percentage. Making a tour of rest-room areas during sampling observations guarantees employee resentment, and this should be avoided. A later discussion of computerized sampling reports will describe another alternative to account for individuals who are missing.

Recognizing Worker Categories and Activities. If the sampling is to be made of functions performed by maintenance men, for example, the observer must first be able to recognize who they are, which is not easy in a large manufacturing plant. Most would agree that the observer should be able to evaluate the activity involved without interrupting to ask. For example, is the maintenance man waiting for access to equipment, waiting for his helper to bring material, or just loafing? There are chances for bias here unless the study is designed carefully and observers selected who can interpret what they see. Some MPA groups prefer to train supervisors to make sampling studies within the supervisor's own area of responsibility, reducing bias of one kind though perhaps inviting another type of bias.

Worker Anticipation of Sampling tours. This can be a significant cause of bias in making some sampling studies. There will be wide variations in how operators respond when the observer is seen at a distance. If employee relations are on a sound basis, and if operators have been given believable explanations of what the study is intended to accomplish, there may be little change from normal activity. If there is an inherent distrust of the motives for making the systematic observations, however, operators can alter their behavior during the period of observation. It is not unusual for signals to be devised that alert adjoining groups when an observer enters the area. Some groups, where there has been a history of labor relations difficulties, have been known to stop work entirely when an observer enters the area for sampling observations.

As those who have made numerous sampling observations report, the close scrutiny from an observer making repetitive tours usually causes a change from normal work habits at first, but this reaction tends to disappear after some time has elapsed. Discarding the observations made during the first few days of a study is often recommended, to reduce the bias from reactions to the observer.

Abnormal Occurrences. In many plants, or in sections within plants, there is a long-recognized surge near the end of a month in order to meet shipping or inventory objectives. Where this occurs, there will likely be a corresponding letdown in work effort after the rush period has passed. To avoid undue bias in sampling results, the observation period should cover one or more complete cycles in which such variations are known to occur.

Bias from Poorly Planned Sampling Objectives. A frequent objective is to identify various conditions of activity or inactivity, for reasons that prompted the study in the first place. It would often be useful to know whether the operators' nonworking time is caused by lack of material, lack of balance in the flow of product during sequential operations, equipment downtime, lack of instructions from the supervisor, excessive group size, or various other reasons in addition to personal downtime. It might be equally useful to classify the working observations in terms of setup and run time, or perhaps productive operations and rework.

Some of these and similar activities can be identified in a sampling study, and some cannot. It is necessary to select and define the activities to be observed so that bias because of difficult evaluations will be minimized.

Planning the Kind of Study Required

Until enough sampling studies have been made to know what is practical to recognize and identify, the activities to be sampled should be kept as simple and clear-cut as possible. The following list of typical work sampling categories and activities may help in planning studies that produce needed information with minimum bias in making the observations:

Survey the Use of Specific Equipment in a Department, to Estimate Available Capacity for Increased Work Load.

1. In use for productive work.
2. In use for make-ready or setup.

3. Not in use, operator present but not working.
4. Not in use, equipment being repaired.
5. Not in use, no operator present.

Identify the Utilization of Maintenance Manpower, to Estimate Possible Savings from Improved Planning and Scheduling of Such Work.

1. Actual maintenance work, including the handling of tools and material at work site.
2. Walking, away from work site, with or without tools or equipment.
3. Waiting, at storeroom.
4. Waiting, for other maintenance personnel to finish a job sequence.
5. Waiting, for other reasons—not personal time.
6. Obtaining information, from supervisor, drawings, etc.
7. Personal downtime.

Identify Functions of Operators in a Fabricating Department, to Indicate where Improvement Efforts Should be Channeled.

1. Productive operations (cutting, drilling, shearing, etc.).
2. Make-ready or setup, including tool insertion, part clamping, etc.
3. Checking parts.
4. Obtaining information from supervisor, drawings, etc.
5. Waiting for material movement.
6. Operator on personal downtime.

Identify Office Clerical Functions, to Evaluate Possible Methods Changes.

1. Typing.
2. Filing.
3. Use of telephone, business purposes.
4. Other duties at desk.
5. Discussions with office personnel, business purposes.
6. Personal delays at work area, including use of phone not for business.
7. Personal delays, in department but away from work area.
8. Not at work area or in department.

Identify Supervisory Functions, to Evaluate How Time can be Made Available for More Effective Reviews at Work Stations. (With assurance to supervisors that sampling observations are to help find ways to relieve them of tasks that interfere with their primary objectives, cooperation can be expected.)

1. Contacting operators at work locations.
2. Contacting operators in office.
3. Contacting maintenance, quality control, others.
4. Checking production parts.
5. Clerical work in office.
6. Telephone conversations.
7. General observations in department.
8. Personal time, in department.
9. Away from department.

Planning the Length of a Study

As previously noted, the cycle of anticipated conditions that would affect results may be a controlling factor in determining the period of time during which a work sampling study should be continued. The number of tours that can or should be made per day may also be a factor. A third factor that enters into the preliminary planning for a study is the number of random observations required. When each of these three interrelated factors has been determined, an approximate length of time for the study will become apparent.

Statistical mathematics may be used as a starting point in estimating the required number of random observations. One of the more commonly applied statistical concepts is embodied in the following equation:

$$Sp = 2\sqrt{\frac{p(1 - p)}{N}}$$

where S = desired precision, expressed as a decimal. (If plus-or-minus 5 percent of p is desired, use .05.)

p = percent occurrence of the activity being measured, also expressed as a decimal. (Estimate at first, using more precise values as the study progresses.)

N = number of radom observations.

This equation applies with a confidence level of 95 percent, as its derivation was based on two standard deviations in the normal curve of Figure 28. In other words, 95 percent of the plus-or-minus deviations from the average have been accounted for in applying the equation. The values of S are applicable as a percentage of p. If 5 percent precision

FIGURE 29.
Alignment Chart for Determining Number of Work Sampling Observations Required.

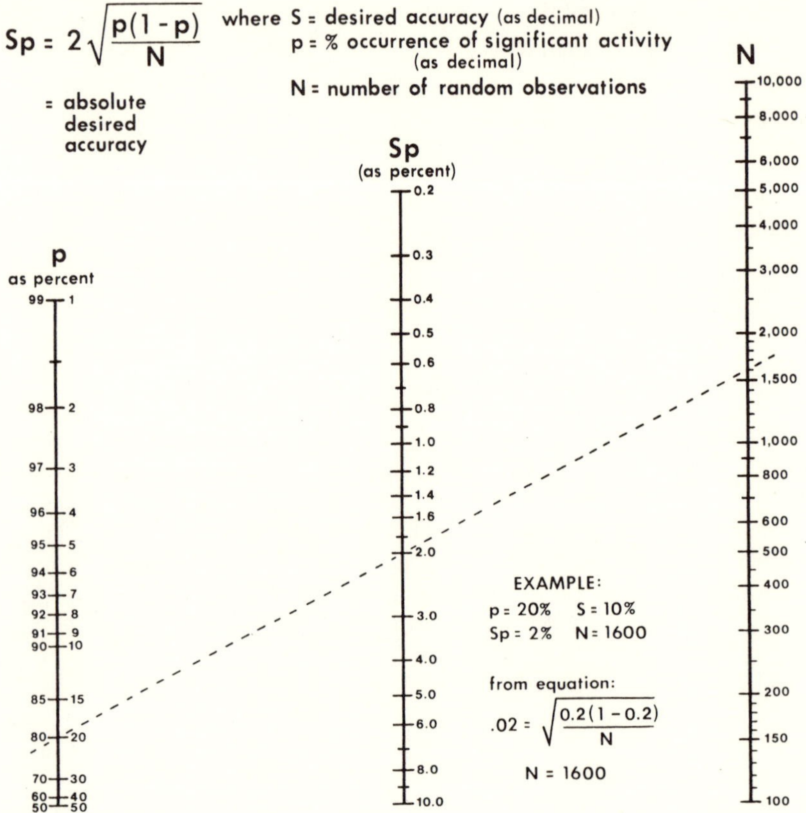

were calculated in deriving a 20 percent nonworking percentage, for example, the latter value could be depended on to be between 19 percent and 21 percent, 95 percent of the time.

An alignment chart such as that in Figure 29 may be used to determine the required number of observations to obtain needed precision for anticipated sampling results. If a nonworking percentage were estimated to be in the 20 percent range, for example, and a precision of ± 5 percent were desired, the statistical error range would be $0.2 \times 0.05 = .01$, or 1 percent. The chart shows that about seven thousand observations would be required. If the section involved one hundred operators and some three tours could be made daily, the study should extend for about twenty-three days. Since this would cover the monthly cycle of variations that might be expected, the MPA group involved might well decide on this as a tentative plan. They would want to lengthen the time somewhat, however, so that observations obtained during the first few days could be discarded for reasons noted previously.

Obtaining Approval

Since the repetitive observations may have an effect on employee attitudes, management's approval is necessary, and this should be followed by explanations to supervisors concerned. What is appropriate here depends on whether work sampling is something new within the plant or whether it has been a recurring and accepted function. In the latter case, a simple notice to supervisors may be all that is needed. If the work sampling concept is new to some of those on the management team, an explanation of the principles involved would be helpful.

How to Make Work Sampling Believable

Supervisors need to understand and believe in the validity of work sampling so that their cooperation can be expected and so they can explain to operators what will be happening. A much-used training program in company K, listed in the appendix, utilized several twenty-minute films of related industrial sequences, along with a hundred randomly spaced signals on tape. For each film, specific activities were defined, and the trainees were asked to check the activity being viewed when a signal occurred. By counting the check marks for each activity, sampling percentages were obtained. The exact percentages were then made known, as derived previously from the films. Invariably, the answers from sampling were fairly close to the exact answers. This exercise, together with a discussion about procedures to be followed and what would be done with the results of the study, served as an effective training program.

Selecting Random Observation Times

If one sampling tour requires twenty minutes to complete, a common practice is to divide the working shift into time brackets of that length and select randomly the times to make the planned number of tours for the next day. An easy way to do this is to write on slips of paper all of the possible time intervals (twenty-four intervals for twenty-minute tours during an eight-hour shift), put the slips in a box, and draw out the prescribed number of slips daily. An alternate approach is to use tables of random numbers to do essentially the same thing.

The Bias Involved in This Way of Making Observations

Some bias is inevitably introduced through such a procedure. An example will illustrate the point. Assume that the significant percentage to be derived by sampling is estimated to be 30 percent, and a precision of ± 10 percent is considered close enough. The chart shows that less than a thousand random observations would accomplish this. Making a hundred observations per tour would require only ten tours. But it is clear that selecting ten starting times at random could easily skew the observations of working conditions such as those shown in Figure 27. With twenty-four time slots to pick from, the ten tours could not possibly bracket all of the significant high and low points depicted by this chart. Instead of the 27–33 percent range of anticipated results, there could easily be a 20–40 percent range—too great to be of much value.

This does not mean that the statistical theory for work sampling application is wrong. It means that the theory calls for randomness of each observational time, not just for the random starting point of a tour that produces dozens of observations in a short interval. Of course, it would not be practical to do this, for a variety of reasons. A little common sense can go a long way to skirt this problem, however. The following true story may illustrate the point.

Management in one large company decided it was necessary to obtain, on short notice, an independent review of working/nonworking percentages at fifteen plant locations. This had to be done in a two-month period, which ruled out taking most of the sequential steps recommended in this chapter. The sampling observations to accomplish this objective were made by two individuals working together, one who went to all locations, and the MPA manager at each specific location. Neither operators nor supervisors were informed of the study (a dangerous procedure, not recommended for general use). It was necessary to count the working and nonworking occurrences in each section and record the data without drawing undue attention. (It should be noted that there is nothing unethical about such an approach, since management has a right to the information. The danger is in potential morale problems, which in this case were avoided by proceeding with caution and not publicizing the results.)

After these introductory comments, we can get to the point of the story. Some eight hundred to twelve hundred observations were made at each plant location over a two-day period. All plant areas were covered. The times selected to make the various tours were such that each plant was bracketed with observations from the shift-beginning to the shift-end. During four ten-minute intervals—after the shift started, before lunch, after lunch, and at the shift-end—estimates of downtime percentages were made by quickly touring as much of the plant as possible. Random selection of times to begin the relatively few tours was intentionally avoided, for the reason noted above. Results showed a wide spread of nonworking percentages from plant to plant, ranging from near zero at one location to disturbingly low figures at some others. But there was convincing evidence that these brief studies had a fairly dependable meaning.

At every one of the fifteen locations except the "100 percent plant," a plotting of at-work percentages during the time span for each tour showed the typical diagram illustrated by Figure 27, and which is to be expected at most plant locations. If it is assumed that such a diagram should result from a valid sampling study, then data from a specific study could not be far off-track unless most of the observations were skewed. And that was deemed highly unlikely in this particular study, due to the simplicity of categories involved.

This example is cited because it illustrates that common sense must be paramount when making work sampling analyses. No problems are seen in the statistical theory, only in applying it to some situations.

Making Observations

The work sampling observer should adhere to previously selected tour times, where possible. If it is necessary to miss a scheduled tour, the randomized selection of starting times will not be affected if an added time is randomly selected for a following day.

Thought should be given to making the recording of observations as easy as possible as well as unobtrusive. Small notebooks serve the latter purpose better than clipboards. While the analyst should have at hand the reference numbers for sampling categories, a prominent listing of the activities being sampled may not be wise, as some will insist on seeing just what is being recorded. The record format can be as simple as a series of letter codes, one for each activity, with a mark made under the proper code for each observation. When operators ask questions about details of the study, it can properly be emphasized that none of the observations can or will be personalized. Conclusions from work sampling relate to groups, not individuals.

The tour paths should be varied if possible, particularly at the beginning of a study when operators may tend to change what they are doing when the observer is seen. Different reference sources suggest somewhat different approaches in determining when to reach a conclusion as the observer approaches an individual or group. Experience suggests that this be done as soon as the person or group is clearly visible during the tour. If there are three in a group, for example, the first glance at each should serve to establish the activities to record. Say that one of the three is working on a large wiring assembly, and the other two are casually talking with each other when first observed. Even if the conversation stops later, the sampling observation should still be "one working and two not working."

If there are only a few activity classifications to remember, a practiced observer can keep in mind the several observations while proceeding through a small area. The entry can then be made at a convenient stopping point. In more densely populated sections, entries must be made more frequently. A technique will be described later in this chapter that will simplify the recording of observations during a tour.

During any work sampling study, there will be repeated contacts between the observer and those whose work activities are being sampled, including their supervisors. A frank explanation that the study is aimed at methods improvement will usually bring suggestions, and these should be recorded as a by-product of the study. The observer will repeatedly see a lack of productivity evidenced by recorded activities, and will develop improvement ideas that should also be cataloged for later review.

Summarizing and Reporting the Results

Manual recording of the observations requires a fair amount of desk work after each tour has been completed. On forms devised for the study in progress, the observer should record results from the completed tour and cumulative results for each activity. The latter step could be postponed for daily handling. It is good practice to maintain a graph, for the sampling activity considered most significant, showing the cumulative percent of occurrence. When the plotted line tends to level out, without continued trends away from a reasonably level curve, this provides empirical evidence that enough observations have been made.

Some references suggest that a control chart be constructed by plotting statistical upper and lower limits on the same graph, with current average percentages in the center. This could be confusing rather than helpful. As previously noted, a sampling tour consists of observations made close to one randomly selected starting time. Referring again to Figure 27, if randomly selected times for three daily tours were near the start of the shift, shortly before lunch, and late in the shift, an average nonworking percentage of 35 percent might correctly be derived. If the three tours the next day were made an hour after the shift, an hour after lunch, and about two hours after lunch, a 20 percent figure could result. Reference to a control chart might arouse unnecessary concern.

Upon completion of the work sampling study, a prompt reporting of results and conclusions should be made to those concerned. With the report should go the constructive ideas referred to above and recommendations for action. Continued cooperation in making future studies requires evidence that something worthwhile can be accomplished. Accordingly, the MPA manager should do his best to see that constructive action is taken.

RATING PERFORMANCE DURING WORK SAMPLING OBSERVATIONS

It becomes apparent to any work sampling observer, when decisions must be made as to whether an operator is working or not working, that there are borderline cases where neither description is fully applicable. Some of the obvious cases would include the following:

- A maintenance mechanic eats a sandwich while clumsily using a wrench with the other hand.
- Two operators divide their attention between casually lacing wiring harnesses and conversing continually with each other.
- A shear operator cleans his glasses while he slowly walks back to the front of his machine after stacking parts on the other side.

In such obvious cases, a way to rate what the observer sees at a glance would be realistic and helpful in arriving at overall conclusions. But attempting to rate other levels of performance through a quick glance is inherently questionable. Such ratings would never be dependable on an individual basis. Without understanding the method involved, and without observing an operator's pace for a longer period, significant errors would likely occur. So it is not surprising that there are differences of opinion as to whether performance rating should be attempted during a work sampling study.

When a decision is made to rate performance during a work sampling study, rating increments are generally in steps of at least 10 percent. Whether the rating concept is adjusted to correspond with that used for the labor control plan in effect is another question. When performance is evaluated during a sampling study, the ratings for working observations are first averaged, then applied to the working percentages derived in the usual way. If the rating of performance is included in a report following the study, some may doubt the validity of results. For this reason, the work-sampling report should include working percentages without ratings, as well as the adjusted percentages after ratings are applied.

MULTICATEGORY WORK SAMPLING

Appendix-listed plants 3, 86, and others have utilized the portable microprocessor shown in Figure 7 to record sampling observations and directly transmit the data for computer summarization. This eliminates many clerical functions otherwise required. A number of separately defined studies can be made at one time. It is possible to enter performance ratings where appropriate to do so. And there is a check by the computer as to whether data entered by the analyst matches previously planned subdivisions for each sampling category.

To illustrate what can be accomplished by using this technique, simultaneous studies could be made of production operators, inspectors, storeroom attendants, and maintenance personnel, with somewhat different activity classifications for each. Another possibility would be to make sampling studies in a dozen or more shop departments, with summary data kept separate for each. Of course, just as many sampling observations are needed as for separate studies, but the number of sampling tours and MPA time involvement would be greatly reduced.

It is conceivable that the same objective could be accomplished with manual inputs to separate formats for each of the designated categories. But those who have made work sampling studies will realize that the confusion involved in attempting to do this manually, added to the massive summary time required, would make such a combination of projects difficult without a way to automate or simplify some of the functions.

As with any computer-aided project, an applicable program is required. Such a program could be developed at specific plants to fit the kind of portable microprocessor used and procedural steps considered appropriate. A description will be given next of how multicategory work sampling was applied at the plants referred to above. After reviewing these steps, the framework for an applicable computer program could be devised.

Specifying Study Parameters for Input Screening

The studies to be undertaken were first planned in detail, along with the activities to be sampled for each category. Then, through an interactive response with the computer program, the following information was transmitted through the computer terminal:

- Study number.
- Codes for each category in the forthcoming study. With the microprocessor pictured in Figure 7, the codes used were C,F,H, or any combinations of these (CF, CC, CH, etc.). Where there was only one category involved, no code was required.
- Numbers for each activity eligible for use with specific categories. If there are ten numbered activities, for example, the eligible numbers for category C might be 1, 3, 4, 7.

- An indication as to whether performance ratings will be applied with specific activities.

Obtaining Random Times for Sampling Observations

Although this could be done manually, the computer was programmed to provide the requested number of random tour times for any number of days. This was done after entering through the terminal the shift starting and ending times, starting and ending times for lunch and break periods, and the estimated tour length. The random times derived by the computer program do not begin during specified break periods but might extend into such periods. It was determined that the accepted practice would be to continue a tour until a break period began, stop the tour at that point, and restart the tour after the break ending time.

Using the Microprocessor to Record Sampling Observations

With the portable unit turned on, the military mode of clock time is first entered. Since the unit's clock time is automatically applied for each succeeding entry, this provides a way for the computer program to determine later the clock times needed for a purpose that will be described.

When observations are made during a tour, keys of the portable microprocessor are depressed to record applicable data, after which the ENTER button is depressed. Inputs can be made in a flexible manner, as illustrated by the following examples:

- An entry of "2" or "C2" or "C2*1*100" or "C2*100*1" is in all cases interpreted by the computer program to mean "category C, activity 2, single observation, 100 percent rating." (A numeral entered first, without the category being designated, caused the entry of category C in all cases. Thus, the data entry for single-category studies was simplified.)
- "F1*5" means category F, activity 1, 5 observations, either 100 percent rating, or no rating intended.
- "F1*2*80" or "F1*80*2" means category F, activity 1, 2 observations, 80 percent performance rating.
- To correct entry errors recognized by the observer, a preceding entry would be disregarded by the computer system if code H, alone, were entered.

Transmitting Stored Information to the Computer System

This was done according to instructions included with the portable microprocessor, following a preliminary input through the computer terminal to designate the study number and observation day numbers. After the data stored in the microprocessor had been transmitted, the computer printed out all of the entries, then specified which of the entries were not in compliance with study parameter instructions. The observer could then follow a specified routine to revise or delete such inputs.

If performance rating values had been entered for category/activity combinations not specified in the parameter input, such values were automatically changed to 100 percent. As a precaution against undetected errors, frequency notations (number of operators observed in a group that were at work, for example) must be below ten, and rating values must be between 40 percent and 150 percent, or the program would list the observations as an error. Following corrections, data for that run were printed out with cumulative sequence numbers, and also stored in a computer file, for later summarization.

If there were a number of tours during the day, with each tour covering the same groups, the observer could ask for a calculation of observation variance for each category, after data from the final tour had been entered. This term was defined as the average number derived by comparing the maximum number of daily observations for a specific category with each of the other numbers of daily observations for that category. To some degree, the variance calculations indicate the number of operators outside of the section, presumably on personal time. If the daily variance is seen as dependable information, it can be stored in the computer file, for later reporting on an average basis.

Obtaining Periodic or Final Summary Reports

At any point during a study, the stored information may be summarized in report format, without deleting or altering the computer file. An example is shown below:

ACTIVITY CODE	NUMBER OF OBSERVATIONS	PERCENT OF TOTAL	STATISTICAL PRECISION	AVERAGE RATING	ADJUSTED PERCENT
1	2030	42.8	.034	81.1	34.7
2	830	17.5	.063	100.	17.5
ETC.					

Obtaining "Time Span" Summary

Upon command, a computerized report can be obtained that makes it possible to construct a graph showing how one or more activities varied during the working shift. Figure 27 illustrates this kind of information. An example of the printout follows.

TIME SPAN LISTING, STUDY NUMBER 17, CATEGORY F

ENTRIES BELOW ARE PERCENTAGES OF TOTAL OCCURRENCES OF SPECIFIC ACTIVITY WITHIN THE TIME SPAN NOTED:

DECIMAL HOURS	ACTIVITY 1	ACTIVITY 2	ACTIVITY 3
7.00-7.24	06	85	09
7.25-7.49	65	27	08
7.50-7.74	80	15	05

If activity 1 in this example had previously been defined as useful work, the above data specifies that only 6 percent of the group was at work during the first fifteen minutes, 65 percent during the next fifteen-minute period, etc.

CONCLUSIONS

Advantages from Careful Applications

Work sampling is a powerful analytical tool that costs relatively little to apply in comparison with the cost of control systems based on time standards.

As previously noted, the technique is applicable to almost any kind of industrial activity. This includes maintenance functions, where labor costs are high and realistic time standards have limited application. Work sampling can be applied to most other nondirect functions as a way to evaluate general methods and approximate manpower requirements. The technique is broadly applicable in direct manufacturing, for purposes that have been described.

When sampling observations are recorded with a portable microprocessor, separate work sampling studies can be made concurrently. By transmitting data from the portable unit into a computer system, clerical effort is minimized, and results are summarized automatically. The reports can include a time-span summary, showing how observations varied during specified time intervals throughout the shift.

Average standards can be derived with work sampling for activities where variations in work content make other forms of work measurement difficult to apply. Examples were noted in chapter 3.

Potential Application Problems

There are problems of believability in conclusions derived from random sampling, but this can be overcome with training programs. Varying degrees of inaccuracy can be caused by operators changing their work habits when the observer is spotted, but human nature is such that this subterfuge becomes tiresome and usually does not continue after a few days.

Observational errors can be made when activities that are difficult to indentify are included in a sampling project. Such errors are heightened by the practical inability of interrupting those observed to ask questions. The validity of pace rating during work sampling is particularly doubtful. The combination of these potential errors, while quite variable and inherently unknown, adds to the statistical error range derived from numbers of samples and percentages of the total sample. The fact that multiple observations made during a sampling tour are not the equivalent of random samples called for in the statistical equation can add to the possibilities for error.

With other forms of work evaluation (direct time study, predetermined times, or performance reporting procedures), trails of evidence can be shown to supervisors, managers, and labor representatives concerning the validity of reported performance levels. With work sampling, the observer has nothing to show except check marks on a record format. With that in mind, and considering the well-documented track record of labor resistance to some control systems, it would seem that depending on work sampling as a basic form of productivity control is to invite resistance over a period of time. When work sampling is used as an adjunct to other forms of control, however, experience has indicated that resistance is not likely to be significant after a suitable introduction.

Fundamental Limitations

The work sampling concept described in this chapter cannot be used to evaluate production methods for specific operations. Since control of methods is a key to labor productivity control, and since pace rating by a glance during the sampling process is not dependable, work sampling is not applicable to the close evaluation of sectional performance levels except perhaps for the simplest of SC/R operations. And since the sampling process is applied to groups, rather than to individuals or individual jobs, there is little that can be provided by a work sampling study to identify specific detracting conditions.

9
Learning Curve Concepts

This chapter begins by taking issue with the terminology in the heading. The improvement that tends to result in manufacturing labor costs, as the output of a product continues, includes contributory effects such as the following: design simplifications; equipment, tooling, and layout revisions; various other methods improvements; rework and scrap reductions; operators' learning; and improved management/staff functions. While the phrase "learning curves" is often used in referring to ways of tracking these combined effects, the term is more confusing than helpful. It will be replaced in discussions to follow with "manufacturing improvement curves," shortened in most cases to "improvement curves."

Embedded within the above list of improvement causes was "operators' learning." Long before the wide use of what this book will refer to as improvement curves, learning curves within manufacturing meant the tracing of operators' proficiency in performing a specific job. We will adhere to that definition. Thus, two subjects will be discussed in this chapter rather than one. Identifiable aspects in both have a relation to time standards and labor productivity control. And, as we shall see, some elements of folklore are found in these subjects.

Improvement Curves—Empirical, Confusing, Questionable, Useful

The Origin of Improvement Curves

It has been widely noted that an article by T. P. Wright, in 1936, served to focus attention on simpler ways to predict future improvement in the

FIGURE 30.
A. Improvement Curves on Rectangular Coordinates.
B. Improvement Curves on Logarithmic Coordinates.
C. Two Kinds of Improvement Curves.

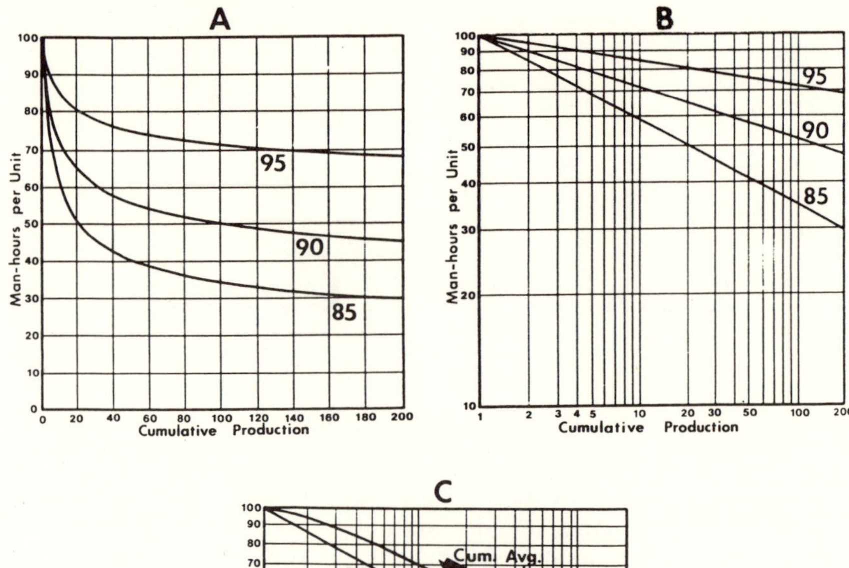

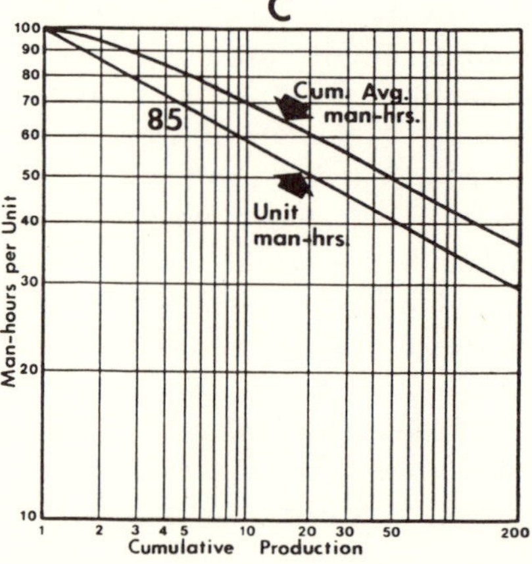

labor cost of manufacturing a product as its output continues (see Nanda and Adler, 1982). Wright's contribution showed that the man-hour cost per order to produce a specific model of aircraft, when plotted as cost versus cumulative numbers of units, tended to follow a parabolic curve like that in Figure 30A. Because parabolas become straight lines when plotted on logarithmic coordinates, as in 30B, the attraction of such a concept for estimating purposes is readily apparent.

Since Wright's article was published, a number of others having access to man-hour cost information for certain manufactured products have submitted analyses of their data for publication. Enough confirmations of the logarithmic straight-line trend have been reported for this to be widely touted as a basis for advance planning, provided the coordinates of the logarithmic line can be defined. Various exceptions to the parabolic shape of curves that show improvement history have also been noted. Since the original concept has become widely applied, at least in defense-related industries, the coverage here will be limited to a discussion of that approach and how it relates to productivity control fundamentals.

Cumulative Average, or Unit Costs?

Two types of improvement curves are shown in Figure 30C. One of these, the straight line, results when unit man-hour costs are plotted as noted above. The other results when cumulative average man-hours are plotted in relation to the cumulative number of units. While there are obvious differences in the shape of the two curves at the beginning, their slope becomes essentially the same at higher production levels. There is a difference of opinion among those who search for guidance in this area as to which of the two ideas more closely represents what has occurred in past examples. Plotting cumulative averages tends to mask discrepancies in the data. For this reason, and because of the inherent simplicity in utilizing improvement curves based on unit costs, the latter way of showing improvement trends has been used more frequently.

D.O.D. Acceptance

Despite the fact that improvement-curve theory is based only on empirical evidence, and despite some of the problem conditions involved in applying it (to be discussed), there appears to be nothing on the industrial engineering horizon that is better suited for utilizing historical data to predict future cost trends. This is particularly true in the manufacture of newly designed and highly complex products, where time standards are likely to be far below actual costs at the beginning of a contract because of design and quality control uncertainties. Many defense-related products fall into this category. The Department of Defense has previously accepted the concept of improvement curves as a management tool and a basis for cost negotiations.

DETERMINING THE SLOPE OF IMPROVEMENT CURVES

Slope Defined as Rate of Cost Increase

The three curves drawn in Figure 30A are all parabolic in shape, but they depict different rates of improvement. Inherent in the algebraic formulas for such curves is the fact that quantities measured on the Y-axis will decrease at a constant rate for each doubling of quantities on the X-axis. When the same curves are drawn to logarithmic scale, as in 30B, this rate of decrease, expressed as a percentage, is referred to as the slope of the resulting straight lines. The use of man-hour, rather than actual direct labor costs, avoids the need to correct for inflation and simplifies the use of time standards in conjunction with improvement curves. Considering the 85 percent improvement curve in 30B, the line beginning at one thousand man-hours—the time required to produce the first unit—extends through 850 man-hours at the second unit, $0.85 \times 850 = 722.5$ at the fourth unit, $0.85 \times 722.5 = 614$ at the eighth unit produced, etc.

Continuing Need for Historical Cost Data

The slope can be derived in a valid manner through the analysis of man-hour records, just as was done by Wright and others. It is not valid to assume that the improvement curve used by one company for a specific kind of product would be applicable in another company, even where a similar product is involved. Differences in management and staff capabilities, types of equipment used, the nature of productivity control systems, and the qualifications of operators can all affect (a) the initial costs in relation to true standards, and (b) the rate of improvement thereafter. While the application of improvement-curve theory makes cost estimating more flexible, it does not change the need for developing and utilizing historical records of actual man-hour costs.

If it is assumed that the logarithmic straight-line function is applicable, the slope and coordinates of the line are established if the initial cost and one other point on the curve can be determined. Deriving two different points would also define the improvement curve. Since various exceptions to the parabolic shape have been reported, however, common sense would suggest that additional points be identified to ensure that the use of improvement curves is sound for a particular application.

The Need to Consider Applying More Than One Curve

Wright's analysis of aircraft cost was based on overall man-hours, as has been the case with much of the confirming data. If improvement curves are to be used in different manufacturing sections, there is less assurance from improvement-curve theory—empirically developed in all cases—that the parabolic function will apply reliably in every manufacturing section.

For example, it matters little to qualified operators of shears, punch presses, or milling machines whether the work to be performed is near the start or end of a production contract, so long as the needed material, adequate tooling, and correct specifications are at hand. And if there is a functioning productivity control system, these basic requirements should be met before shop orders are issued to feeder sections. Time standards are meant to be realistic and achievable for production quantities that are typically involved. There may be little reason why operators in some feeder departments cannot meet the time values, even on new work. A sectional performance level in such departments, where 100 percent is an acceptable target level for operators, might remain at a somewhat lower level, depending on the labor productivity control system that is in effect. In other words, there may be no real basis for using improvement curves rather than time standards plus an adjustment factor for cost estimating in selected feeder sections.

If there are subsequent design changes that require rework or repeated operations, or if machining shapes and tolerances are difficult to achieve, there could certainly be more delays and rework at the start than at later production stages. In any case, however, the improvement process in most feeder sections is expected to differ appreciably from that in component assembly or final assembly. Exotic product designs may involve considerable delays or rework in assembly departments at the start of a new production process. If designs are in a state of flux, there may be material shortages. To illustrate the point, one plant, whose work involves the manufacture of complex, state-of-the-art electronic devices, applies improvement curves having a 95 percent slope in feeder sections and slopes of 88 percent and 85 percent in assembly departments.

THE STANDARDS INTERCEPT POINT

By itself, an improvement curve having a predetermined slope can be used to predict the rate of cost decrease in direct labor during the manufacture of successive products, and that is about all. If either the initial production cost or the unit cost at any production level is known, the curve will predict the estimated cost at various levels of cumulative output. But there can be delays and other problems in obtaining unit man-hour costs for products that have a long manufacturing lead time. And it will often be necessary to derive estimated costs before actual production begins. To utilize improvement-curve theory in a flexible manner requires determining a fixed relation between time standards and the logarithmic curve. It should be noted that standards on complex products of unusual design may not be finalized until after the completion of several units. The point on the improvement curve where time standards are historically met is referred to as the "standards intercept."

Use of Standards Intercept for Estimating

It has been typical within the aerospace industry to develop cost estimates by assuming that time standards are attainable on 80–85 percent improvement curves at a production level of a thousand units (Nanda and Adler, 1982; author surveys). Various intercept points are used by other organizations as a basis for cost estimating. As emphasized in previous chapters, sound measured day work standards reflect good shop conditions. They do not include allowances for rework, avoidable delays, poor methods, or other detractors which the improvement curve implies are likely to exist at the start of a new production contract. From the standards intercept point, one estimating technique is to "back up" on the logarithmic line to whatever lower production level the estimate is intended to cover. Or, for higher production quantities, the path on the curve may extend beyond the intercept point.

To illustrate this, let us say that a man-hour estimate is required to manufacture a product when fifteen units have previously been completed. Assume that the time values for all required operations total 2500 man-hours. From the 85 percent curve, such as that in Figure 30B, an initial labor cost of one thousand man-hours would dwindle to 522 hours for the sixteenth product, and about 198 hours at a standards intercept of one thousand units. The estimate for the sixteenth product then becomes 2500 × 522/198, or 6,591 man-hours.

Utilizing the 95 percent curve shown in 30B, with a standards intercept point at the hundredth unit of production, the estimate would become 2500 × 815/700, or 2,910 man-hours. The wide spread between this value and that noted above illustrates the importance of correctly identifying both the slope and standards intercept point when this estimating procedure is applied.

ACCOUNTING FOR BREAKS IN PRODUCTION

If complex manufacturing processes were interrupted for an extended period of time and then started again, a setback in the improvement process could be expected. Such interruptions are not uncommon in defense-related manufacturing. There have been attempts to develop routine procedures that can be followed to account for breaks in production when improvement curves are used for cost estimating. One such procedure is described by G. Anderlohr (1969). An appendix-listed plant has developed a chart, based on his article, which specifies the loss in accumulated "learning" when production breaks occur. This can be illustrated by referring to the previous example in which 6591 man-hours were estimated for the sixteenth product. If a one-year interruption occurred, the chart would indicate a retention of only 20 percent of prior "learning" experience. Only three products would then be figured as completed previously, rather than fifteen. The estimate for the sixteenth product would be calculated as if for the fourth, and the resulting estimate becomes 9,116 man-hours rather than 6,591.

PROBLEMS INVOLVED IN THE APPLICATION OF IMPROVEMENT CURVES

Although there is a mass of literature regarding improvement-curve theory, the detailed ways in which specific organizations apply the theory is not generally publicized because of competitive situations. However, there is enough information in published articles and in my own detailed studies to list some questionable aspects that appear to exist.

Conflicts with Tested Productivity Control Principles

The proper application of time standards involves methods analysis. When time values are issued, this implies that there is a sequence of operations or procedures which can be followed to produce a part or make an assembly, provided operators are supervised adequately and given proper training. To say that the performance ratio for assembly operations on a new product is as low as 38 percent after a production level of at least sixteen units (2,500/6,591 in the previous example), and to say that this ratio will remain low for hundreds of such repetitions does not speak well of the control system that is in effect.

To illustrate the point, consider the various operations required to completely manufacture a newly designed steam turbine in a modern facility. Before shop orders are issued to the floor, the necessary tooling would be on hand and listed on the route sheets. Designs would be firmed up and drawing copies furnished as required. Material needs would be identified and made available to operators through adequate control. The necessary operations would be listed in sequence, with time standards. If an advanced measured day work control system were in effect (to be described later), supervisors would know what the performance of individual operators was, in relation to standards, in time to ask questions and help solve problems.

The sectional performance ratios for such work would be somewhat below the 100 percent target level, for various reasons. Perhaps a 75 percent ratio could be expected at first, increasing to around 85 percent after a half-dozen units had been completed. This is not just conjecture. It is what has typically been observed where control systems were effectively applied.

When products being manufactured are on the cutting edge of technology, it is understandable that there could be long delays for inspections, frequent rework to make design revisions, and other detracting conditions not included in time standards. Here the 85 percent improvement curves and standards intercept points at production levels of one thousand might conceivably apply. The point to be made, however, is that management should be very slow to base cost estimating decisions on improvement curve applications without thorough derivation and testing of the steps involved.

Obtaining Data to Define Improvement-curve Slopes

It is often the case that work is being done in a specific section on a mix of products. To accumulate actual costs for a specific product at different levels of production requires a sophisticated time reporting system. Yet that is necessary if data for improvement-curve slopes is to be meaningful. Because of the difficulties in obtaining valid data, it is tempting to adopt the slopes that other companies are known to apply. And there are also temptations to minimize the differences in improvement-curve slopes within various plant sections or for different types of work within sections. Taking such approaches can provide misleading and inaccurate information.

Failure to Derive or Define Standards Intercepts

Before comments are made along this line, attention is directed to Figure 31, which may help to illustrate certain points. The block diagram on the left portrays a mix of detracting conditions that could reasonably be expected to exist when the average performance ratio for operators within a manufacturing section was 50 percent in relation to target standards. That happens to be the estimated performance ratio derived from a 90 percent improvement curve, standards intercept at one thousand and production level at the tenth unit. We will assume that the work involved is done within a department where component assemblies are produced for different products. Given a 50 percent performance ratio, the time standard would fill only half of the eight-hour working time. We will also assume that time values are listed on route sheets, but the performance level of individual operators is not evaluated in relation to the standards. While not an effective basis for productivity control, this is the case in various plants, including some that utilize improvement-curve theory. The estimated percentages in blocks A-E of the diagram are explained as follows:

Delays Not Related to Learning. Numerous work sampling studies have shown that operators in such departments typically develop habits leading to excess downtime in the range of 20 percent above allowances in the time values. Such delays can include late starts, early quits, other

FIGURE 31.
Performance in Relation to Standards at Two Production Levels.

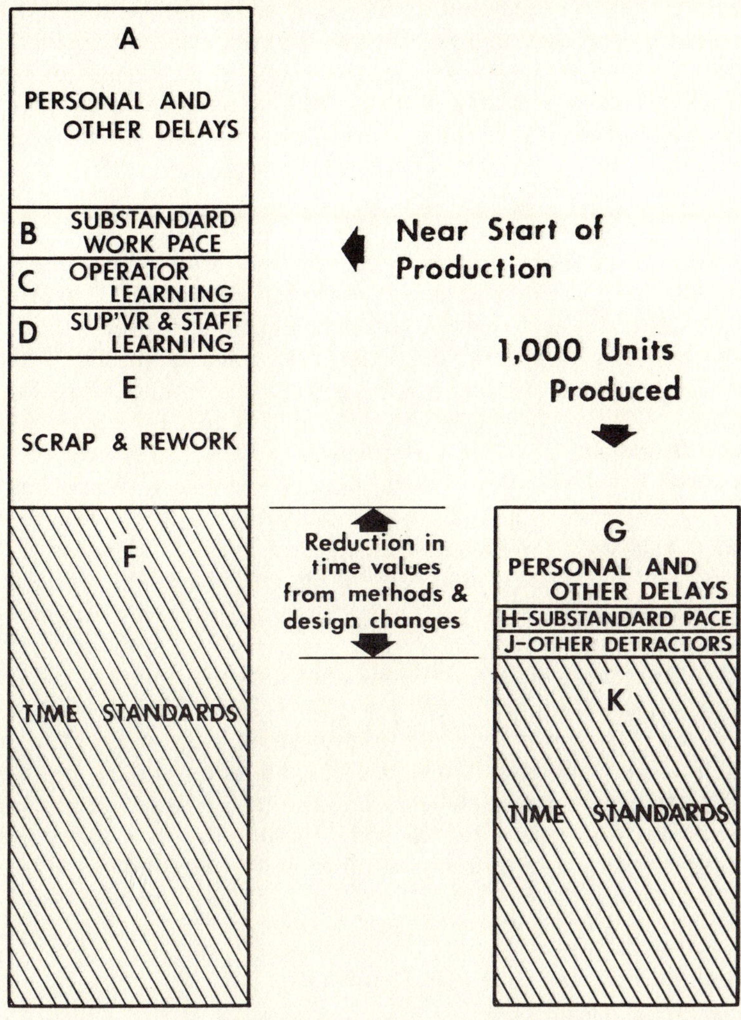

personal downtime, and perhaps some delays from lack of material or other reasons. This is shown by block A, which has no relation to operator learning and is the result of ineffective productivity control.

Lower Pace Level, Not Related to Learning. Block B (5 percent) is estimated to be the reduced pace level that goes along with ineffective control. This also has no relation to operator learning.

Detracting Conditions that Can in Time be Avoided. Blocks C, D, and E represent losses due to operator learning deficiencies, supervisor or staff deficiencies that may occur at the beginning of a contract, and rework or scrap that can eventually be minimized.

Consider next the diagram at the right in Figure 31, which is the performance level determined from the improvement-curve slope and standards intercept point. The operators' inefficiencies are shown in blocks G and H as remaining at the same 25 percent level, because this is the same department as before, with the same degree of productivity control. Since the control system involves no systematic way to question the reasons for failure to meet time values, we would expect to see other losses that have not been included in the time values (block J). The sectional performance ratio is 65 percent, even though the time value established at the production level of ten units has been met. The reasons for the lower time value lie in design and methods improvements during the several years of production required to reach the intercept point. Some of the conclusions that might be drawn from this illustration are as follows:

Vague Procedures. The literature relating to improvement curves generally refers to the standards intercept point as a step in estimating, but without recognizing the fact that properly maintained standards are subject to revision over a lengthy production interval because of design revisions and improvements. Different time values would produce different estimates when applying the steps described above. The intended procedure remains vague.

Lack of Transference. Just as was noted for the improvement-curve slope, deriving the standards intercept point for specific curves involves the analysis of historical data which many plants are not likely to have available. To use the one thousand-unit value or any other, simply because it has been used elsewhere, is no more valid than to choose an improvement curve slope for the same reason. Variation in labor productivity control effectiveness is another reason for this lack of transference.

Indefinite Effect of Breaks in Production

For many manufacturing organizations, job-lot production is a way of life, and breaks in producing a specific design come after each job lot is completed. Time values are established so they can be met for quantities typically produced, and they are met if sound productivity control systems are in effect. There are always some problem conditions that tend to lower sectional performance ratios, such as equipment breakdowns or material shortages, but these have no inherent relation to breaks in production. The standards are commonly divided as to setup and run time, so that necessary changes in setup need not detract from the performance level.

As products increase in complexity, there is understandably some learning loss on the part of operators, supervisors, and staff when production breaks occur. The example given previously, in which a year's lapse in production continuity was said to cause an estimated increase from 6,591 to 9,116 man-hours (38 percent), would seem to be extreme, provided control systems were in effect to specify the operations required and assure that material was on hand. Organizations using the improvement curve for estimating would be expected to accumulate data concerning the effect of production breaks within their own manufacturing departments.

Need for Adjusting Improvement Concepts to Account for Similar Prior Production

Just as there may be some loss when production breaks occur, there will be an advantage to gain when a new product design is introduced following or concurrent with the manufacture of similar products. In the previous example of steam turbine production, a new design was said to make little difference in sectional performance ratios. The literature dealing with improvement curve concepts does not specify systematic ways to account for the effect of prior experience.

Using Improvement-curve Guidelines for Staffing

The estimating procedures described previously could be applied as a basis for staffing departments to handle planned work loads. If this were done, Parkinson's "law" comes quickly to the forefront: "Work expands so as to fill the time available for its completion." This has been recognized in the literature (Nanda and Adler, 1982) as a possible reason for some of the evidence submitted concerning the validity of improvement-curve applications.

CONCLUSIONS, IMPROVEMENT CURVES

There have been too many published validations of the improvement-curve concept not to view this as a potentially useful technique for cost estimating or manpower planning, if tailored to fit existing conditions within specific sections. Most organizations involved in manufacturing defense-related equipment have embraced the technique, and the Department of Defense has previously endorsed it.

Questionable aspects of improvement-curve applications include the slope of such curves for work within a section, standards intercept points for different types of work, extra allowance calculations for breaks in production, and the effects of prior experience when followed by new products that are similar. There are ways for a specific plant to derive the factors required for improvement-curve applications. The fact that such derivations may not be possible without changes in man-hour reporting systems, and may not be possible in a short period of time, tends to encourage borrowing some or all of the slope/intercept/production-break applications from other companies. This can lead to serious estimating errors.

Some of the results from improvement-curve applications in current use, such as production quantities required before standards can be achieved, or the added allowances for breaks in production, differ widely from practices followed in LC/LR manufacturing where valid labor productivity control systems exist. This tends to raise questions as to whether plants that make use of improvement curves for manpower staffing may be following a self-perpetuating path in doing so.

The day-to-day application of improvement-curve concepts described in this chapter is largely within defense-related industries. Other manufacturing locations, which have no doubt applied historical data in some manner for cost estimating, would do well to investigate whether logarithmic improvement curves can serve their needs in a more flexible and dependable manner.

Operators' Learning

BASIC CONCEPTS

A Fundamental Difference between Improvement Curves and Operator-learning Curves

With some exceptions, the literature dealing with what we have termed improvement curves implies that it is conceivable for man-hour cost reductions to continue indefinitely along the parabolic curve. Assuming an 85 percent slope, for example, the man-hour cost for a specific aircraft at the ten-thousandth unit might be figured at 85 percent of the cost for the five-thousandth unit. Since the manufacture of aircraft and similar complex products rarely approaches such levels, the improvement trend for that production level and type of manufacturing remains theoretical. The concept is believable, however, because of the history of design, tooling, and methods improvements that have taken place in such industries. For learning by operators, on the other hand, there is clearly a performance limit that will be reached for any given manufacturing method. That limit may be partly set by equipment involved, and partly by the known physical limitations of hand and arm motions.

Two Stages in the Learning Process

As noted by Hancock, the process of learning how to perform a task includes two stages: (1) threshold learning, consisting of learning a sequence of events to be performed; and (2) reinforcement learning, during which repetition of the task creates improvement in the ability to perform. Hancock has shown in experiments that the reinforcement process tends to follow a parabolic curve when plotted as cycle time versus number of repetitions, just as was illustrated in Figures 30A and 30B for overall manufacturing improvement. If necessary to do so, reinforcement learning can be quantified, using predetermined time analyses and specified procedures (Hancock and Bayha, 1982). This is not required for product cost estimating, since operator learning is embodied within the manufacturing improvement curves that were previously described.

Correlation between Methods Improvement and Learning-time Reduction

The steps proposed by Hancock bring out the fact that complex hand movements, such as difficult grasps and positions, cause a greater increase in reinforcement learning time than do the simpler motions. Since the complex motion increments consume more time at any stage of learning, it has long been recognized that methods analysis should be aimed at minimizing the need for them. Uses of bell-mouthed guides for positioning, or fixed placement of parts between operations to eliminate jumbled grasps, are just two of many techniques to remember in developing better methods. The point to be noted here is that work simplification not only reduces motion times after learning is complete, but also acts to reduce the learning time involved.

Ways to Minimize Threshold Learning

Threshold learning times will of course be variable, depending on factors such as the following: length and complexity of the operation, capabilities of the operator, prior experience on similar work, and the effectiveness of training that is provided. The latter point is particularly subject to neglect in many instances because it can be postponed when supervisors become occupied with other duties. Some of the tested ways to facilitate the learning process are as follows:

Operator Instruction Cards. For SC/R operations, needed motion-pattern instructions can usually be recorded on one card. Plant 69, listed in the appendix, has for many years required that the detailed motion pattern be posted for each manual operation, along with photographs of the correct workplace layout. The 4M DATA system, described in chapter

6, provides a way to automate the Get/Place motion descriptions for each hand.

Sequence Instructions. Written sequence data for LC/LR operations may be used when the work involved is lengthy and complex. Plant 110 used a key operator to prepare such instructions as the first of large electrically wired control boxes was produced. At plant 19, sequence instructions for relay-instrument assembly were prepared by MPA analysts, with illustrations, as a step in time standards development.

Audiovisual Training. Utilizing slides that are changed automatically along with taped instructions, such programs have been applied at plants 5, 31, and various others to guide operators making complex assemblies. Less expensive than closed-circuit television or films, such units can be actuated by operators at successive work stages. The use of earphones makes it possible to work without disturbing others.

Training Personnel. At plant 47, where some instruction was needed at the beginning of each new production run on lengthy paced assembly lines, key operators were effectively used for training during limited periods.

Training by Supervisors. It is normally the supervisor's job to provide necessary training. If the feedback of performance data can be handled at short intervals, as described in a following chapter, a routine can be established through which the supervisor knows where instructions are needed.

THE QUESTION OF EXTRA ALLOWANCES FOR LEARNING TIME

Wage Incentives

As will be noted in chapter 11, learning allowances are required for a period of time when new operators are made part of a group that is covered by a group wage incentive plan. With the basic wage rate guaranteed by incentive systems that are applied on an individual basis, there is no cause for new employees to receive learning allowances before they can become proficient. However, there may be problems when experienced operators, who have been receiving bonus pay regularly, are required to begin work on new jobs where a period of learning will be necessary. If such changes in assignment are made on the basis of seniority, learning allowances should not be required.

Measured Day Work

In measured day work applications, where performance ratios are derived both for individual employees and for a supervisor's section, there are situations where job learning causes a reduction in both operators' and sectional performance ratios. The question arises as to whether learning allowances should be developed and applied in such cases, much as was noted for new operators where group wage incentives are in effect. It was the general consensus within measured daywork plants listed in the appendix that this should not be done, for the following reasons:

Variations in Ability and Prior Experience. Because of the wide diversity in operators' abilities and experience, the arbitrary application of learning allowances cannot be dependable. Many qualified operators can perform at the 100 percent level on new jobs, right from the start. Arbitrary learning allowances would hinder achieving standard performance in such cases.

Camouflaging the Problems. Learning allowances tend to hide problems that exist. When a supervisor sees a low performance ratio, he should be expected to investigate the cause and seek to correct it. In the case of poor methods or delays caused by new job assignments, training by the supervisor is called for, rather than allowances to camouflage the problem.

Answering Questions about Low Productivity. As lower sectional performance ratios are questioned by management, such questions can be answered by identifying the amount of new work or new operators that may have been required within the section. Chapter 14 shows how this can be done routinely.

Cost of Applying Allowances. The application of operator-learning allowances in a dependable way would be a time-consuming and costly MPA function that should be avoided wherever possible.

How Time Standards Reflect Learning Requirements

Time standards should be based on the performance level that can realistically be expected after threshold learning, given the combination of operation cycle time and typical production quantities involved. For example, a four-hour operation at appendix-listed plant 30, to produce a complex wiring harness where order quantities are in the range of thirty to forty units, will never be done with the same methods/pace finesse that could be expected at plant 83 for wire insertion in fluorescent light fixtures on a paced conveyor, and where order quantities are in the thousands. If direct time study is used as a basis for standards, a qualified analyst will handle the obvious differences through performance rating. If 4M DATA (computer-aided MTM) is used for standard data development, the built-in simo-chart adjustments that MTM provides for low-volume operations may not suffice to account for the hesitations, repeated motions, and occasional fumbling that will not be recognized or included in predetermined time analysis for complex LC/LR operations. A separate adjustment factor, determined through prior comparisons with direct time study, may be necessary in such cases. The 4M DATA system applies such factors automatically, as directed.

THE NEED FOR WORK ASSIGNMENT FLEXIBILITY

A significant point which does not seem to be discussed in references that deal with the learning process is the need for supervisors to be given enough flexibility in making work assignments so that there is a reasonable chance of minimizing the amount of learning required by operators involved. To illustrate this point, three examples are noted below:

SC/R Operations on Paced Lines

It is sound practice to balance the division of work on paced lines, specifying the precise grouping of job elements for each work station. But requiring that the predetermined grouping of elements be followed without change assumes two conditions that are rarely true: (1) that the standard time content of each element has been precisely determined; and (2) that the operators to be assigned are equally experienced and otherwise qualified. Many plants find it is practical to give supervisors some flexibility in shifting the recommended balance to compensate for differences that exist in the experience level of operators.

The Possible Effects on Learning Costs of Centralized Production Control

For nonpaced operations of any length, some flexibility is needed in the assignment of jobs to operators by a supervisor. There are various reasons for this, such as equipment loading, material availability, and the need to have jobs available for prompt assignment. But one of the primary reasons for such flexibility is to facilitate the assignment of specific jobs to those who can handle them best. For example, if there is one operator in the group who performed a complex operation on a previous job lot, then it would minimize learning costs if that operator could be assigned the same work on parts just delivered to the section. But if that operator has a few more hours of work before completion of another job already started, there will be a delay before the optimum matchup between an experienced operator and available work can be made. If tight scheduling requires that some other operator be assigned to the new work, there could well be a 20 percent added cost due to the learning time involved. And added costs could extend throughout the section if inflexible priorities required that the first available operator be assigned to the highest priority job lot on hand in the section. The needed emphasis on minimizing work-in-process inventory costs should not overshadow a recognition of the added labor cost from increased learning time.

Maintenance Craft Flexibility Versus Learning Costs

A somewhat similar point could be made about work done by plant maintenance, which is often the most costly indirect hourly function within a manufacturing plant. Because of highly restrictive labor agreements in the past regarding the work boundaries of craft groups within a maintenance department, new plants have tended to minimize the number of craft designations. In some cases, there may be just two specialized groups within maintenance: mechanical and electrical. This provides needed flexibility of assignment, which should be retained. But there are nevertheless the same learning periods required to become proficient in crafts such as plumbing, carpentry, hydraulic systems, etc., as has always been the case. A sound management objective would be to retain the advantage of flexible assignments when emergencies occur, or for short sequences in all work, but also to retain the needed specialization on nonemergency jobs by assigning specific individuals to handle work for which they are best trained. A following chapter will enlarge on this point.

CONCLUSIONS, OPERATORS' LEARNING

Although a number of useful training aids are available to shorten the process of threshold learning, supervisory attention is the most basic requirement. In considering the shape of learning curves for a given method during the process called reinforcement learning, it is clear that there is an ending point, unlike the theoretical concept of manufacturing improvement curves. There is a correlation between various methods improvement goals and the goal of learning-time reduction, which adds to the possible savings from applied work simplification. While extra allowances for learning time by newly assigned operators is common practice in group wage incentives, learning allowances can be a handicap in measured day-work applications, and they should be unnecessary for individual wage incentives.

It is important to recognize that direct supervisors require some flexibility in selecting jobs for specific operators, if learning time and other delaying conditions are to be minimized. Centralized production control systems for LC/LR work, while a necessary scheduling function, cannot substitute for supervisory judgement in the work assignment process.

Trends toward reducing the number of designated crafts within plant maintenance provide flexibility in assigning personnel to perform emergency jobs or short craft sequences, but learning requirements are still a significant factor to be considered in making craft assignments.

10
Selecting and Preparing for a Productivity Control System

Recent industrial history contains many examples of labor productivity control systems that have been successful in reducing costs, and many others that have failed and been discarded. It is difficult to look behind the scenes to know all of the reasons for success or failure. As we said in chapter 2, however, there appears to be a set of interrelated principles that must be considered and acted upon if any control system is to be effective at the outset and remain so as the years pass. At the risk of being somewhat redundant, these management principles are listed again, along with comments as to why they cannot be ignored if a firm basis for control is to be established.

DEVELOP CLEAR AND FAIR IDEALS

The rules of fair play must extend throughout the management team. As those who are responsible for achieving positive results work toward such a goal, there are inevitable temptations for some to ignore the concept of fairness in dealing with operators. Safeguards against this should be established. In all plants within company K, as previously noted, basic employee relations principles are summarized on framed plaques for all to see. Of course, fairness must work both ways, since some employees are like some of those in management when working relationships appear threatened. Procedural rules governing the rights of both labor and management need to be written down. The content and interpretation of such rules are often subject to labor/management negotiations.

Applying a control system that seeks a fair day's work may require certain rules that appear questionable to some. An example previously cited is the practical impossibility of allowing worker-originated methods improvements to be exempt from revisions in time standards. To allow for such exemptions would be to open a Pandora's box of claims and counterclaims about the origin of ideas, and maintenance of standards would in time become impossible.

Establishing a suggestion award program is one way to reduce unfairness in such cases, but there can be problems with this. Company B, noted in the appendix, received as many as ten thousand suggestions per year at one major plant during a start-up period. It was necessary to reply to many of these that the idea involved was already in use in other departments and could not qualify for a full award. Administering any suggestion award plan fairly but effectively is often a costly procedure. A number of plant locations, including many of those listed in the appendix, have discontinued such programs for this reason.

A conclusion to be drawn is that adhering to everyone's concept of what is fair in the administration of a control system may not always be possible. But establishing ways to maximize fair play is an essential management policy.

SELECT QUALIFIED PERSONNEL

The point here is an obvious one. A vacancy may be filled by upgrading from lower classified jobs, in which case well-defined procedural rules usually must be followed. Where employee selections are made from outside applicants, the available choice depends largely on wage rates for specific job classifications. For most of the appendix-listed plant locations, job evaluation procedures required to identify specific labor grades involve a joint effort by representatives from the MPA and employee relations departments. It is a periodic responsibility of the latter group to survey area wage rates for equivalent job classifications. By assuring that wages within a specific plant are competitive with area rates, there is a reasonable chance to select new employees who are qualified.

In all cases, the supervisor where a vacancy is to be filled should be given a chance to reject the applicant where there is cause to do so. Normally, a specific and fairly short time interval is established as a designated trial period. After such a period, acceptable reasons for potential discharge become more stringent, often following procedures that have evolved through labor/management negotiations.

PROVIDE JUSTIFIABLE STAFF

The functions of what we have chosen to call an MPA group have been discussed in previous chapters. It would be helpful if it were possible to suggest applicable ratios of MPA personnel to operators covered by the productivity control system. Attempting to do this would be misleading, however, because of wide variations such as the scope of assigned duties, status of standard data compilations, type of control program, competency of staff personnel, or the nature of problems involved in administering the system. Appendix-listed plants 61 and 67 had MPA/operator ratios of 1:35 because of massive problems in administering a group wage incentive system. Plant 6 successfully utilized ratios of about 1:75 to handle individual incentive applications. Plant 69 used ratios of approximately 1:50 at the start of a measured day-work control program, gradually reducing this to about 1:75 as their highly effective control application continued for many years. Plants 18 and 83, with a number of paced lines and relatively simple operations, applied measured day work successfully over a long period with an MPA/operator ratio of less than 1:100.

The tendency here is to view the cost of such MPA involvement as an added cost in applying a productivity control system. This overlooks a significant point. As previously indicated, many of the appendix-listed plants found that MPA analysts could regularly generate about three times their annual salary in cost reductions through methods improvement savings.

STANDARDIZE WORKING CONDITIONS

Lighting, heating, ventilation, safety requirements, adequate maintenance of equipment, provisions for operators to sit while working—all require due consideration and appropriate action for a control system to be fully effective. For example, it has long been recognized that the cost of chairs with footrests and adjustable backrests is a sound investment. Where practical, the operators should be able to sit or stand alternately, without being forced to work in a strained position. Sound working conditions should be so prevalent that they rarely need to be considered in developing individual time standards.

DEFINE WORK REQUIREMENTS

The usual procedures for handling this basic control principle systematically include the following: a routing function for specific shop orders involving sequential, nonpaced operations; operator instruction sheets for SC/R operations; line balancing specifications for paced operations; engineering drawings where applicable; and detailed instructions where the combination of routing data and engineering drawings do not provide sufficient information. Some of this data may be kept on file in shop sections where the work will be done. The routing information for LC/LR operational sequences is typically issued, along with drawing copies, in a "job pack" which accompanies the issued material as it proceeds through the shop from operation to operation.

Route sheet preparation is a responsibility of the MPA group for most of the appendix-listed plants, although the preparation may involve inputs from other groups, such as manufacturing engineering. There is generally a complete bill of material, followed by a condensed description of sequential operations. The time standards for each operation are listed in terms of setup and the per-piece operation time, or "run time." Operations are numbered, and the combination of shop order number plus the operation number provides a basis for information feedback to permit tracking of the order status from start to completion.

Computer inputs of routine information serve both to print the route sheet copies and set up a data base for production control and material control follow-up. In many cases within appendix-listed plants, this data base is also used, in combination with information transmitted in other ways, for the periodic reporting of sectional and operator performance records. Along with routing data, one or more punched cards for shop-order and operation-number identification may be issued during the various steps of informational feedback by operators. Such cards would be retained in the job pack envelopes.

CONTROL MATERIAL AVAILABILITY

As already noted, it is not within the designated scope of this book to cover procedures for material control in terms of computerized techniques, inventory control functions, material flow systems, hardware storage within user departments, etc. A following chapter will review some of the feedback techniques that are essential in knowing the status of material in process. Reference sources listed in the appendix cover basic aspects of material control. The subject is one in which there is little mystery involved but much needed attention to details. Labor control systems will fall short if material is not readily available when jobs are assigned. And direct supervisors will not find time to handle their necessary duties in productivity control if they must continually look for needed material before or after work assignments are made.

MAINTAIN SOUND PERFORMANCE STANDARDS

This principle is essential to the long-term success of any control system. Because of multiple and significant uses for time standards, their application has become widespread within industry. As noted previously, the fact that very approximate standards will suffice for some of the applications tends to obscure the fact that labor productivity control will suffer unless there is reasonable precision in developing production targets used to evaluate operators' or sectional performance, to balance paced lines, or to serve as the basis for bonus calculation in wage incentive systems.

PLAN MANPOWER REQUIREMENTS

Personnel requirements for handling projected work loads efficiently can be predicted on an approximate basis through reference to marketing forecasts and orders already received. The MPA group may properly be assigned responsibilities for coordinating such predictions, applying man-hour estimates, and recommending sectional manpower levels. Minor variations in manpower requirements can be handled through departmental transfers, normal personnel turnover, occasional overtime, vacation scheduling, or inventory fluctuations. The costs of major changes in manpower levels should be evaluated, so that such steps are taken only when justified.

The point to remember is that a departmental group cannot perform efficiently unless there is sufficient assignable work at hand. To restate this more emphatically, operators will tend to reduce their performance level intentionally unless they perceive clearly that there is enough assignable work to avoid force reductions.

While there are costs involved in using inventory buildup as a way to level the work load, just as there are costs in manpower fluctuations to accommodate load changes, these disadvantages need not apply in large groups such as plant maintenance, toolmaking, or janitorial functions. To some extent, low priority construction work can be postponed to level the maintenance work load. This may also be true for toolmaking projects. In all of these functions, a portion of the work load can generally be handled on a contract basis during normal periods, so that minimal crew sizes can be supplied with adequate work during slack times.

CONSIDER WHETHER WAGE INCENTIVES ARE JUSTIFIED

Judgment is required here, and it should be based on a thorough understanding of both potential savings and potential problems. It might be helpful at this point to describe a type of work in which wage incentives could properly be considered, and another where incentive applications would clearly do more harm than good.

An Example where Incentives Could be Helpful

Consider first a manufacturing organization having about three hundred direct operators and producing a limited range of mechanical and electrical devices. The product line has been fairly stable over the years, with moderate growth in output from year to year. Much of the work is manual in nature, with very few operations in which machine cycle time controls output. Although the plant is approaching its capacity limitations, based on how operators have performed in the past, management believes that a continued increase in production requirements is likely to occur.

This plant is privately owned. It is managed by the principal owner, who has developed close and trusting relations with employees. Wage rates are slightly below the area average, and a few of the more skilled operators have reluctantly left to seek better-paying jobs. The plant is fairly modern in its application of manufacturing information data, but time values have largely been estimated in the past. Wage payment has always been on a day-work basis, and this is reflected by leisurely working habits on the part of most operators.

The manager of this plant, whom we shall assume to be familiar with wage incentive principles, could properly give serious consideration to installing a financial incentive plan that would help meet his production targets without an increase in plant size, and which could serve to keep operators from leaving for "greener pastures." Assuming that the owner/manager is familiar with administrative problems involved in the installation and maintenance of such a system, and assuming he would stay closely involved in dealing with potential problems, there is a good chance that a wage incentive plan could succeed. Establishing a small staff group to review methods and develop sound time values would be a first step and the chances are that this function would pay for itself by developing improved methods as jobs are analyzed. Since the basic plant equipment does not involve a large maintenance function, the manager would not face a major problem when those within maintenance began to observe some operators earning wages near their own rates of pay.

Where Wage Incentives Should Not be Considered

Next, consider a large facility where there are over a thousand employees involved in all phases of low-volume, complex electronics manufacturing. The equipment in use often controls an operator's work pace. Order quantities are generally low to begin with but may increase at intervals. There is considerable rework as minor defects are found or design changes are introduced. The rate of learning how to perform jobs efficiently is different in feeder sections from that in departments where electronic assemblies are put together. Time values have been established for this work based on a proficient learning level. Performance reports range from low percentages at the beginning of a new type of work to higher levels when order quantities increase.

Clearly, the application of a wage incentive plan at such a plant would involve many problems. Delays such as those occasioned by rework, material shortages, waiting on inspection, or reference to instructions would generate allowance claims that could easily be exaggerated. If time standards were correctly based on full knowledge of how jobs should be performed, there would be a wide discrepancy in wage earnings, leading to dissatisfaction and pressures to loosen the standards. A following chapter will indicate many other reasons why the application of wage incentives to work of this kind would be difficult to administer on a continuing basis.

This is not to say that measured day work would be equally unsound for work at such a plant. With supervisory involvement, failure to meet standards could lead to the identification and correction of problems, which is the pathway to improvement.

Typical Questions That Should Be Asked

In these two examples, we have shown where wage incentives might be helpful, and where they would be impractical. There is a wide gap between the two situations. In considering where incentive systems could properly be applied within that gap, the following questions would be applicable:

- Would improved performance appreciably reduce potential overhead costs?
- Could most of the plant personnel be covered by an incentive plan in a practical manner?
- Does the work involve relatively few unavoidable delays that would require special allowances to make incentive earnings possible?
- Do most of the operations require a relatively short learning period by those in appropriate job classifications?
- Can most operations be performed by individual operators, or by small groups of the same size that stay together? Or, if variable group activity is required, are the potential hazards of group wage incentives thoroughly understood and considered to be avoidable? (See chapter 12.)

- Does the work consist largely of manually controlled operations, not on paced lines?
- If there is a labor union involved, can its representatives be expected to accept the principles of wage incentive administration without undue resistance?
- Are existing wage rates such that they can properly serve as incentive base rates, without being reduced to lower values?
- Does the plant manager thoroughly understand what his responsibilities would be in upholding the integrity of an incentive application?

If the answer to all of these questions is "yes," there is a good chance that an incentive program can succeed. If the answer to some of them is "no," contents of the following chapters will help to explain why there may be potential problems in making an incentive system function as intended.

DEVELOP METHODS IMPROVEMENTS

This principle implies a continuation of methods analysis and improvement, not just a short-term approach. One reason for continued emphasis lies in new technology, which is being created with increasing frequency. A plant that does not stay abreast of available tools, equipment, and techniques may soon find itself outdone by competitors. Methods analysis must also stay abreast of the product design changes that are commonplace in most industrial organizations. A third reason for emphasizing methods improvement on a continuing basis is the fact that the ultimately low-cost technique rarely comes at first try. Invariably, one idea can build upon what has been done before. There seems no end to what can be achieved through continued questioning of the many aspects that constitute effective manufacturing methods.

As already noted, the scope of this book does not include a detailed discussion of manufacturing engineering technology. But the subject of methods is everyone's business, and much can be achieved through simple and inexpensive changes. However, ideas that appear simple upon fruition may not be generated without systematic review. While direct supervisors and other managers generally have the inherent ability to improve production concepts, their preoccupation with managerial details often precludes a sufficient depth of study. Consistent improvement usually calls for specialized staff personnel who have specific assignments for analyzing and upgrading methods.

INDICATE TARGETS FOR ACCOMPLISHMENT

In a sense, manufacturing route sheets that show setup and each-piece time standards for required operations are a listing of targets for accomplishment. The same could be said for a car dealer's service guide that spells out average repair times. But unless an auto mechanic realizes that both the shop foreman and customer are aware that there will be only a two-hour charge for a specific repair job, that job could easily stretch to an afternoon's work. And unless an operator knows that the time values on route sheets are being specifically compared with actual performance time, either through wage incentive bonus calculations or through other forms of performance reporting, then the time values on route sheets are likely to be ignored.

Going a step further, assume that the auto mechanic knows that a customer who brought in a vehicle at 8:00 A.M expects to have the several items totaling four hours of work completed by noon. Usually, the work will be done on time. Similarly, an operator may be assigned several jobs having time values that total about four hours, which are expected to be completed during the morning work period. This target for accomplishment becomes more definite and more likely to be achieved. Chapter 14 will enlarge on these points.

SUPERVISE TO ACHIEVE PRODUCTIVITY AND QUALITY OBJECTIVES

A survey of various plants listed in the appendix that have applied group wage incentive systems in manufacturing would have shown that their ratios of operators per supervisor were much higher than such ratios where measured day-work control systems are in effect. That is because incentive supervisors depend on group leaders to handle most job assignments and related details. A chapter that follows will describe problems faced in administering these control systems effectively. Many of the problems were closely related to the lack of clear communication between operators and representatives of management. Evidence to substantiate this will be given later. For now, let us emphasize the point that adequate direct supervision should be provided if productivity control systems are to become and remain cost-effective.

EVALUATE INDIVIDUAL PERFORMANCE

Unless supervisors have a dependable, systematic way to find out where productivity problems exist, they cannot be expected to manage properly. And unless operators know that their supervisor is aware of their performance in relation to standards, measured day-work operators can in many ways camouflage their lack of effort or methods effectiveness. Of course, a control system involving individual incentives must by its very nature have a dependable performance reporting system. A following chapter will discuss the pros and cons of various performance-reporting techniques.

When group wage incentives are established, bonus payments are based on the group's collective performance, although operators within the group often work on individual job assignments. As will be discussed later, this inability to evaluate an individual's performance on specific jobs is a fundamental disadvantage in maintaining effectiveness of such control plans.

It is necessary to deduct significant unavoidable delay times from actual times in reporting performance ratios for operators. This holds for measured day-work as well as for wage incentives. There should be a check by supervisors on the claims for such allowances. Chapter 14 illustrates one way of doing this effectively.

EVALUATE SECTIONAL PERFORMANCE

Most of the appendix-listed plants report sectional performance ratios on a weekly and cumulative basis, without making allowances for delay times. There may also be a second ratio reported with allowances deducted, as noted above for operators. Within listed measured day-work plants, these two percentages were typically referred to as follows: Performance Ratio, Unit Management (PRUM), and Performance Ratio, Operators (PRO). The periodic reports for sections in which wage incentives are involved may call for identifying the extent of day-work and "average earned rate" applications, which for obvious reasons should be minimized.

PROVIDE MANAGEMENT COORDINATION

As emphasized previously, no productivity control system is likely to be successful over an extended period without top management's full understanding and support. The manager at an appropriate level in the organization must go further than to provide a responsible staff and delegate authority. From time to time, the manager should be expected to take an active part in reviewing performance reports, making sure that they are reliable, and coordinating steps for improvement when the need is indicated.

11
Wage Incentive Concepts

OBJECTIVES

A wage incentive application can be said to have three primary objectives, as follows:

Methods Improvement

Competent MPA analysis, prior to the evolution of individual standards, serves to screen the general methods involving equipment, plant layout, and material handling. The development of time standards and standard data involves the analysis and identification of detailed methods such as the use of tools and fixtures, feeds and speeds, workplace layout, and motion patterns by the operator. In the course of such analysis, considerable improvement can be expected even before the motivation through wage incentives.

Minor Reductions in Direct Labor Cost

A low-task performance level ("normal") is defined through the application of time standards. Since the wage rate is generally guaranteed below that level, normal performance becomes the minimum acceptable level, if only by implication. With a "full sharing" incentive plan (to be defined), direct labor costs may be reduced to the extent that low performance can be identified and raised to that level. Although the concept of normal is properly derived as a percentage of the more readily identifiable "high task" performance level (i.e., average incentive pace), it may be assumed that normal differs little from the performance level before incentives are applied. With a full-sharing incentive plan, there are no reductions in labor cost after the low-task level is reached. Thus, direct labor savings with such a plan are not expected to be significant.

Reduction in Overhead Costs

Increased performance above the established low-task level, which is anticipated when incentive plans are soundly implemented and properly maintained, results in greater production from existing equipment and plant space. To the extent that sales volume increases accordingly, overhead costs per product unit are reduced. Since various nondirect groups within the plant can be expected to continue their functions without growth proportional to the increased output by direct operators, further overhead cost reductions are possible.

TYPES OF INCENTIVE PLANS

Task Levels

In Figure 32, line ABC defines the typical full-sharing incentive plan. Line ABD illustrates a partial-sharing plan. Despite wordy phrases often cited to define "normal," as the term is used in control plans of this type, there is no way to stipulate what the normal performance level should be except through training and experience. There are variations, as illustrated previously by data in Figure 5, taken from widely accepted training material. For the ABC system to be successful, however, the low-task level called normal should be set so as to provide a bonus-earning opportunity sufficient to motivate the operators who will be involved. Many would agree that this will be achieved if qualified and experienced operators can earn an average bonus in the range of 25 percent above their base wage when working without undue physical effort.

If normal is designated as 100 percent, which is typically the case, incentive pace would be in the 125 percent range. A more logical but less common approach is to apply the 100 percent value to the expected average level (incentive pace), in which case normal might be labelled 80 percent. With line BC extending through the zero point in both cases, there would be no difference in the full-sharing concept.

Variations in Framework

During the period after wage incentive plans came into vogue, there were numerous variations in their framework. Some of the more intricate

FIGURE 32.
Typical Wage Incentive Plans.

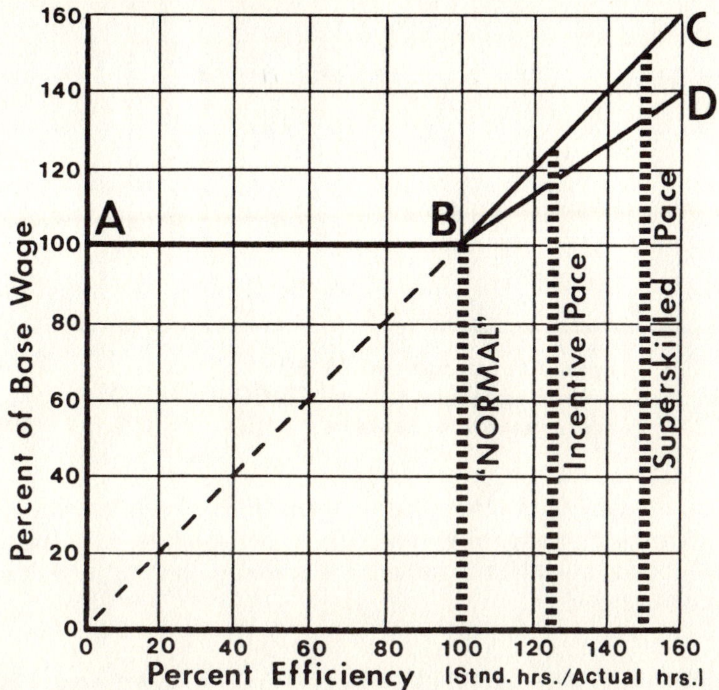

variations have been discontinued in favor of simpler concepts. For example, appendix-listed company K applied incentives in past years which involved an increase in the base rate of 11 percent at point B, with the line to C at a full-sharing slope, and with pace levels defined in terms of somewhat lower percentage values. This framework, intended to motivate workers strongly, was in time revised to the ABC pattern of Figure 32.

Other variations have continued despite what would appear to be extreme differences. The base wage rates at appendix-listed plant 53 were about half those of other area plants, but bonus earnings began at 50 percent of normal and continued as a full-sharing plan. This approach was successful for many years. Despite these and other differences in the framework of specific incentive systems, the ABC concept of Figure 32 remains widely accepted as a fair and workable plan.

Simple piecework plans omit the guaranteed rate shown by line AB. Variations of framework within other incentive plans include a downward shift of point A, Figure 32, with respect to day-work rates for nonincentive jobs. Other variations were developed by pioneers in the field, whose names were attached to specific pay plans (Gantt, Halsey,

FIGURE 33.
A Scale to Illustrate Labor Productivity Changes.

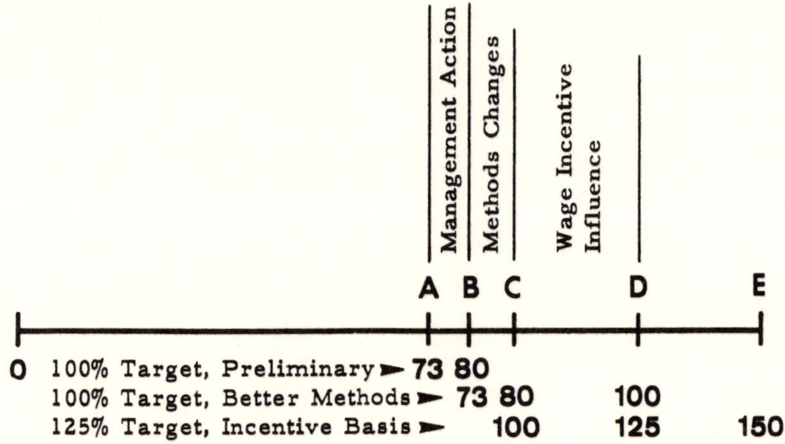

Emerson, Bedaux, and others. See Carson, 1958). With general recognition that the plan shown by line ABC is both simple, fair, and commonly applied, we shall not burden the reader with a detailed description of other types.

AN ILLUSTRATION OF WHAT INCENTIVES ARE MEANT TO ACCOMPLISH

Some of the expected gains in wage incentive control systems come from motivation of operators, but a large part of the gain comes from systematic methods analysis not directly associated with the application of incentives. It may be helpful to illustrate this point in the following way:

Initial Efforts to Improve

Let us say that product sales by plant X are on the increase, and management recognizes the need to get more output from existing plant facilities. We will assume there are competent supervisors involved but no MPA functions or time standards. With reference to the simple diagram shown in Figure 33, the existing productivity level is assumed to be at point A. The 73 percent figure at this point can be viewed in relation to a desirable and fair performance target, which could properly be referred to as the 100 percent basis.

When the need for increased production was recognized, there would no doubt have been meetings with supervisors, discussions about how to improve, and perhaps a few veiled threats. These efforts would probably have smoothed out some of the existing problems. We might assume that material availability improved; supervisors began making work assignments in advance; operators began starting work sooner after the whistle blew; and closer attention by supervisors caused some reduction in excessive personal downtime. There would likely have been little change in work effort or general methods, however, since work habits become hard to change after a long period of acceptance. It would seem reasonable to estimate that the efforts of management could have raised the level of operators' performances to point B on the scale, or about 80 percent of a valid target.

Improvements from Methods Analysis

Let us say that this improvement was not enough to meet sales forecasts, and a small MPA group was brought into the picture for the announced purpose of implementing a wage incentive system. At the insistence of the MPA manager, the first step in this direction was to survey overall methods, in cooperation with supervisors and managers involved. Next, the operational methods were evaluated during a period of time standards development. Through changes in equipment layout, material handling, fixture design, combination of operations, feed or speed revisions, reduction of delay intervals, and other improvements, it was possible to raise the performance level to point C, before the application of incentives began. This required no particular increase in working effort or pace. Although assumed to be a 10 percent improvement, this point can still be viewed as an 80 percent level from the standpoint of operators' performances.

Derivation of Task Levels and Time Standards

Through previous experience and additional training, the MPA group learned to identify an expected level of working pace and operator-controlled methods that represented what was considered attainable on an average basis with financial motivation. This high-task level was labelled 125 percent. A lower-task level of 100 percent was also identified and referred to as "normal." This included 5 percent allowance for unavoidable delay times and 10 percent for personal time and fatigue. We might assume that operators were currently taking about 20 percent nonworking time for the three reasons noted, but working somewhat above the performance level built into the low-task standards. Thus, their net output might well have been at the 80 percent point on the second scale of the diagram, redefined as 100 percent in the new wage incentive arithmetic. Training films were obtained to illustrate the normal performance level.

Effects of Wage Incentives

A wage incentive system was introduced, similar to that defined by line ABC of Figure 32. At the start of the program, most operators were skeptical, realizing that earning a meaningful bonus involved appreciably more output than before. As they became familiar with the methods on which standards were based, however, some produced at a higher rate. Once the reality of bonus earnings became clear, most of the operators increased their relatively low performance level. Some produced near the rate indicated by point E on the scale, which would be attainable by very skilled operators. A few would occasionally exceed this level, which tended to indicate a time-reporting problem or a methods change not yet accounted for by time values.

Some of the operators would barely exceed the level of normal, feeling that the amount of extra bonus was not worth reduced personal delays or extra effort. Despite the fact that incentive normal was pegged at a low-task level, not much could be done to require a better performance, since the working pace above a designated normal is inherently voluntary. When individual performance levels were consistently below normal, however, with the base wage guaranteed, prompt supervisory action was required to find and correct the reasons.

With sound time values, revised as methods were changed, the average performance level of the group could be expected to fall near point D on the scale, which is about 25 percent more production output than expected with MPA methods analysis but without time standards applied as part of a control system. There is no direct labor saving here, since the full-sharing wage incentive plan illustrated by Figure 32 was applied. There is the cost of time standards development and maintenance to consider, although there are many other potential uses for standards, as previously noted. The big savings in this illustration occurred in preliminary methods improvements, followed by a reduction of overhead costs. Included in the latter was the cost of added equipment and plant space that would otherwise have been required.

Extending the Example to Consider Other Factors

In view of common experiences with wage incentive applications, several other conditions might be illustrated by continuing briefly with the preceding example.

Knowing that some direct operators earn nearly 150 percent of base pay, with little outward appearance of undue work effort, those in nondirect labor sections would soon realize that their wages were less than that of many operators, despite their higher job classifications. Skilled maintenance personnel, often in the highest labor grades, are quick to resent this fact. Time standards and direct incentive applications are not practical for most plant maintenance repair work, as a later chapter will indicate. (Some attempt to apply incentives indirectly to maintenance, awarding a fixed-size crew the average bonus percentage of direct operators, provided the crew continues to maintain shop equipment. But there are obvious problems with such an approach.) The chances are that maintenance personnel in the plant would begin taking a much more relaxed attitude in performing their duties. Comments would be heard such as: "Why should I work hard when those unskilled people are paid more than I am?" The same discrepancies would become apparent to other highly skilled employees such as toolmakers. Although incentive applications are possible here, they tend to become after-the-fact applications that soon drift toward controlled bonus levels.

Reactions could also be expected from other groups of employees such as storeroom personnel, inspectors, clerical personnel, material handlers, and others in nondirect categories. With human nature being what it is, there would likely be some reduction in work effort within such groups. A later chapter will describe ways in which MPA analysts can review methods in nondirect functions and develop sound productivity control concepts. This becomes more difficult, however, when wage incentives apply only to direct operators.

Later Problems

As a year or so passes, and as methods changes continue to be introduced, it is almost inevitable that some slippage in the precision of time standards will occur, before changes are recognized and time values revised. Even with MPA auditing of standards, it would be unusual if the 125 percent average, which was assumed in the previous example, did not increase by about 5 percent without a corresponding increase in output.

To conclude the extension of our previous example, it would also be expected that the revision of standards to correct for methods changes would be resisted whenever the reason for change was not clear to those concerned. Increased involvement by labor representatives and more MPA and supervisory time spent on grievances would be strong possibilities.

HOW WAGE INCENTIVE SYSTEMS ARE MAINTAINED

When operators are told by their employer that they will be rewarded monetarily if they produce more, some basic questions are bound to arise about how time standards are set, how the reward will be calculated, whether standards will be revised arbitrarily, what happens if machine cycle time controls the working pace, what happens if an operator cannot meet the standards that are set, or whether standards believed to be incorrect can be challenged. While there may be variations in how questions of this kind are dealt with in specific incentive applications, it is necessary for the operators concerned to be assured of fair play if they are to respond as anticipated.

As indicated by line ABC or ABD in Figure 32, a basic wage rate is guaranteed. This does not mean that questions won't be asked if the low-task time values are not met. As in the preceding example, continued fall-downs would be cause for investigation and remedial action. But operators should be given assurance that the incentive system does not take away rights they have had in the past.

Policies Regarding Time Standards

How the time values are established, and the kinds of allowances that are included, should be explained by supervisors. Patient answers to questions are helpful, as MPA analysts make contacts in the shop. Unless standards issued to the shop floor are specifically designated as temporary values, assurance should be given that they will not be changed except when methods are revised. This can be tempered by the willingness to restudy time values that the supervisor involved considers to be incorrect. Typically, the standard developed by a new study will replace the old one, whether it be higher or lower. There should never be restrictions on MPA audits to check for methods revisions.

There is an inherent dilemma in guaranteeing that standards will not be changed until provable methods changes are introduced. If MPA mistakes are made in standards derivation, which is of course possible from time to time, there can be runaway bonus earnings. The same result can occur if operators develop methods improvements. But if the performance reports indicating such earnings are commonly used as a signal to "invent" methods changes so a new study can be made, operators will soon learn to respond by controlling output to avoid sending such signals. Some MPA managers are known to apply this rule: If a supervisor requests the restudy of a time value thought to be "tight," then another standard time within the same section can also be selected for restudy.

An attempt to circumvent this dilemma by one company is shown by the following paragraph printed on carefully developed operator instruction sheets which are routinely issued: "*The approved method is as shown on this form, and no change in method may be made by the employee without securing approval of the company as indicated by the issuance of a revision.*" No doubt the best way to guard against major problems from loose standards is through systematic auditing, as previously recommended. That must be done if deterioration in standard times is to be avoided.

Machine-controlled Operations

The question of machine-controlled operation cycle times is often a matter for concern. If extra allowances are applied so the operator involved can earn a bonus, this tends to defeat the purpose of an incentive system and causes resentment on the part of those whose bonus must be earned by extra effort. On the other hand, an equipment operator on day work, surrounded by others who can earn a bonus, may cause more machine downtime than if on an incentive basis. This is one of many points to be considered in determining whether a wage incentive system should be implemented in the first place.

Day Work within an Incentive Area

There will likely be other kinds of operations, including those for which time values have not yet been developed, to which only a day-work rate is applicable. These should be minimized, since dayworkers surrounded by incentive operators earning extra pay can be counted on to produce at substandard levels. There will be temptations to apply "average earned rate" to calculate bonus percentages when incentive work is interrupted by conditions not the fault of an operator. Again, this should be minimized or avoided entirely.

INDIVIDUAL AND GROUP WAGE INCENTIVE PLANS

When an incentive plan is first designed, a significant choice to be made is whether bonus earnings are to be calculated on an individual basis or on a group basis. There is wide agreement that individually applied incentives tend to bring about an increased response from those to whom the opportunity for bonus earnings has a special appeal. On the other hand, peer pressure from group members can raise the performance level of some who might not otherwise respond. This section will describe briefly the differences between individual wage incentive plans and group plans. A following chapter will deal with advantages and disadvantages that have resulted in the past from each type of system.

Individually Applied Wage Incentives

If operations are performed by individual operators, without the need for reassigning such individuals to work on jobs that require more than one person, it becomes fairly routine to evaluate individual performance levels in relation to standards. Ways of handling the necessary reporting details will be covered in a chapter to follow. Performance ratios are calculated as total standard time (usually in hours or fractions thereof) divided by actual time. If there are unavoidable delay intervals, the approved deductions are made from the denominator of the fraction. If there are nonstandard work requirements, such as extra stock to be removed from bad castings, the added time may be deducted as a delay, after authorization, or an estimated standard time may be added to the numerator, after MPA review. The net performance ratio is applied to the base rate for calculation of bonus earnings, although the arithmetic may be more involved in order to account for any time spent on daywork jobs or where average earned rate was authorized in special cases.

If practical, incentive earnings should be calculated on a daily basis, so that failure to meet the low-task standards during specific days does not act as a deterrent to work effort on successive days. In practice, a weekly calculation is more likely to be the case, as in various appendix-listed plants. This serves to minimize the amount of checking required to estimate the standard hours accomplished on incompleted operations or job lots.

If there are multi-operator crew sizes on specific types of work, without ways to cover with time standards the work assignments of each, incentive calculations must of course be pooled for the group. This does not necessarily involve the concept of group wage incentives which will be discussed under a following heading. An operator could be assigned to work three days on one-man jobs and two days as part of a two-man crew. The weekly accounting process would be more complex, but the individual basis for wage incentive administration could be retained.

Group Wage Incentives

When groups are performing a related type of work, whether or not the operators involved are required to work together in performing specific operations, management may elect to apply the wage incentive concept on a group basis. A group leader is selected to act as a "straw boss" in apportioning work. The rate of pay is a fixed percentage higher than others within the same labor grade. He or she may be responsible for assuring that required material is on hand, or for training new operators. A group leader is not a management representative and is expected to perform work within the group. The percentage of time required for specified group leader functions is estimated, and the remaining percentage is applied as actual working hours, along with others in the group, to be used in the calculation of incentive pay in the manner described previously.

All employees within the group, including the group leader, report to the sectional supervisor, at least in theory. There are inherent management problems with this arrangement, as will be noted in a subsequent chapter. Because many of the functions normally handled by supervisors are delegated to group leaders, the crew size an incentive supervisor is expected to handle may be quite large. In appendix-listed plants 61, 67, 38, and others, crew sizes in the range of forty to fifty operators per supervisor were common, with several groups being involved.

The introduction of new operators into a group causes a proportional reduction of efficiency until the operators are trained, and this arbitrary reduction in overall group earnings is unacceptable. Accordingly, in plants referred to above, it was common for allowances based on assumed learning curves to be established by MPA representatives for each new employee within an existing group. However, such allowances did not act to raise earnings of new employees during the learning period.

Labor grades within a group must be controlled so that they are in approximate relation to the skill levels required to perform work handled by the group. This was accomplished in plants 61, 67, and others by a yearly MPA analysis of shop orders assigned to each group during a previous interval. In plant 38, this function was simplified by computer analysis of job classifications that had been applied on all route sheets during MPA development of the initial routings.

Step Incentives

This term, borrowed by the author from several appendix-listed plants where the system to be described was applied, has commonly been referred to within industry and industrial engineering literature as "measured day work." It is a form of wage payment involving a calculation of incentive bonus earnings through the averaging of efficiencies over a period of time such as a one-month to three-month interval. Wage payments for the next period of time are figured as for other incentive systems, but with changes in bonus earnings being made in designated steps of 5 or 10 percent. There is nothing hidden about the wage incentive nature of this concept. It is simply another of the many ways that incentive plans have been applied over the years. To refer to this system as day work, given the meaning of that term during the many years that incentive systems have been widely applied, is a misuse of terms. Yet current IE literature still gives the long-standing name to this specific incentive concept. So that there will be no confusion in the reader's mind, our use of the term "measured day work" in this book has absolutely no relation to what we are now referring to as "step incentives."

Incentives Applied to Operators on Paced Lines

Although a group of operators is inherently involved on paced assembly lines, this does not fall within the category of group wage incentives, as discussed above, unless management chooses to utilize group leaders. Lengthy assembly lines are much less suited to the application of wage incentives than are manual operations fully under the control of individuals. Two reasons can be cited: One is that incentive pace is inherently voluntary, and it takes only one on the line to cause problems. The other reason is that measured day-work performance levels for SC/R operations are on a par with what can be achieved with wage incentives, so long as measured day work applies on a plant-wide basis. As previously noted, this was demonstrated in plant 18 when line speeds remained the same on hundred-operator assembly lines after the incentive system was discontinued. Close observations at appendix-listed plants 69, 83, 36, and others, all of which apply measured day work for assembly-line operations, have served to reinforce this conclusion.

That Questionable Word

The term "normal" has been used in this chapter as it is customarily used in describing wage incentive systems. To the extent that a low-task performance level may have existed in a specific plant before application of wage incentives, it is understandable that such a level might be called normal. The word conveys a psychological message. It tends to assure management that any level of performance above normal is acceptable. It seems fair to consider the longstanding use of this word as a promotional technique to assist in the application of a wage incentive plan.

There is a particular problem when this word is allowed to extend beyond the area where wage incentive psychology must be emphasized. Some industrial engineers, who may have had experience where wage incentives were applied, have been taught to believe that an operator should not be expected to work above the low-task level of incentive normal when the job is paid on a day-work basis. Yet they would only have to open their eyes at most supermarket checkout counters, or at a busy fast-food service counter, or perhaps at a muffler installation center, to realize that people often work at or above true incentive pace when the wage payment plan is day work. It may not be overstating the point to suggest that the current definition and use of "normal" can be termed wage incentive propaganda.

12
Wage Incentive Limitations and Problems

This chapter will no doubt be controversial. It is intended to cover some of the negative aspects that are ignored or glossed over in the literature describing wage incentive systems. Those who are familiar with monetary incentives which seem to be functioning properly will tend to equate comments about wage incentive problems with symptoms of mismanagement. That may be true to some extent. But there are many recurring problems which are inherent in the systems themselves, rather than being primarily related to managerial or staff ineffectiveness. And where mistakes do occur in the administration of incentives, it is often the case that corrective action is more difficult because of the industrial relations climate engendered by necessary wage incentive functions.

Under the heading that follows, several reasons usually given for considering incentive applications in the first place will be listed and discussed. The comments that appear in this section will largely be generalities, with logic to support what is presented. A following section of the chapter will deal with actual situations that have occurred in specific plants where wage incentives were applied. The basis for conclusions in that section consists of my own close observations at some thirty-three plant locations within several different companies. Since most were large plants, involving an extremely wide range of manufactured products, the sample size in relation to the total number of incentive applications within the United States is not insignificant, either in plant population or types of manufacturing.

THREE TYPICAL REASONS FOR CONSIDERING WAGE INCENTIVES

There is a wide disparity of opinion between those whose industrial experience has primarily been where wage incentives were applied, and others who may have been exposed to labor productivity control systems that do not involve financial incentives. What some may label folklore, others might consider to be factual information. Thus, as stated above, the following attempt to sort facts from folklore will be controversial. But the case histories that come later will help to buttress what is listed here. (To avoid a one-sided viewpoint, the same approach is taken in chapter 13, which deals with the measured day-work system of control.)

Opinions about Day-work Performance Levels

Can a fair day's work be obtained consistently, for various types of work, when the wage payment is on a day-work basis? Or, as many believe, is some form of financial incentive necessary to achieve this valid management goal?

Folklore. While paced assembly lines or paced equipment indexing can raise day-work performance for SC/R operations to a reasonable level, better results can be achieved by allowing operators to establish line speeds based on a full-sharing wage incentive plan. For nonpaced work, operators paid on a day-work basis tend to function at low performance levels, well below incentive normal.

Factual Observations. As previously noted, several long assembly lines in a major appliance plant were converted from a valid incentive control system to measured day work, with no change in line speed. After this step was taken, there were fewer line stoppages, due to improved managerial control made possible by a better labor relations climate. Close observations of paced operations in other manufacturing plants, where there had been a long history of wage incentive applications, indicated that the methods/pace level at such locations was clearly inferior to that on paced lines in a number of measured day-work plants within the same company. Careful methods analysis is much easier without the distrust of incentive operators, who tend to view changes as a cause for reduced bonus opportunity. The automobile industry in this country long ago discarded wage incentive concepts.

Within a plant involving LC/LR work, where wage incentives apply to most operations, the performance of those who are assigned to day-work jobs is understandably low, for reasons such as the following: (a) the strong implication that a fair day's work is expected only of those who receive bonus pay; (b) the fact that methods have probably not been analyzed or defined clearly for such work; and (c) the lack of a systematic way to evaluate performance, since time standards have not been applied. As stated before, this has no bearing on the performance level that can be expected in a well-managed measured day-work plant, entirely separate from any form of wage incentive application.

For LC/LR operations, it is true that effective measured day-work control is more difficult than where methods and pace on short-cycle operations can be evaluated quickly. Without prompt awareness of problems that arise (which would tend to come at once from incentive operators who want to earn their usual bonus), corrective action may lag. A variety of data collection methods in current use, however, help to improve supervisory awareness of individual performance levels. Chapter 14 describes a newly developed technique in which operators on LC/LR work know clearly what is expected; supervisors can track performance levels at intervals during the shift; and problem conditions can be spotted in time for corrective action.

When the maintenance of time standards deteriorates in any form of control plan, operators may tend to camouflage loose standards by working at a lower methods/pace level. In a wage incentive system, it may be difficult to prove methods changes so as to revise time standards. In measured day work, there should be no restrictions on restudying any job.

The Demonstrated Response to Incentive Applications

What performance level is to be expected with control through capable direct supervisors, having staff assistance for production and material control, but without a control system based on work measurement? What cost reductions, if any, will a sound wage incentive system produce? Will such savings continue? Will alternate control systems produce more savings, or less?

Folklore. The industrial engineering definition of "normal pace" begins as follows: "The work rate ordinarily used under capable supervision but without the stimulus of an incentive-wage-payment plan. . . ." It is generally found that a carefully applied wage incentive plan results in average performance levels about 25 percent above this so-called normal. With a typical incentive plan, direct labor costs remain the same for performance levels above normal, but major savings can occur in the allocation of overhead costs to product costs because of the increased production level. With sound maintenance of standards, this level of savings can be expected to continue indefinitely.

Factual Observations. The possibility of a 25 percent average improvement in operators' reported performances, compared with what could be expected without time standards or an effective control plan, is a reasonable estimate, although some of this might be due to generous allowances for unavoidable delays. There are two things that may be considered either poorly stated or lacking in the longstanding definition referred to. One, which has previously been noted, is use of the word "normal" to define a low-task performance level that is below what would be acceptable in a manufacturing plant where a valid control system is in effect. The other thing wrong with the above definition is its strong implication—almost a definite assertion—that wage incentives are required to raise a low-task performance to an acceptable level.

Salesmanship is necessary to make any labor control system function effectively. But there seem to be a number of industrial engineers and managers, whose background has primarily been within plants where incentives were applied, who have succumbed to their own sales efforts. They truly believe that a wage incentive system is the only pathway to achieving a fair day's work. Since this book attempts to show more than one path toward that objective, it seems appropriate at this point to discuss three components which, as most would be expected to agree, combine to produce the improvement that can be gained with a sound wage incentive plan. These components are as follows:

- Operator-controllable methods improvements.

Some may be identified during the process of time standards development and either communicated to operators or reflected in the rating of performance. Others of a minor nature, which will in time be developed by operators themselves, are often not sufficiently provable to warrant new studies.

- Reduction in avoidable downtime.

This category includes late starts, early quits, excessive time for personal breaks, waiting for work assignments, waiting for material handling, delay time in finding needed material, time-out for conversations at the work site, waiting for inspection, etc. It is a rare work sampling study that does not record 20 percent or more of such avoidable downtime in manufacturing departments that do not have in effect a sound labor productivity control plan.

- Increased working pace.

The potential here will vary from zero on machine-controlled or process-controlled operations to sizeable increases for some manual operations. Most industrial engineers would be expected to agree that the work ethic of past years, when many operators responded to wage incentives with a high pace level, is not as prevalent in this country now.

These three categories combine in some proportion to produce an increase in average reported performance because of the response by operators to a wage incentive system. The total average increase is commonly found to be in the range of about 25 percent, when the system is applied correctly in a suitable environment. Can we also estimate the contribution to this amount by each category? The reader is urged to do this, based on his or her previous experience. Then compare the estimates with those of the author, which are as follows:

Operator-controllable methods improvements	10 percent
Reduction in avoidable downtime	10 percent
Increased working pace	5 percent

It could be maintained that the concept of incentive normal includes methods improvements which should be developed and implemented by the analyst prior to taking a time study. This would imply that the analyst—not the operator—will find all of the possible shortcuts before or during the work-study process. It is unlikely that this will occur except on relatively simple operations. Of course, there are major methods advances which manufacturing or MPA engineers develop and implement, requiring new studies to derive applicable time values.

Estimates as to the effect of the three listed categories will vary, based on what each individual believes he or she has observed. But the chances are that most estimates for the third category will be low, which is not the equivalent of "extra effort for extra pay"—the frequently used phrase applied to describe what wage incentive systems are intended to accomplish. And if the reader's estimates are anything like those noted above, it should be clear that improved labor cost control does not necessarily depend on the existence of a wage incentive plan. With about 40 percent of the total improvement contributed by methods upgrading, and another 40 percent from a reduction in delay time, there are other control systems that can accomplish similar results. They will be described in chapters to follow.

The last point to contend with in the previous listing of folklore is the assertion that wage incentive improvements can be expected to continue indefinitely. Unfortunately, recent industrial history does not bear that out, as will be illustrated later. Reasons are listed below as to why deterioration is difficult to prevent. Some of these reasons have already been noted, and the effects of others will be pointed out in a section to follow.

- The "pocketbook effect":

  Fluctuation in earnings because of product changes;
  Less bonus opportunity because of machine-controlled work;
  Inequalities between various operators' earnings;
  Unwarranted claims for extra allowances.

- Increased resistance to methods analysis:

  General opposition to any change affecting bonus earnings;
  Resistance to changing job assignments;
  Controversy concerning work sampling.

- Gradual loosening of time standards:

  Greater influence by organized labor;
  Resistance to standards auditing;

Precedents set by occasional management concessions;
"Quotas" set by operators, to camouflage loose standards:
Early quits, late starts, excessive downtime.

Opinions About How Wage Incentives Can Reduce Costs

Is there likely to be a reduction in direct labor costs? To what extent will overhead costs be reduced? Can this be expected to continue as the work load fluctuates? To what extent will wage incentives applied to direct operators affect cost control within nondirect groups? Will increases be needed in certain nondirect or staff functions?

Folklore. With day-work performance often in the 65 percent range (where normal is pegged at 100 percent), there will be a sizeable reduction in direct labor costs up to the 100 percent level, even though increases in performance above that level will not cause further direct labor savings. Increased production will be possible with essentially the same equipment and plant space. Fewer direct supervisors will be required, since the incentive pull substitutes for much of a supervisor's duties. The overhead percentage applied to product costs to account for other nondirect, staff, and management personnel will be reduced in relation to increased output by direct operators. Forms of incentives can be applied to certain nondirect functions, if necessary to reduce wage inequalities.

Factual Observations. When referring to day-work operations, it is important to qualify the conditions that surround them. Day-work operators may in fact work at 65 percent of normal when surrounded by other operators responding to a wage incentive plan. But this has no relation to day-work functions within a separate plant where a valid nonincentive control plan has been applied.

Remember that incentive normal, if established with the usual incentive allowances, is a low-task performance level that can be achieved through sound management and supervision. If preincentive performance levels are appreciably below such a level, the plant is not ready for wage incentives, since the required performance increase to earn a meaningful bonus will be too challenging for successful application of the system. What is probably needed in such cases is frequent work sampling to identify where lost time is occurring, along with management follow-up to reduce detracting conditions. Remember also that incentive normal is a subjective concept, established as discussed in a previous chapter. If time study is begun when performance levels are well below what a fair starting point for the incentive bonus should be, there will be strong tendencies to set loose standards in the beginning. The usual form of financial incentive plan, such as line ABC of Figure 32, produces little or no direct labor savings.

If there are appreciable numbers of machine-controlled operations within the plant, one of two results can be expected: (a) either the operators involved will tend to slack off in their manning of the equipment, because of obvious inequalities in earnings capabilities; or (b) an appreciable incentive allowance must be built into time standards for the operations. In both cases, direct labor costs for such work are likely to increase in relation to what could have been achieved prior to introduction of an incentive plan.

Depending upon the number of operations in which machine time is an appreciable percentage of total operation time, additional equipment and corresponding floor space will be required for increased production, unless there is already an excess of such equipment. In neither case will capital outlays be reduced in proportion to the reported increase of operators' performance. There may be some reduction achieved in product overhead costs for such nondirect functions as maintenance, material handling, janitorial duties, storeroom personnel, inspection, etc., though again not in proportion to the increased performance level of operators.

There will be a guaranteed resentment on the part of such personnel when direct operators are able to earn a sizeable bonus and they are not. Inevitably, this will affect their morale and work habits, decreasing the possible savings in overhead cost that wage incentives are thought to provide.

As previously noted, frequent attempts have been made to extend the incentive concept to such groups. This will be discussed briefly in a following chapter. To generalize here about such approaches, it is fair to say that they are difficult to maintain on a sound basis as production demands rise and fall. In any case, such applications would negate much of the overhead savings generally attributed to financial incentives for direct labor. This is not to say that forms of indirect cost control are impractical, when based on careful analysis and prior experience. But there is a big difference between control procedures that can be readjusted as conditions change, and wage incentive agreements that set firm precedents. It is easy to go up in maintenance wage rates, for example, and very difficult to go down.

As the next section will emphasize, experience has shown that a reduction in the number of direct supervisors, on the assumption that they will have less to do when operators "take care of themselves," is a sure way to hasten deterioration of the system. To mention just one of the reasons, a supervisor who does not have time to monitor claims for extra allowances to cover "unavoidable" delays, will soon find stacks of these claims to be signed off at the end of the week, and many will likely be exaggerated.

It is true that certain managerial, staff, and office functions may not have their basic work loads changed appreciably if production levels increase in the shop as wage incentives take effect. On the other hand, there will be a requirement for more MPA personnel than with nonincentive controls, added steps to process wage-payment arithmetic, and a probable increase in the functions required of industrial relations personnel.

Salaried personnel are not likely to resent bonus earnings by direct operators, and office clerical personnel may feel somewhat insulated from what happens in the shop. One exception to this may occur when direct supervisors find that higher classified direct operators, some of whom may be drawing a bonus of 30–40 percent, are earning more than the supervisors themselves. Should the question arise as to whether direct supervisors can properly be covered by some form of financial bonus based on their performance, it is clear that this must never be related directly to wage incentive earnings by operators. The next chapter of this book will discuss in detail some of the basic responsibilities of direct supervisors.

Another point to consider, when analyzing how wage incentives for direct operators might reduce overall costs, is the fact that production requirements are not always on the increase. The work load usually goes up and down. If such fluctuations have occurred frequently in the past and are likely to continue in the future, the prospect of layoffs will affect how operators decide to work in relation to the low-task level called normal.

Conclusions About Reasons for Considering Wage Incentives

When SC/R operations are performed on paced conveyor lines or their equivalent, the experience of many companies indicates that a fair day's work can be achieved without financial incentives, assuming an absence of incentives elsewhere within the plant. The same applies to machine or process-controlled operations. For other work, it is generally conceded that methods analysis, time standards, and a sound wage incentive plan can often lead to a performance level roughly 25 percent above that expected when supervisors are unassisted by a systematic control plan.

Contrary to the typical view of "extra pay for extra effort," observations by the author indicate that most of the improvement tends to occur with little average increase in working pace, being due primarily to improved methods and reduced amounts of avoidable delays. This suggests that there can be other control techniques to consider for achieving equivalent results.

Financial incentives, such as those depicted by line ABC in Figure 32, are unlikely to reduce direct labor costs beyond what can be achieved by competent supervision and management. There are possible increases in such costs through reduced performance (or unproductive bonus applications) on paced operations, machine-controlled operations, or day-work jobs. There are strong possibilities for increased direct labor costs if an incentive system is allowed to deteriorate, which can occur for a variety of reasons.

The amount of overhead costs allocated as a percentage of product costs can be reduced when increased production results from the response to wage incentives. This is more likely to occur if there is an expanding market for the plant's output. The amount of overhead cost savings will be reduced to the extent that the morale and work habits of nondirect employees are affected because they do not share in bonus earnings.

To emphasize a point made earlier in this book, the term "normal pace," or "normal," is misleading. Given their long-standing definitions, these terms are applicable only within the boundary of wage incentive applications or promotional discussions.

CASE HISTORIES OF WAGE INCENTIVE PROBLEMS

The purpose of this section is to describe serious problems that have been observed in the administration of wage incentive systems within some thirty-three different manufacturing locations of three different companies. Since this is a form of industrial history, two quotations seem appropriate at the beginning. The first is from Oscar Wilde: "History is merely gossip." Some of what follows may fall into that category, but most of it does not. I have contacted each of the thirty-three locations for at least a week, functioned as a consultant for months at several of them, and discussed with industrial engineering and manufacturing managers the causes of various problems. The other quotation, from Santayana, explains itself: "Those who cannot remember the past are condemned to repeat it."

Group Wage Incentives

A number of the plants referred to relied primarily on group incentive applications. Each group involved from ten to twenty operators who performed related LC/LR operations. The group leaders, although initially selected by management, were not part of the management team. They reported to sectional foremen (referred to in this book as direct supervisors). The group leaders were authorized to assign specific jobs to operators, train personnel as required, and see that material and tools were available. The estimated time required for such functions was covered by corresponding allowances, and group leaders were expected to perform work on production operations when not occupied by such duties. Their base rate was slightly higher than that of operators within the group. H. B. Maynard (1971) provides a more extensive description of how group wage incentives are intended to function, and lists some of the potential problems involved. The paragraphs that follow summarize specific problems that were observed, and an attempt is made to explain their causes.

Subsidies when New Operators Were Assigned. Because new operators assigned to any group require learning time, it was necessary to provide man-hour subsidies during the estimated learning period so that the groups' bonus earnings would not be adversely affected. This was a planned administrative function, not related to deterioration in the system. The point is brought out here, however, because these subsidies increase direct labor costs associated with group incentive systems.

Diminished Supervisory Influence. The direct supervisors tended to work through group leaders, rather than by contacting individual operators. This was partly due to the large number of operators per supervisor and partly because it was the group leader who generally could provide or obtain needed information. As supervisors became more insulated from contacts with operators, group leaders were perceived by operators to have more authority. Management's viewpoint in employee relations tended to be replaced by the viewpoints of group leaders, which included ways to maximize or protect bonus-earning opportunities.

Hidden Performance Times for Individual Jobs. The group system inherently involves pooling of total man-hours worked by the group for weekly comparisons with standard man-hours on completed operations. It was not possible for the supervisors or MPA analysts to know the performance ratios of individual operators or operations. Those within the group could spot the tight and loose time values and were quick to ask for a restudy of the former.

Resistance to MPA Analysis. As group leaders became more "in charge" of events within their section, sound wage incentive administration became more difficult. MPA analysts were asked to show definite reasons for making time studies, and work sampling studies were resisted strongly. As a confrontational attitude developed along these lines, labor union representatives took a very active part.

Burdensome and Unproductive MPA Duties. There were grievances to analyze and attempt to settle. On the final day of each week, MPA analysts were kept busy checking the percent completion of operations still in process, reviewing extra allowance claims, and handling other paperwork requirements.

Difficulty in Proving Methods Changes. As noted in previous chapters, a methods change often affects various elements of a study in ways that are difficult to prove. The grievance process became heavily loaded with cases along this line. As arbitration came into the picture, management's viewpoints were not always upheld. Since standard data was the basis for establishing most time values, the data gradually became less reliable because of "creeping methods changes," and this affected future time standards.

Inflated Bonus Earnings, or Controlled Make-out. In one large plant, where a strike-prone labor union was involved, conditions such as those noted above led to frequent group earnings in the 200 percent range. At other large plants, rather than draw attention to such gross inequities, the path taken by most groups was to set arbitrary ceilings on earnings. This could be done by a combination of greatly increased downtime (late starts, early quits), along with the "banking" of completed job cards. If the cards were not needed one week to reach the established wage ceiling, group leaders simply stored them until later. Production control functions were affected. Dual accounting functions were involved weekly as standard practice—once by the group leader before pay cards were turned in, and once by the accounting department. Weekly performance ratios remained almost exactly the same for specific groups. In some of the plants, it was unusual to go into a department forty-five minutes before quitting time and find anyone working. Since the average group make-out was far above normal, and since an incentive system inherently lets operators decide how much bonus they choose to earn, supervisors lacked a practical control. Labor problems hindered systematic auditing of standards.

Invalid Claims for Unavoidable Delays. Another way to control the make-out was by submitting claims for extra delay allowances. Some were valid and some were not. Without frequent contact between direct supervisors and the many operators under their control, there were obvious loopholes in the approval process.

Massive Grievance Claims. Increased labor union involvement, brought about in large part by wage incentive arguments, led to frequent grievances, arbitration procedures, and some strikes. Occasional unwarranted concessions by plant management, to avoid work stoppages, set precedents that tended to make enforcement of procedures by MPA representatives ever more difficult.

Greatly Increased Direct Labor Costs. The drifting toward chaotic conditions, as above comments indicate, greatly increased the labor costs for manufactured products.

Final Results. It must be realized that neither plant nor corporate management stood idly by while the conditions fueled by group wage incentives ran their course. But with strong labor unions, contractual agreements to revise time values only when methods changes could be proved, lengthy operation cycle times that helped mask creeping changes, and the lack of actual job performance time data, incentive systems of this kind became a burden that could no longer be tolerated. The same labor unions were involved at plants within the company where individual incentives were applied, leading to labor relations difficulties and increased problems in maintaining those systems. A policy was adopted to drop wage incentives entirely at all new plants, substituting forms of control to be described in a following chapter. All wage increases at existing incentive locations were negotiated on a day-work basis, and there were several negotiated changes to a nonincentive control plan at such plants.

A final paragraph is needed to stress still another disadvantage in wage incentive applications. When wage rates become inflated for reasons such as those noted above, it is very difficult to negotiate reductions in total wages, even when the incentive system is abandoned. Some companies have in recent years had sufficient evidence of inflated wage rates to negotiate reductions (steel and automobile companies, for example). In the case of the plants referred to above, most of the changes to another form of labor cost control were made through a lump-sum payment to affected employees. Memories of past bonus earnings, often without extra effort, do not provide fertile ground for any form of renewed labor productivity control. Most of the manufacturing activities within this company that were previously covered by wage incentives have either been sold or moved to entirely new locations. The failure of group wage incentives, along with recurring problems in managing other wage incentive systems, were contributing factors in decisions to take such steps.

Step-incentive Applications

Four of the appendix-listed plants applied step-incentive control plans, generally on a group basis but without group leaders. Described in chapter 11, this form of control has illogically been called "measured day work" in the literature. As noted, the incentive basis for wage steps that are supposedly involved in these systems has no relation to the measured day-work control plan referred to in this book.

Understandably, there is a strong tendency for wage steps to go up and not down. When an operator is paid a fixed wage for a long period, there is "hell to pay" if it is lowered for an equally long period. At the four plants referred to, the wage rates tended to remain at higher levels, once those levels were reached, despite the usual design revisions, methods changes and employee turnover. No attempt will be made here to assign reasons for the lack of bonus fluctuations, as the facts speak for themselves. Wage systems at these plants were negotiated to a measured day-work form of control, as the term is defined in this book.

Individual Wage Incentives

The first part of this chapter discussed advantages, limitations, and disadvantages of individually oriented financial incentive systems. When such systems are properly applied, it is less likely that some of the inherent problem conditions noted above for group incentives will be encountered. Wage incentive systems applied on an individual basis can be maintained, despite problems that occur, or they can deteriorate through possible combinations of MPA ineptness, management neglect, resistance by organized labor, or fluctuations in work load. Under headings below are given several examples of how systems of this kind either were administered without deterioration, or revitalized after becoming ineffective.

Appendix-listed Plant 6. With the same labor union as at several of the above plants where group incentives were applied, the MPA and management team at this plant of about two thousand operators were periodically challenged through grievance procedures when revisions in time standards were made because of minor methods changes. However, it had always been standard practice for MPA analysts to film at least one cycle of each operation on which time studies had been made for standard data development. When questions came up, it was necessary only to locate the film segment involved and review it with those who did not understand the reasons for change. For at least twenty-five years, this plant was able to continue the incentive system without major problems.

Appendix-listed Plant 104. Changes in equipment and processes at this plant location of company H, without adequate maintenance of standards, had led to excessive bonus earnings in one section, typical earnings in a second, and no bonus earnings in a third large department. The inequalities had caused labor turmoil. Through a series of discussions with a representative of the national union involved, it was agreed that a new beginning was in the best interests of the overall labor force. New standard data brought about changes that improved labor relations and increased output.

Appendix-listed Plant 94. In this privately-owned plant, an old incentive plan had deteriorated through lack of maintenance. Bonus earnings were low, as was the performance level. With a solid basis for trust between management and the workers, it was possible to overhaul the incentive program to the advantage of all concerned.

Appendix-listed Plant 18. This large major appliance plant utilized predetermined times as a basis for developing methods and standards. While there were no insurmountable problems in revising standards as methods changed, the perceived grievances brought about by wage incentive applications helped to cause frequent assembly-line delays and numerous plant work stoppages. A negotiated buy-out of the incentive plan, leading to a measured day-work application with time values at the approximate level of incentive make-out, greatly relieved the labor unrest previously encountered.

CONCLUSIONS ABOUT OBSERVED INCENTIVE APPLICATIONS

Inherent problems were encountered in maintaining group wage incentive systems. There were hidden job performance times and diminished supervisory contacts with workers. Group leaders tended to manipulate incentive principles, encouraging resistance by organized labor to the revision of time standards when methods were changed. Direct labor costs increased to excessive levels. Although step-incentive and individually applied wage incentive systems were less difficult to administer, they also caused employee relations problems. Incentive concepts in one large company were eventually replaced with alternate control procedures.

One example has been noted in which MPA personnel within a large plant utilized films of operation cycles to resist grievances related to time standards revisions. Another example showed how predetermined-time applications assured the maintenance of standards, but incentive concepts still caused labor unrest. Two additional examples described briefly how individually applied incentive systems could be brought back to life despite major deterioration that had occurred.

13
Measured Day-Work Concepts

Three different levels of measured day-work control will be described in this chapter and in chapter 14, based on long-term analysis of control plans in over sixty of the measured day-work plants listed in the appendix. It is important to recognize that results which can be expected to occur depend to a large extent on the degree of control that is in effect. To facilitate the discussion, names and acronyms have been assigned to each of the three levels. Their basic concepts are listed in Figure 34.

WHAT'S IN A NAME?

Before discussing different levels of control, there is a need to recognize the confusion that continues to exist when the name "measured day work" is applied. Prior to about 1960, industrial engineering literature illogically defined measured day work only in terms of what this book has referred to as a step-incentive plan. In a 1963 *Industrial Engineering Handbook*, definitions coordinated by the American Society of Mechanical Engineers (ASME) gave two separate meanings for measured day work, one as day work with time standards and the other as a step-incentive system. Sure enough, a control plan by that name was described one way in one chapter and a different way in another chapter. In a 1983 *Handbook of Industrial Engineering*, comments in one chapter begin by indicating that measured day work "pays the employee's hourly rate, but output is measured and controlled objectively." Next comes the statement: "Measured day work is a widely used incentive program."

As previously noted, the name used within a plant to designate a specific staff group may have little significance, since functions assigned to the group will become clear in a short time. But the name applied to a control plan will often affect an operator's perception of what the system is intended to accomplish. If an inexperienced operator were to hear the phrase "measured day work" while being trained, the words might be shrugged off. But an operator who has been exposed to various plant environments could have a reaction such as the following: "Day work? Oh, that's what was in section B3 where I worked last, and where the employees goofed off half the time because they got no bonus. But if it is measured, then that must mean we will be working harder and not getting paid for it!"

Another employee's reaction might be something like this: "Measured day work? Sure, I know about it. We had that system at an electronics plant. Everybody ended up with a 30 percent bonus. But you say we don't get a bonus! How come?"

The measured day-work control plan we are concerned with here must be totally divorced from wage incentives, so as to avoid problems discussed in the last two chapters, which are inherent with financial incentive plans. In attempts to search for a better name, one company tried calling it the "PC system," for "productivity control." But that word "control" has a harsh ring to it, at least to operators. Another possibility is to use one of the names and acronyms in the heading of Figure 34, depending on which level of control is being applied. But these are cumbersome, intended for definition rather than for general use. Two other possible names are noted below, for consideration:

Methods and Productivity Management System (MPM). The management process, by direct supervisors and others, needs to be stressed in this control plan that does not involve financial incentives. But "management" and "control" would likely end up in a tie vote if operators were asked to give their opinions.

Methods and Productivity Improvement System (MPI): No doubt a better substitute for the term "measured day work" will be found in time, but this is the one we shall use within this chapter and the next. It stresses three key words:

> *Methods.* By eliminating the roadblock of wage incentives, methods analysis can be pursued with less resistance, and methods training can be emphasized. The ability of any manufacturing organization to remain competitive is closely related to the significance it places on methods development.
>
> *Productivity.* The general meaning of this word is so widely accepted as a valid objective—nationally as well as by industrial organizations—that its inclusion in the name for a control plan would not likely be objectionable, even to operators.

Improvement. This seems to be an appropriate action word. The need for continued methods improvement is understandable and acceptable. "continued productivity improvement" might raise some eyebrows, but training sessions with operators can make clear the fact that productivity will advance as better methods are applied, and the pace of operators is not expected to rise beyond the level of rhythmic, natural motions.

Need for a Better Name than "Time Standard," or "Standard," or "Time Value"

These three words or phrases have been used interchangeably so far, and there is not much wrong with them. They are straightforward and honest in their implications. But perhaps the MPI system (as we shall begin calling it) needs a bit of the salesmanship that has been applied in wage incentive terminology with the word "normal." In discussing MPI, that word must be avoided, since it has long been defined as a low-task work level that has connotations of being the level that exists before a control system is applied. Since the MPI performance target must definitely be at a higher level than incentive normal, we must use that word only within the context of financial incentives. No more—at least not in this chapter or the next—will the words "normal," "high-task," or "low-task" be applied. But a meaningful word could be used to replace the somewhat pompous and time-worn phrases noted in this paragraph's heading. There may be one that is suitable.

A dictionary defines the word "norm" as "average, mean, median, par, or standard." It is a noun that is given about the same meaning as that adjective we said would not be used. If "norm" has at times been applied as shorthand for "normal," at least that usage has not yet made its way into most lists of industrial engineering definitions. So consider replacing "standard time" with "norm" when discussing the MPI (measured day-work) system. We shall do that, but feel free to stay with other terms if you prefer.

IMPROVING AND DEFINING METHODS

Differences between the three levels of control noted in Figure 34 will become apparent as basic concepts within the MPI control plan are discussed. Methods improvement is a key point in each of the three levels. There are two primary reasons for emphasizing methods analysis:

- Work measurement must be based on a definite method. If this is a method that can easily be improved upon, the norms that are established will not represent a fair day's work; costs will be unnecessarily high; and inequities in work requirements will become apparent to operators.

- Unless ideas are continually being generated for methods upgrading, there will be little chance of getting from the MPI control plan one of its primary advantages—an ability to implement methods changes without the inherent resistance from operators that tends to exist where wage incentives are applied.

Ways of promoting progress in methods development have been covered at length in various references, including those noted in the appendix. A brief summary is given here. Some of the recommended procedures follow.

Systematic Analysis over a Broad Range

It is often worthwhile to diagram the existing methods in some clear-cut manner, so that a questioning approach can be taken effectively. Operation charts, flow process charts, or man-and-machine charts may be applicable. A questioning process is the next step. To do this systematically involves taking the "4P" approach:

Question the PURPOSE. Is an operation required because of improper previous operations? Would the operation be necessary if subsequent operations were different? If the original purpose of the operation was to give sales appeal, is this reason valid? Would the operation be unnecessary if tools and equipment were OK?

Question the PART. Use better or less expensive material? Join parts better? Make machining easier? Can the design be simplified? Are tolerances and specifications reasonable and clearly defined? Could material be used that is less expensive or more economical to process? Is the material economical in both size and condition?

Question the PROCESS. Can an operation be changed to simplify others involved? Can manual operations be done mechanically? If done mechanically, should more effective equipment be used? Can the equipment be operated more effectively? Can setup time be reduced? Is machine capacity being fully utilized? Are better holding devices required?

Is material utilized most effectively, with minimum waste? Are causes of rejects being corrected? Are inspection methods OK? Can working hazards be reduced? Are lighting, temperature, and ventilation OK? Housekeeping?

Question the PLANT LAYOUT. Can the time to pick up material be reduced? Is material placed in position for the next operation? Can reaches and moves be shortened? Replace manual handling with mechanical equipment? Make better use of existing facilities? Is walking minimized? Are storage areas satisfactory? Are service centers close to production areas?

Other Methods Analysis Techniques

Motion Study Using Predetermined Motion Times. This step can be taken, where called for, as a continuation of the systematic analysis process noted above; or it can be an adjunct to the process of establishing standard data to derive norms. As previously indicated, the 4M DATA system for computer-aided MTM–1 applications provides "improvement indices" that suggest how a method can be further improved.

Direct Time Study. A methods review by the analyst should always be the first step involved when making a time study.

Work Sampling. This is an economical way to get data concerning the activities of a group, to assist in finding where improvements can be developed.

Operators' Involvement. While suggestion award plans require close follow-up to be effective, they remain a possible way to promote employee interest in the productivity improvement process. An approach called "quality circles," to be discussed in chapter 16, involves structured groups of selected employees who meet regularly to help solve problems that often relate to manufacturing methods.

Cost Improvement Programs, with Stated Goals. A team approach, aimed at reducing costs on a broad basis, can strongly promote methods improvement objectives. Such an approach would typically consist of: (a) cost reduction objectives for each functional group of management and staff representatives; (b) regular meetings to review proposals and assure action; and (c) a periodic report concerning the status of each proposal. The MPA manager can properly be assigned to coordinate this approach.

BASIS FOR NORMS WITHIN THE MPI SYSTEM

Just as in a wage incentive system, MPI norms are not revised unless the basic methods are changed. In all cases, 100 percent is the targeted average performance level when there are no unavoidable delays. Realistically, this tends to become a performance ceiling, which emphasizes the fact that norms should be established carefully by MPA analysts. In general, the work measurement concepts described in chapters 3–7 are fully applicable. There is no adequate way to describe on paper a specific level of performance on which norms should be based. However, some of the concepts involved are listed in italic as follows and subsequently discussed.

Norms for MPI are intended to reflect *good shop conditions.* They represent the performance level of a *qualified operator,* working under *capable supervision,* to produce a *defined output of acceptable quality,* when following *an acceptable method.*

Good Shop Conditions

A competent supervisor strives to maintain good conditions in his section, barring unforeseen circumstances. Of course, such conditions may not always exist. For example, delays can occur due to a lack of material, or because of equipment downtime. The output of affected operators will be reduced accordingly, but the supervisor will be expected to know the reasons and take steps to correct the problems. Action to follow up and correct detracting conditions will be much less likely to occur if broad allowances are applied within the norms to cover such delays. Another reason for omitting allowances for infrequent delays is that they would have the effect of loosening the norms when good shop conditions exist.

Qualified Operator

This phrase implies a fully-trained individual, with needed skills, who knows how to perform the work. If an operation is both complex and new within the section, there will understandably be some learning time. If there has been a turnover of personnel, this also may be a cause for reduced performance levels by operators concerned. Making these conditions apparent, both to the direct supervisor and to his superiors, is preferable to camouflaging them with arbitrary learning allowances.

Pace Expected under Capable Supervision

Just as there is no universal benchmark for the pace level expected in wage incentive systems, so also will the performance level defined by MPA norms be adjusted to fit conditions at specific plants. Don't be misled by data that may accompany films originally developed as guidelines for wage incentive applications. As discussed in chapter 3, the venerable and much-used SAM rating films show a wide spread of ratings for wage incentives, depending on allowances used and the percentage applied to define incentive pace. The ratings suggested by these and similar films have no inherent relation to MPI performance ratings. That is a matter for individual plants to determine, through input from the MPA staff and experienced management representatives.

Although an attempt to define pace levels in writing can never serve as a clear explanation, the following summary may be helpful:

Expected MPI working pace IS characterized by:

- Brisk performance,
- Reasonable effort,

- A performance level that can be averaged by a qualified operator,
- Allowances for personal time and unavoidable delays.

Expected MPI working pace IS NOT:

- Easy-going,
- Unduly tiring,
- The top level at which a qualified operator can work,
- Inherently the equivalent of any specific wage incentive task level.

Defined Output of Acceptable Quality

The expected output for assigned work should be communicated to operators so it can be understood clearly. One way to do this is through a listing of hours per part, plus setup time, although calculations are required for this to be meaningful. A better way in many cases is the listing of norms in terms of setup time plus parts per hour. The best approach, wherever practical, is to provide each operator with a clear-cut schedule, in advance, listing expected production during a specified interval (concept OSPE/SIS of Figure 34). The following chapter describes a way to do this without paperwork calculations by the supervisor.

During the initial expansion of MPI systems within one company, a few managers insisted on making the production targets available to supervisors but not to operators, reasoning that the norms tended to set production ceilings which qualified operators might otherwise exceed. Not only does such a policy involve elements of unfairness, but it is self-defeating. Without giving operators a clear indication of what is expected, there is no sound basis for indicating to them that there should be an improvement when performance is found to be below the target level, and it was found that taking such an approach for a year or so established precedents that were very hard to change.

MPI norms are in no way intended to detract from compliance with quality specifications. Thus, they should include time for planned inspection intervals. While provision should be made for authorized delay allowances when unplanned quality problems occur, there should also be assurance of needed follow-up to correct the reasons for such problems.

An Acceptable Method

This last item in the preceding list of concepts for MPI norms is meant to emphasize the fact that the method on which norms are based is just as significant as when developing time standards for wage incentives. In the latter case, a poor initial method opens the door to improvement by operators and runaway bonus earnings. With MPI norms, operators may improve upon the method but hide the fact by working at a lower pace. In both cases, the MPA analyst may in time correct the problem by revising the time standard or norm. But the sequence of events in both cases tends to undermine each system to some extent and affect the morale of operators who feel entitled to the reward achieved by their own ingenuity.

Review of Newly Established Norms by Line Supervisors

As will be covered in a following section, the reporting of average performance ratios for a supervisor's section is a key step in the administration of MPI systems. Direct supervisors are an integral part of management, and the performance norms should be developed with their active participation and support. In actual practice, complete checking of how the norms are derived is rarely practical because of time limitations. Thus, the checking may evolve into such functions as: (a) review of conditions on which time studies or predetermined time analyses are based; (b) review of performance rating in time studies; and (c) occasional questions about specific norms.

SUPERVISORY FUNCTIONS WITHIN THE MPI SYSTEM

The Span of Control

Supervisors within an MPI control plan are relied on for close contact with operators, to see that norms are met or to assist in correcting the problems involved. Thus, there is a somewhat lower limit, compared with wage incentive plans, to the number of operators which one supervisor can manage effectively. This number will be higher where routine, repetitive work is performed and lower where there is less repetitive or precise work involving the interpretation of drawings or quality control interactions. A typical ratio of productive employees per direct supervisor can be expected to range from about 15 to 40, depending on the type of work involved.

Direct Supervision

MPI supervisors are expected to be in direct contact with operators. To shorten the management path, to provide operators with clear explanations of management policies, and to avoid problems discussed previously in connection with group wage incentives, the use of group leaders or assistant supervisors is not recommended. However, operators may be assigned as justified to perform work such as setup, material handling, or training.

Management within a Framework of Procedures

The MPI supervisor is manager of his section, but with certain constraints. He must conform with personnel policies, assign work to meet scheduled commitments, see that design and quality specifications are met, and supervise to meet established norms. This is not unlike the requirement of managers at any level, who must also work within a framework of procedures.

A Difference that Exists

In a control plan based on financial incentives, there are time standards that define an expected level of performance, and there is enough bonus in the picture to motivate operators so that most will want to achieve that level. (As we have said, such standards are often adjusted to a lower performance level, where the bonus begins, but the effect remains the same.) Some are less motivated by extra earnings, choosing to work below the average level, while others will apply a combination of added effort and methods effectiveness to work above average. Supervisors who manage an incentive section without group leaders have obvious responsibilities, such as assigning work to meet schedule requirements, training operators, controlling quality, assuring that material is available, and handling employee relations problems; but they don't have much to worry about in terms of achieving a fair day's work. The bonus percentage takes care of that if the system is maintained properly.

In a measured day-work control plan, which we have chosen to call the MPI system, there are also time standards, referred to herein as norms, that are developed so that 100 percent defines the target point of a fair day's work. Even though there is no inherent relation between the target performance level in the two systems, let us assume for the moment that they have the same average performance objective. This would be realistic, since average incentive pace can generally be achieved largely through working at a reasonable pace for a full shift (less allowances) and utilizing proper methods. If the plant starts out with MPI and has no incentive background, operators will not have to break away from old habits. Their pay rate should be such that they are properly compensated in relation to other area plants.

FIGURE 34.
Basic Concepts in Three Levels of Control.

OSPE/SIS: OSPE, PLUS SHORT-INTERVAL SCHEDULING	OSPE: OPERATORS' & SECTIONAL PRODUCTIVITY EVALUATION	SPE: SECTIONAL PRODUCTIVITY EVALUATION	
X	X	X	1. Careful development and communication to operators of methods and time standards for specified operations.
X			2. Clear communication to operators of the expected output during appropriate, short-term intervals.
X	X	X	3. Close supervision to achieve productivity targets.
X	X		4. Reliable reporting of individual operators' performance in relation to time standards.
X			5. Short-term feedback of how individuals perform in relation to standards, along with problems encountered.
X	X	X	6. Longer-term evaluation of how direct supervisors are meeting sectional productivity targets.
X	X	X	7. Manpower planning and control, so there will be a balance between the scheduled work-load and available man-hours.
X	X	X	8. Emphasis on problem correction and methods improvement by all concerned, to benefit from the climate for improvement which the system can help establish.
X	X	X	9. Close follow-up by general management, to spot weak points and see that they are corrected.

The Need for an Added Supervisory Tool

But training will be needed; monitoring of work habits will be required; and there will often be frequent delays to identify and control. These functions will fall on the shoulders of the direct supervisor. He can depend on paced operations for assistance, if there are such, but that is often not the case. To some extent, the supervisor can and should be out in the work area as much as possible, with eyes open to spot problems; but a direct supervisor has many functions to handle that will require attention, and operators don't want a "policeman" standing guard all the time. The supervisor will need help in some orderly way if he or she is to manage effectively.

Consider now the SPE column of Figure 34. Items 1, 3, and 8 are clear-cut and have been discussed above to some extent. But they are like "motherhood and apple pie," to use an old cliché. We read here that norms are published for operators to see; the supervisor tries to get all concerned to achieve these targets; and then he or she goes about correcting problems and smoothing out methods. But can a supervisor know clearly and promptly just who has not been meeting the targets, particularly when LC/LR operations are involved? And can operators be depended on to identify in retrospect the conditions that may have caused problems? With perhaps twenty-five or more operators in the section, and with many other duties for the supervisor to perform, there will probably be negative answers to these two questions.

Items 6 and 9 are checkup functions that put the supervisor on the spot, without providing real help. Item 7, manpower planning, is a staff activity that provides a chance for matching manpower with man-hours, but does not help the supervisor see that labor productivity is under control. Looking realistically at the SPE version of the MPI system, we could say that it describes little more than sound management without having norms at all. The operators on LC/LR operations will soon come to realize that their boss, acting alone, is unable to keep track of whether specific individuals are meeting the norms shown on manufacturing information. Of course, periodic sectional performance reports may give supervisors a reason to try harder. But after the first year or so, when it becomes evident that not much attention is being paid to the norms by operators or supervisors, there will be less emphasis on maintaining them, and a deterioration can be expected.

A Partial Answer for Upgrading MPI Results

Attention is directed next to the OSPE column of Figure 34. This shows an added feature that can be used to assist supervisors in the management process. It involves a reliable reporting of individual operators' performance levels. Ways to accomplish this will be discussed later. Even weekly reports of this kind give the supervisor a management tool that is badly needed. He or she will be able to contact the low performers, ask what the problems have been, and emphasize that any delaying conditions should be reported immediately, for follow-up. Operators are just like all of us! When they know that the boss knows their performance level, there will be an improvement. Of course, a delay in getting performance data means that most of the questions asked by the supervisor will refer to what happened a week ago, but that is better than nothing. For SC/R operations, daily performance reports are practical, and the next chapter will describe a technique for accomplishing this where LC/LR operations are predominant.

A More Complete Answer

To consider a third, more advanced and more effective system for MPI control, consider the OSPE/SIS column of Figure 34. To those who may be familiar with a tedious, paperwork form of short-interval scheduling by supervisors that has been around for many years, let us say at the outset that this is not being proposed. Neither are we referring to the centralized and computerized form of production scheduling that may sometimes be referred to incorrectly as short-interval scheduling, when it merely lists jobs that have priority and for which material should be at hand. Such information is needed, but it does not substitute for detailed planning and follow-up by direct supervisors. A description of MPI control with OSPE/SIS functions will be left until the following chapter.

How a Supervisor Might Describe MPI to a New Employee

At this point, it may be helpful to outline some of the topics that a competent MPI supervisor might be expected to emphasize in a discussion with a new employee who is to begin work in his or her section. The wording that follows is in a conversational mode:

"Susie, I know you've been told we have a system here called methods and productivity improvement, and you're probably wondering what to expect. Well, it's really a simple thing. The emphasis is on better methods. This includes what you might call major methods that you and I can't do much about—the equipment we have and the tooling that goes with it. But there is a lot both of us can do to improve the minor methods that really have a major effect—things like learning the very best way to perform an operation, how to use both hands effectively, how to locate batches of parts so that reaching them is easier, or getting hold of them is easier—that sort of thing. You'll find that methods improvement usually means making jobs easier to perform, and that is what we both want to concentrate on.

"Now take that other word, productivity. You know roughly what it means, of course. It's what keeps us in business along with the competition. But maybe you didn't realize that methods affect our productivity more than anything else. That's why the two words are combined as a name for this MPI system. Of course there are other things, like staying on the job without too much conversation or idle time. But if you keep an eye on those things, and you really try to smooth out the manual methods on your jobs, there is nothing about this word productivity that is going to bother you.

"Maybe there is one other point I should mention, though, and that's to ask you to help me keep the different kinds of delays under control—the equipment problems that sometimes occur, or the problems in locating material, or having to wait for an inspector to show up—things like that. Just do your best to think ahead and avoid delays. But if something does come up that looks like it might last, say five minutes or more, be sure to look me up, pronto. Don't feel you are snitching on anybody. It's my job to keep those delaying conditions from happening repeatedly. My section has a productivity report each week, and delays are the big reason why I'm not doing so well right now. So keep that in mind, please!

"You will be seeing a few guys or gals that are called an Awareness Group—Methods and Productivity Awareness. Their job is to help us all in looking for better methods, and to develop what we call norms, so our productivity level can be measured—yours and mine both. I get reports each week telling me how our section is doing. My boss sees that report, and he's not too happy with it right now because of the delays. I also get a weekly list covering each operator in the section, showing how their productivity looked for the previous week. I'll pass along your figures from time to time. They may be a bit low as you learn the ropes, but you'll do better as you get a feel for the methods to use.

"The point to remember in this productivity thing is that it is the average value that counts. Nobody claims these norms I mentioned are perfect for all conditions. If there is a subassembly that has to be adjusted before you can insert it into a main assembly, then the norm for your job is going to be a bit on the tight side. If it is a continuing problem, you let me know about it. I'll get it corrected, and also make out an allowance to cover your delay time. But try to average out in relation to the norms. It is the cumulative figure that my boss is more interested in, and I look at things the same way.

"As you know, the pay here is above average for the area, and that helps us get above-average operators. They don't have trouble meeting the norms, as long as all of us can keep those delays under control. Now come with me over here, and I'll show you how to enter the information about each job that is started and completed. . . ."

THE MOTIVATION OF AN MPI CONTROL PLAN

Each person who works for someone else wants to know what is expected. Correspondingly, each manager needs to know what should be expected of those he or she directs. Such concepts are basic. Just as they apply to operators and their supervisors, they are also applicable within successive levels of management. If the general supervisor is not achieving productivity targets for his various sections, the manufacturing manager will want to be made aware of significant problems, so that constructive assistance can be provided.

Industrial psychologists have identified and named a number of motivational influences that affect an operator's reaction to his or her job. Some of the names applied are job enrichment, job enlargement, hierarchy of needs, motivation-hygiene theory, and management by theories X and Y. The MPI system does not rule out the application of such concepts when appropriate, but neither does the system depend on them for labor productivity control. The fundamentals that successful

MPI applications do require are a team effort to improve methods, the planned assignment to operators of a fair task, a feedback of results to identify problems, and follow-up to correct problem conditions.

Comments about Negative Motivation

The term "folklore" has been used in this book a number of times as a way to highlight questionable viewpoints. Under the heading of "motivation," it might not be amiss to point out some of the widespread folklore about negative motivation on the part of those whose job it is to work in manufacturing plants. This is particularly significant in a discussion of control plans that do not have the tested motivation which comes from earning extra pay for improved performance.

Ever since Charlie Chaplin, in the movie "Modern Times," performed his stunt of trying unsuccessfully to keep up with a fast-moving conveyor, a number of industrial psychologists, media personalities, editorial writers, and others have apparently accepted as gospel that the work in a manufacturing plant is much like Chaplin's scene. It is claimed frequently that the jobs which operators must endure are inherently boring to them, and that society is amiss in not putting an end to such travesty.

Several questions might properly be raised about those who speak or write along this line: Have they ever been inside a manufacturing plant? Have they made a serious effort to extract opinions from representative operators about boredom (as distinguished from other perceived grievances)? Or, do they realize that what interests (or bores) a college professor, for example, might differ from the tastes of a high school graduate with little or no working experience? In order to make a point here as quickly as possible, the following comments are listed for consideration by the reader:

- Realistically, most manufacturing jobs require careful attention to detail. The current, needed emphasis on quality control makes this even more understandable to operators.
- Trends in the United States are toward LC/LR operations and fewer SC/R jobs.
- There is broad flexibility in the design of many operational sequences, with job enlargement being a possibility when justified.

  Many industrial engineers are known to have strong opinions, based on their experience, that those who gravitate toward the simpler, short-cycle, repetitive operations do so because they can think about other things while working, or chat with associates, unbothered by the need for concentration requiring mental effort.
- Most plants have procedures for selective bidding by employees, aimed at eventual transfers to work of their own choosing.

- Compared with such jobs as store clerks, fast-foods attendants, auto service station personnel, shoe salesmen, telephone operators, office typists (the list can go on and on!), most manufacturing jobs are much more varied and challenging.

The points just made may not be particularly significant in relation to the broad subject of labor productivity control. But the general conclusion seems worth noting, in a discussion of motivation as related to the MPI control plan, that the possibility of negative motivation is often distorted.

TAKING ACTION WHEN THE NEED IS INDICATED

It is important for an organization that applies the MPI system to resist taking action the "easy way" when a specific operator consistently falls below the performance level of established norms. To take the easy way would mean basing disciplinary action directly on the fact that targeted performance levels were not achieved. Such an approach would be an open invitation for strong labor resistance to the derivation and maintenance of sound time values, which has all too frequently caused the downfall of wage incentive systems in the past. When operators are not meeting established norms, however, it remains the supervisor's responsibility to find the reasons and correct them.

Conditions Not under the Operator's Control

The reasons for poor performance may prove to be conditions such as material not available when needed, defective material, tools or equipment in poor condition, or balance lacking between interrelated operations. Corrective action may be taken directly by the supervisor in such cases, or it may be necessary to call for action by staff specialists involved. In any case, the direct supervisor should follow up until the problem has been handled effectively.

Methods that are Largely Controllable by the Operator

Are the proper equipment or tools being used? Can the time spent in getting or disposing of parts be reduced by changes in the workplace layout? Can setup time be reduced through instructions and training? Are cutting feeds and speeds correct for the material involved? Is the operator using both hands effectively? These are just some of the questions that supervisors would be expected to ask in searching for reasons why job performance is below established norms. The assistance of MPA personnel can properly be requested to find the answers. If conditions along this line are identified, training and closer supervision may be called for.

Working Pace and Continuity

When delays or incorrect methods are ruled out as causes of poor performance by operators, the supervisor may determine through observation that an operator is away from the work station much of the time, interrupting jobs for frequent conversations, or working at an unacceptable pace level. Supervisors should be expected to follow up such situations until they are corrected, making clear that a fair day's work will be a condition of employment. It is obviously not possible to spell out the detailed steps to be taken in such cases, as these will vary according to the policies of specific companies. In taking disciplinary action, however, specific employee deficiencies should be emphasized, rather than the failure to meet established norms.

It is fair to expect that operators remain on the job for the prescribed interval, apply sound methods, and work at a reasonable pace. The supervisor should have no hesitation in undertaking follow-up to achieve these fundamentals. A prerequisite would be for plant management to confirm such a policy and provide the necessary assistance and support.

PERFORMANCE REPORTING PRINCIPLES

We shall leave to the next chapter a discussion of ways to implement the reporting process required for categories OSPE and OSPE/SIS in Figure 34.

Weekly Performance Reporting

Described below is a typical way to develop weekly reports necessary to implement the SPE concept of Figure 34. This approach would be applicable where there is in effect a standard cost system of accounting, which does not require the reporting of actual man-hours for completed operations. It involves comparisons between the actual man-hours worked within a section during the week, and man-hours for the norms of operations completed during the week. This form of weekly performance report is practical for sections involving production release completion times which are relatively short. The data will become approximate or even misleading when completion times are longer, since actual hours included in the report will not be the same hours that are worked on jobs completed during the week, for which norm values were accumulated.

Even though a weekly reporting process developed in this general way cannot be used to define the performance level of individual operators, the identification of specific detracting conditions that occur throughout a section, along with the estimated or actual time for each, provides a basis for including on the report a meaningful performance ratio for the average performance of operators in relation to norms. It is also possible to identify specific detractors as being outside of the sectional supervisor's area of responsibility, resulting in a slightly higher ratio for the section than for the overall management process. Examples are shown below of typical detracting conditions.

Detractors which Supervisors Should Attempt to Minimize

It will be recognized that there are shared responsibilities in many of the occurrences noted below. A separate listing of the man-hours, by category, can assist in necessary follow-up by management.

1. Extra setup, caused by production scheduling, lack of needed material, or machine conditions. (Actual time.)
2. Defective machines or defective tooling. (Estimated additional time for that reason.)
3. Parts cannot be processed by established method because the specified tools, fixtures, or equipment are not available. (Estimated extra time.)
4. Extra operations resulting from purchased material found to be defective. Examples: machining castings to size, sanding operations on steel, etc. (Actual time.)
5. Material having substandard machinability, either not according to specification or substituted to expedite the order. (Estimated extra time.)
6. Work performed on equipment other than that originally specified, caused by production scheduling or machine conditions. (Estimated extra time.)
7. Time lost waiting for material, equipment repairs, etc. (Actual time.)
8. Any expense operation normally performed by indirect personnel, but which has been temporarily assigned to a direct operator in order to expedite the manufacturing process. Examples: unusual material handling, cleanup, minor repairs to jigs or fixtures, etc. (Actual time.)

Detractors Not within the Control of Direct Supervisors

Controlling the following categories of man-hour cost within a section may be considered a responsibility of the management staff, or management at other levels:

9. Operations required, but not part of the listed manufacturing information data covered by norms. (Actual time.)

FIGURE 35.
Subdivisions for Performance Reporting.

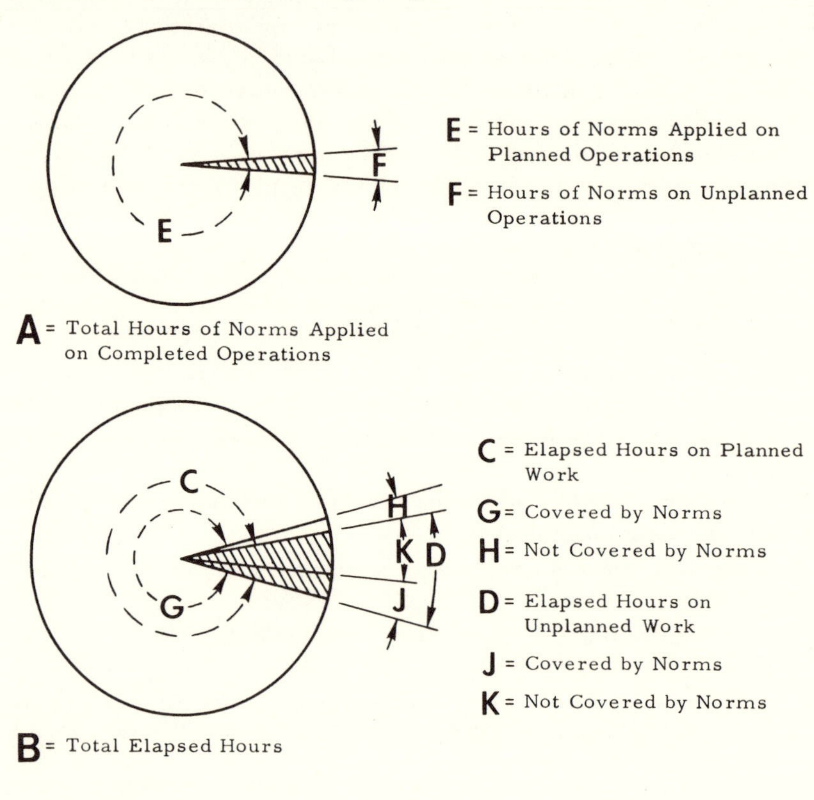

10. Nonsaleable orders, authorized for experimental purposes or for other departments. (Actual time.)
11. Extra work due to changes specified by the engineering department after manufacturing information was issued. (Actual time.)

Three Performance Ratios

Figure 35 illustrates graphically the information that could properly be used to prepare weekly performance reports. The actual man-hours of detracting conditions (unplanned work) would comprise segment D. Where practical, the MPA group could apply norms on some work of this kind, which would require a division of D into segments J and K. The norms so applied comprise segment F of Figure 35. There are three performance ratios which can then be derived, as follows:

Performance Ratio, Operators (PRO). This is calculated as A/(G + J + X), where X is the estimated or actual man-hours for items 1–8 above, or their equivalent, when not part of J. The ratio serves to evaluate how the operators performed on all jobs covered by norms, whether or not some of this work consisted of jobs not included by the original manufacturing information. The PRO ratio does not include in its denominator the estimated actual hours for detracting conditions which the supervisor agreed were not under the control of operators (unless norms were applied to portions of such work by the MPA group).

Performance Ratio, Unit Management (PRUM). This ratio is calculated as E/(B − H − Y), where Y includes estimated or actual man-hours for items 9–11 or their equivalent, when not part of J. The ratio is not reduced if there is an occasional omission of norms on operations in the manufacturing information. However, there would be less significance to the ratio if item H is an appreciable amount. The ratio is also not reduced by detracting conditions over which the supervisor clearly has no direct influence or control.

Performance Ratio, Operations Management (PROM). The calculation here is E/(B − H). An objective is for norms to be established on all planned operations called for by the manufacturing information, in which case H would become zero, and both the PRUM and PROM ratios would have more significant meanings.

Summary of Detracting Conditions. A second part of the typical weekly performance report can properly consist of a total man-hour figure, by section, for each general category of detracting conditions, such as those suggested by items 1–11 above.

Report Preparation and Limitations

As previously noted, this method of performance reporting usually involves some mismatch between data in the numerators of performance ratios and data in their denominators. When production-release manufacturing times are relatively short, the errors involved will tend to average out, particularly when trends are charted or when cumulative figures are developed. For more lengthy production cycle times, this reporting technique may be misleading except on a cumulative basis. As has already been emphasized, the reporting of what happened on an average basis a week ago gives managers a picture of how the direct supervisors are managing their section, but such reports do not assist the supervisors in identifying problems that should be corrected. There are systematic techniques which serve that purpose, however, and they will be described in the following chapter.

MPA analysts should not be burdened with the preparation and issuance of reports. That is a data processing or accounting function. A way will be required to record manually the man-hours for detracting conditions, subject to supervisory approval and coding. Other data necessary for the performance summaries can often be derived from a computerized data base, with data processing being used for preparation of the reports themselves.

ADMINISTERING THE SYSTEM

For the MPI system to function as intended, it must have strong support from the plant or manufacturing manager. Adequate support will include the following:

Delegating Responsibility for Follow-up

It would be appropriate to select one individual to monitor key aspects of the system and see that they are handled correctly on a continuing basis. Normally, this would be a function of the MPA manager. His or her organizational status should be consistent with the need for contacting those closely involved, to determine whether procedures are being followed. A periodic MPI compliance and status report to the manufacturing and plant managers, required as a routine function, would be a practical way to get action when responsibilities within the system are being slighted. Duties of such a coordinator should include the following:

Monitoring the Reliability of Performance Reports. The chapter that follows will describe daily reporting functions. A procedure for weekly reporting has been described above. In both cases, supervisors have responsibilities to define, code, and follow up variances from norms, as they occur. The coordinator should be expected to make random checks to see whether this is being done thoroughly, on a fair basis, and with prompt checking to reduce the variances.

Maintenance of Norms. Establish an auditing procedure. Follow up to assure the correction of standard data and individual norms as methods are revised. Keep a record of annualized savings from such changes, as illustrated by Figure 4.

Manpower Planning. See that planned manpower levels are sound, and that the plans are followed.

Action where Performance is Low. Evaluate reasons for low sectional performance ratios. If not due to the influx of new operators who require training, determine whether action is being taken by those concerned. Assist in establishing realistic improvement goals. Provide records to show whether such goals are being met.

Training Programs. At the start of the MPI program, thorough training is important, and the need for training will continue.

Assistance in Supervisory Follow-up. Provide MPA assistance to supervisors in identifying the reasons for low performance, and furnish methods instruction as required.

Employee Relations

The MPI system involves people working together to meet clearly defined objectives that are fair to all concerned. Management should see that the element of fairness remains constantly in the picture. Generating a spirit of cooperative methods improvement is an objective to be sought constantly, not only within the management/staff organization, but by supervisors in their relations with operators.

14
How to Upgrade Results from MPI (Measured Day Work)

With paced assembly lines or equipment, the short-interval scheduling concept noted in Figure 34 is automatically applied, since operators know exactly what is expected of them at specific intervals, and the supervisor can see at a glance whether the designated plan of action is being followed. This chapter will explore ways of upgrading MPI control functions, when applied to LC/LR jobs or nonpaced SC/R operations, so that the same motivational concepts are in effect to a limited extent.

EVALUATING THE PERFORMANCE OF INDIVIDUAL OPERATORS

Combining Data Inputs for Two Purposes

As indicated by Figure 34, both of the steps that lead toward the objective of upgrading MPI results require reporting performance ratios for individual operators. Inputs from the shop floor that are necessary to accomplish this involve much of the same information that is also used for centralized production and material control functions. These two sets of inputs should obviously be combined. The scope of data collection typically required to satisfy combined requirements is shown by Figure 36.

The somewhat limited amount of information listed in Figure 36 implies that what is not listed can be found by cross-reference from a computerized data base. For example, the setup and per-piece norms should be identifiable from shop-order and operation numbers. The asterisks are intended to suggest that start/stop times for delay intervals,

FIGURE 36.
Typical Inputs for Production Control and Performance Reporting.

REQUIRED FOR PRODUCTION CONTROL FEEDBACK	FOR REPORTING OPERATORS' PERFORMANCE	
	X	Operator identification number.
	X	Section identification.
X	X	Shop order number, or equivalent.
X	X	Operation number.
	X	Clock time, date, and shift.
X	X	Action involved (start, delay*, complete, etc.)
	X	Code for type of delay*.
X	X	Pieces completed, or percent completion.

along with codes to designate reasons for the delays, require either supervisory inputs or authorization, if performance reports based on such data are to be realistic.

Electronic Data Collection

Various kinds of electronic data collection devices can transmit information of this kind from the shop floor to a data processing center. Included are the following:

Input Device Reads Keypunched Card and Accepts Other Keyed Data. The card may identify only the shop order, with operation numbers entered separately, or the job pack may include a card for each operation. Provision can be made for real-time testing of the input data by a central computer program. If the data is not acceptable, this will be indicated. For example, an input to the effect that operation 3 has been started before operation 2 was shown to be completed may be rejected as an error. With devices of this kind, the time of day is recorded automatically, and necessary calculations are made by the computer program to develop elapsed times.

Input Device Reads Mark-sensed Card and Accepts Keyed Data. Functions involved may be essentially the same as noted above.

Shop Data Terminals, for Keyed Input. These are the familiar terminals with viewing screen and printer, for two-way communication with the central data system.

Advantages and Disadvantages. It has been observed that equipment of this kind can serve the purpose for production control inputs, where the needed inputs are few and errors are not critical. However, errors in data input for performance reporting at a number of plant locations were such that the resulting reports had little value. This was true despite intensive efforts to train the operators, and despite screening of the data through a real-time program. The reasons for such errors could be detailed at great length. A few of the many input problems include the following:

- Improper designation of partial completions as the shift ended.
- Rework requirements for one or more parts after the corresponding operations for other parts had been completed.
- Frequent selection of the wrong operation cards or shop-order cards.

W. A. Smith (1967, 1968) spells out in detail the problems that have been encountered along this line. Other disadvantages in the use of electronic data collection equipment by operators are:

- With input from an operator directly to the data center, the supervisor is left in the dark about what has happened, until it is too late to ask questions or correct problems.
- Since the equipment is expensive, the number of units must be limited. Excessive lost time occurred when operators left work stations for a round trip to the input units, with conversations along the way.
- Excessive time was required for supervisors to make approximate corrections each day on printouts of questionable data which had been entered the previous day.
- Having operators enter delay codes and start/stop delay times was unreliable. A separate, manual procedure was necessary, requiring supervisory approval. Since the records were generally batched until the end of a shift, the supervisor had little opportunity for adequate follow-up.

Manual Records for LC/LR Operations

Shown in Figure 37 is a card format on which the operators in one plant recorded manually the information needed for production control and performance-reporting inputs. LC/LR manufacturing was involved, with an MPI control plan. Supervisors made work assignments by entering data on the left side of the cards before the shift began. When possible, a full day's work was indicated at that time. As the work was started, operators were expected to record either the shift starting time or the time for completing a preceding job. Also entered in advance by operators were the norms specified by manufacturing information. Ac-

FIGURE 37.
Format for Manually Entered Performance Data.

NAME SS NO. DATE

SHOP ORDER NO.	DRAWING NO.	ITEM	OPER. NO.	MACH. NO.	PCS. COMPL	CLOCK TIME	DEC. HOURS	NORM PER PC.	TOTAL

tual man-hours and norm totals were also entered. If delays were encountered, the reasons and time lost were recorded at the bottom of the cards. At end of shift, partial completions were estimated and recorded. Actual hours and the hours for norms plus delays were totaled by operators. It was possible for supervisors to check work progress during the shift by reviewing cards at the work sites.

After checking partial completion data and recording this for the next shift, supervisors delivered the cards to the data processing center. Here the pertinent information (not including the operators' subtractions and multiplications) was keyed for computer processing during the night shift. This formed the basis for both production control inputs and weekly MPI performance reports. The latter report provided performance ratios on a sectional basis, as described in the preceding chapter, along with the average performance ratios of individual operators.

Advantage. Operators were required to look at the norms and make a comparison with actual times. They knew this information was available during the shift for review by their supervisor. With significant data entered by supervisors, and checked to some extent as operators referred to manufacturing information, there were fewer errors. The weekly reporting of individual operators' performance ratios, while not error-free, served the purpose noted by category OSPE of Figure 34. There was a big saving in equipment cost that would have been required for electronic data collection units, and operators did not waste time walking back and forth to use such equipment.

Disadvantages. Clerical costs were involved on the part of both operators and their supervisors, and written data had to be keyed into the computer system. It was possible for a supervisor to evaluate an operator's performance at intervals during the shift, but calculations were required to do so. Since there was no procedural way to require such reviews, and no way to check whether they had been made, the strong tendency was to wait until the end of shift before reviewing performance levels. This card-record system cost less to apply and accomplished more than would have been possible with electronic data collection, but it provided only a step toward the OSPE/SIS category of Figure 34.

Manual Records for SC/R Operations

When the work involved is repetitive, even though not paced, effective MPI control becomes much easier. There are often counters on equipment such as punch presses, and the only records needed to gauge performance in such cases are readings of the counters along with the norms involved. At plants 69 and 83, for example, supervisors were able to apply the OSPE/SIS category of control systematically, and performance ratios at both locations were consistently in the 100 percent range. However, since the trend in U.S. manufacturing is toward LC/LR work, ways of upgrading MPI control remain an elusive goal in many cases.

THE OSPE CATEGORY OF MPI CONTROL, WITH SHORT-INTERVAL SCHEDULING

Limitations of Centralized Scheduling

The remainder of this chapter deals with what we have continually been referring to as LC/LR operations—jobs with longer cycles that are less repetitive. For such work, some managers seem to be convinced that effective centralized scheduling and material control systems are sufficient aids to supervisors in getting the most out of an MPI control plan.

An industrial engineering definition of scheduling is: "The prescribing of when and where each operation necessary to the manufacture of a product is to be performed." There are often successful attempts to accomplish this, with a necessary degree of tolerance, through centralized computer manipulations of a data base that includes information such as shop-order due dates, operations and time standards (norms), material requirements and material receipts, shop sections where each operation is to be performed, labor man-hours to be loaded in each section or subsection, status reports from the shop floor, etc. Because of the many variations that will always occur in LC/LR manufacturing, it is necessary for the centralized scheduling process to have a considerable amount of tolerance. One of the reasons why that is necessary has already been noted: the need to assign specific operations to operators who have done such work previously and thus do not require a costly learning period. Other obvious reasons are the usual variations in operators' performances with respect to norms, the unforeseen delays that occur from time to time, machine capacity limits, and unanticipated rework requirements.

Although centralized scheduling and material control functions are essential in meeting shipping-date commitments, essential for sound inventory control, and an aid in reducing some delays that might otherwise occur, they cannot serve as the basis for getting operators to deliver a fair day's work. That must remain the direct supervisor's job in the MPI system of control. And it has been found that detailed scheduling by the supervisor of jobs for individual operators to perform, with follow-up at reasonable intervals to identify and correct problems, is a way to maximize what can be accomplished with MPI. A technique will first be described that gets results by forcing supervisors to do that, but is so objectionable from a labor relations and supervisory viewpoint that it is often discarded after a short period of application.

Manually Applied Short-interval Scheduling

For many years, there have been a number of management consulting groups whose specialty has been the implementation of a control technique that is given various names by the groups involved, but which can be referred to by the generic name of "short-interval scheduling (SIS)." I have observed a dozen or more of these applications closely within different plants, different companies, and after the involvement of four different consulting groups. Each of these applications was essentially identical as to the concepts involved. The basic aim was to require that supervisors manage their section closely in the following ways: Schedule work for each operator, based on time standards; check at specified intervals to see whether the schedule is being followed; account in man-hours for all of the noncompliance reasons; and follow up to correct such reasons.

As noted by Mitchell Fein (1972), the basic objectives of SIS are nothing more than sound management principles, not something new or different. However, it cannot be considered good management practice to require that supervisors dilute their overall effectiveness with lengthy clerical procedures and repetitive questioning of operators that soon becomes confrontational. In all of the observed SIS applications, negative aspects so outweighed positive results that the systems were either dropped entirely or reduced to impotence after a short period. But much was accomplished while the procedures remained in effect. Rather than write these applications off as something to avoid at all costs, which is the viewpoint many have elected, it should be worthwhile to examine the detailed approaches taken, discover what encouraged improvement, and decide how to accomplish the positive results without negative aspects. That is what the balance of this chapter will attempt to do.

In each of the applications referred to, a full-time "coordinator" was utilized, reporting to the manufacturing manager or equivalent. The coordinator's function was to counter the inherent resistance of busy supervisors to clerical record-keeping and repeated questioning of operators. Required daily functions of each supervisor included these steps:

- Written daily schedules for each operator of job assignments and completion targets, calculated on the basis of what we are now referring to as norms.
- At intervals of about two hours, the supervisor was required to contact each operator, review performance in relation to the schedule, determine reasons for any negative variance, and revise the written schedule if necessary.
- The supervisor was required to list all man-hours of negative variance with reasons for each occurrence, balancing the estimated variance times with falldown man-hours.
- The supervisor was responsible for taking some follow-up action on each variance, preparing a written summary of the corrective action in each case. Copies of the daily summary went to higher management and to the coordinator.
- Through copies of the schedules and variance reports, the coordinator was able to determine whether each supervisor was adhering to prescribed steps. There was sufficient management backing so that the listed steps were closely followed during an initial period.

Advantages and Disadvantages

In most cases, the positive results included a marked increase in performance by operators and a reduction of delaying conditions. Negative aspects should be apparent from the preceding list of steps. There was too much clerical effort, and there were unnecessary confrontations between supervisors and operators in checking the adherence to schedules and making revisions. As indicated previously, the negative points became so objectionable that the systems did not remain intact for long. In today's era of clerical automation, two hours per day of writing, rewriting, and manipulation of figures will be resisted by those with managerial responsibilities. And operators will resist the repeated and often unwarranted questioning which these systems demand.

PLANACODE—PRACTICAL SHORT-INTERVAL SCHEDULING

I have developed and helped to apply within appendix-listed plant 19 a method of short-interval scheduling that eliminates most of the clerical requirements, stresses planning rather than confrontation, yet retains features that help to maximize what an MPI control plan can accomplish. A 48 percent improvement in overall performance ratios was reported within a four-month period after the system went into effect. Given the name PLANACODE for reasons that will be apparent, the system's scope and limitations have yet to be determined. A description in some detail will be given here, not to imply that the new technique is thoroughly tested in all respects, but to suggest a path for future development by others.

Objectives

As this application is described, the reader is urged to keep in mind the following essential points which variations of the technique should be expected to include:

The Planning Function. A way for supervisors to plan operators' job completion targets during the working shift, quickly and without clerical entries, so that operators can see and understand the targets for accomplishment, and so that revisions can be made easily as conditions change.

Graphic Reporting of Job Performance. A way to portray in graphic form, for operators, supervisors, and others to see, the performance in relation to norms at intervals during the shift.

Reasons for Variance. A way to identify, as reliably as practicable, all of the reasons for lack of compliance with the work plan, so that problem conditions can be followed up. This must be done without alienating the operators and with minimum clerical effort.

Job Status Identification. A method of identifying job carry-over man-hours, so that reliable OSPE reports can be developed periodically (see Figure 34), even though there may be a two-shift continuation of jobs, or if an operator's assignment is changed before a job has been finished.

Automated Data Collection. Computer-aided techniques for data collection will serve the purpose of production control feedback as well as MPI performance reporting. Such a system must be reliable, inexpensive, and conserving of operators' time.

Computerized Performance Reporting. Completely computerized performance reports, including both weekly and cumulative data, with detracting conditions summarized and coded, and with a way to show whether or not the supervisors have been accounting for detracting conditions.

Bar-coded Labels Applied to Job cards

The job card is illustrated by Figure 38. A bar-coded label was produced automatically, utilizing information from the computerized data base. This label provided sufficient information for job assignment. The example shows section, work center, order quantity, and total standard hours on the reference line of the label. Work order and operation numbers are shown on the bar-coded line.

After applying the label to the card, a half-inch cut is made on the top edge of the card, utilizing a scale corresponding to the total norm-time involved. (If norm-time is greater than the length of the shift, no

FIGURE 38.
PLANACODE Job Card.

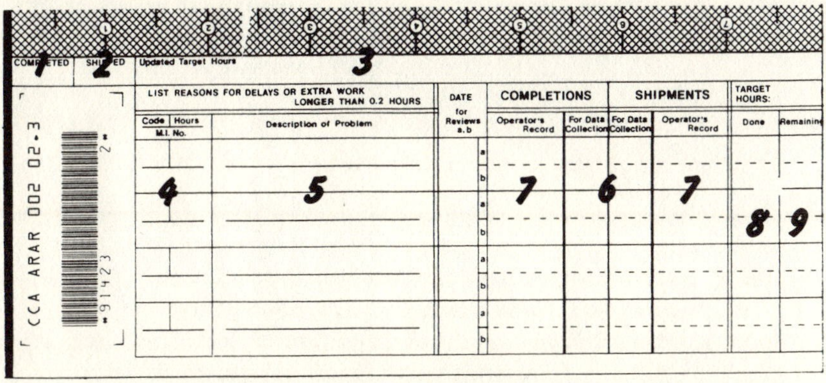

cut is made.) These preliminary steps were carried out in a data processing area. While the two clerical functions involved some ten seconds per card, they were insignificant compared with data collection savings through a process to be described. (Equipment could be obtained to apply the labels automatically.) In any case, the supervisor was not involved at this point. After preparation, the cards were delivered at night to the desks of the section supervisors involved, along with a printout of manufacturing information for order quantities ready for assignment.

Job Assignment by Supervisor

The key PLANACODE step involves a graphic display of card lengths at the left of the slit on the top edge. Figure 39 shows insertion of a single job card into the plan-rack for a designated operator. In Figure 40, various cards have been inserted, representing in graphic form a full day's work for one operator. The racks function to space the cards as if each had been cut entirely at the designated scale length. Yet the cards remain full size, for minimal record entries and later use as will be described. The sequence of cards in the rack can easily be changed. With or without PLANACODE, the job assignment process is inherently a direct supervisor's responsibility. Placing cards in the rack involves less time than a conversation.

Feedback Records by Operator

On the job card of Figure 38, the operator will enter a single check mark in space 1 when the listed order quantity has been produced. There will be a second check in space 2 when the order quantity has

FIGURE 39.
Inserting Card into Plan-rack.

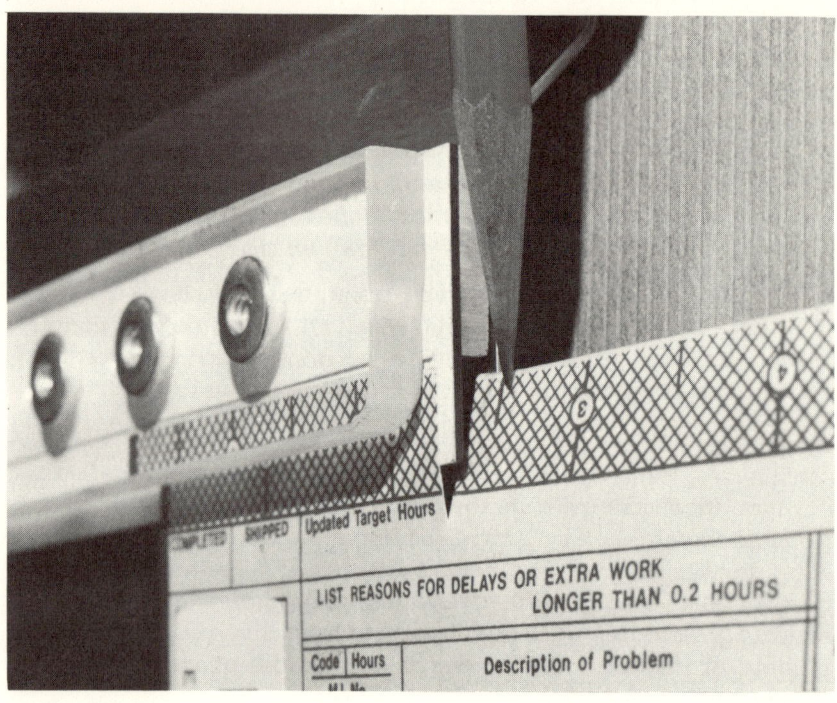

FIGURE 40.
Plan-rack, Showing Graphic Picture of Completion Targets.

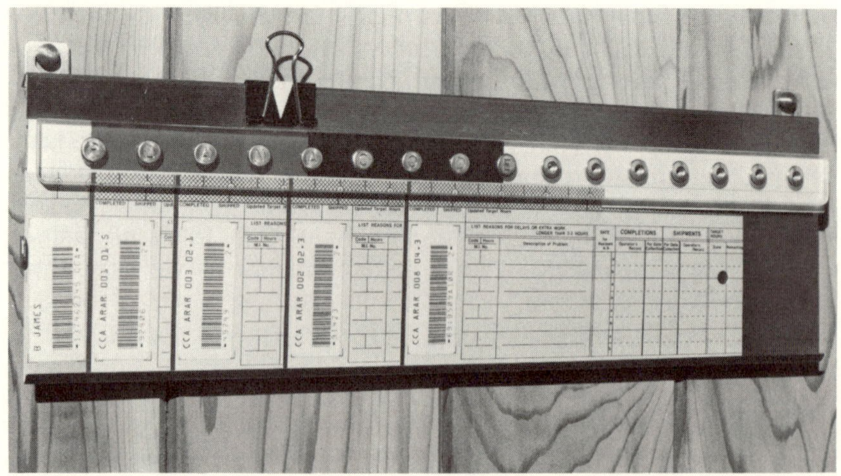

been inspected and "shipped" to the next work station. The operator will record notice of necessary delays in space 5, along with the delay time. (The supervisor should be contacted if his action is needed.) If there are partial completions at the end of a shift, this will be noted in space 7. The format for required feedback records can of course be adjusted to fit existing conditions.

Indication of Short-interval Work Target and Work Status

Screw posts on the plan-rack are separated by one hour of shift time, and four-hour segments of the shift are color coded. As Figure 40 indicates, the result is to show clearly, for reference by operator and supervisor, the work completion targets for any specified period of time. At intervals during the shift, the supervisor will move a spring-held pointer to show the work status at previously designated times. This can generally be done by glancing at either the entries in card-column 7 or the progress of work in process. The equivalent of a daily performance report for each of four operators is illustrated in Figure 42 and 43 by the location of pointers at end of shift. A total of 7.6 norm-hours was completed during the eight hour shift by the first operator, 8.3 by the second, 6.7 by the third, and 8.1 by the fourth. (Weekly reports described below are based on collected data, not on where the pointers were located.)

Entries for Variance and Partial Completion

At the shift-end review, in some cases summary entries will be required by the supervisor. In column 4 of Figure 38 will be entered a variance code and decimal hours involved, when the variance from norms during eight hours is greater than a half-hour. Figure 41 illustrates how a two-digit code can be applied for typical conditions that occur. For carry-over jobs, the approximate figure to show remaining standard hours will be entered in column 9. Since this entry is on the last job card, the spaces are visible without shifting cards. The supervisor will then mark in space 3 where the card should be cut when next assigned. "Paperwork" by the supervisor involves only these minimal entries, plus movement of pointers. (After a training interval, the latter function could be done by operators.) The supervisor would no longer need to prepare a "turnover report" to line up his or her counterpart on the following shift, as would likely be required if the status of all jobs in process were not clearly shown.

FIGURE 41.
Example of Coding Detracting Conditions to Show Responsibility, for Weekly Reporting.

		PRIMARY RESPONSIBILITY OF OPERATOR AND SUPERVISOR	*PRIMARY RESPONSIBILITY OF SECTIONAL SUPERVISOR*	*NOT THE PRIMARY RESPONSIBILITY OF SECTIONAL SUPERVISOR*
1. DELAY, MATERIAL NOT AVAILABLE	1. Stock-out, storeroom		X	
	2. Floor stock not available		X	
	3. Wrong material sent		X	
2. DELAY, REQUIRED INFORMATION LACKING	1. Engineering drawings			X
	2. Manufacturing information			X
	3. Methods description		X	
3. ADDED WORK WITHIN PLANNED OPERATION	1. Bad parts or material		X	
	2. Equipment or tooling problem		X	
	3. Extra setup		X	
4. ELECTRICAL REWORK, PLANNED OPERATIONS 5. MECHANICAL REWORK, PLANNED OPERATIONS	1. Defective purchased material			X
	2. Defective mat'l, other section			X
	3. Work in this section, other oper.		X	
	4. Work in this section, same oper.	X		
6. REWORK, UNPLANNED OPERATIONS				X
7. EXPENSE ASSIGNMENTS	1. Work-place meetings			X
	2. Q.C. meetings			X
	3. Safety meetings			X
	4. Medical			X
	5. Training		X	
	6. Cleanup, mat'l hdlg., etc.		X	
8. OPERATOR DEFICIENCY	1. Normal learning not complete		X	
	2. Performance level below norm	X		
9. NORM ENTRY MISSING, FIRST SETUP OR RUN-TIME		-	-	-

Bar-code Data Collection

Instead of operators walking to a data collection point at repeated intervals during the shift, an assigned person toured the area at the end of shift, using a portable bar-code reader. Figure 42 shows the equipment involved. Wanding the bar-coded label on a job card, with no partial entry afterward, signified completion and forwarding of the order quantity. When partial or variance entries were required, this was done after wanding the respective labels, using a wristband as in Figure 43. Experience to date indicates a time requirement for this purpose of about one minute per operator, which compares with the estimated fifteen minutes per operator that would be necessary for the walk/talk time to input at a central point what is shown by the average requirements illustrated in Figure 40.

Experience has also shown that data collection errors with the new technique are infrequent, largely because of supervisory checking, bar-code reliability, and the fact that one or more trained individuals made

FIGURE 42.
Use of Portable Bar-Code Reader to Record Job-order and Operation Numbers.

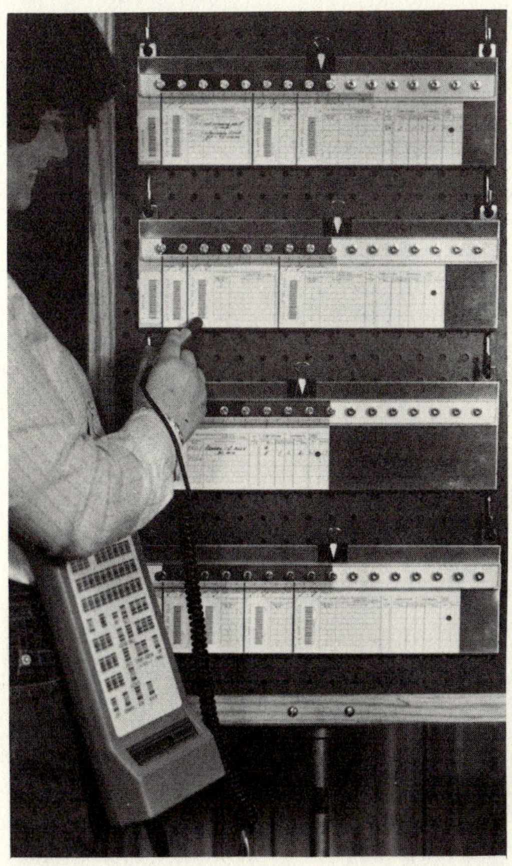

the inputs rather than numerous operators. This is not the case with usual forms of electronic data collection, as noted previously. If there is a second shift, any new assignments can be added without disrupting the first-shift display of cards. Then, after data collection has been finished, completed job cards are removed. (They can be used as message cards to follow up detracting conditions.) The plan-rack is rearranged by shoving assignment cards to the left.

Automated Reporting

The primary function of PLANACODE is the visible, greatly simplified SIS routine described above. The system goes much further than typical

FIGURE 43.
Method of Entering Variance and Partial Completion Data with Portable Bar-Code Reader.

short-interval scheduling applications, however. Collected data is fed electronically into a computer terminal. Figure 44 illustrates a system flow chart, which could be revised as necessary to fit specific plant conditions and requirements. Where PLANACODE was first applied, the following outputs were obtained from computer processing of collected information:

- Job completion data, for production control uses.
- Automated weekly performance reports showing the performance ratios of individual operators, with four-week running averages.
- Automated weekly sectional performance reports, with four-week running

FIGURE 44.
Example of Information Flow for PLANACODE Application.

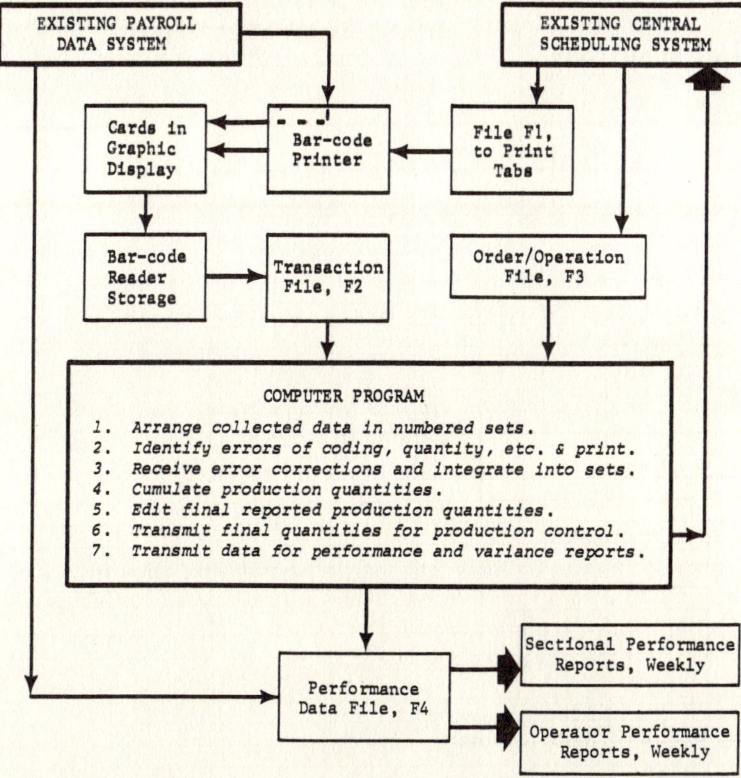

averages, based on valid comparisons between standard hours and actual hours worked. Such reports included a tabulation of variance hours for the week, by designated codes.

- Automated reporting of the percentage of variance hours not accounted for by individual supervisors. This, together with the visibility of plan-racks, obviates the need for a system coordinator, or "policeman," which has been observed to be a full-time requirement with SIS applications of a clerical nature. (The MPA manager can properly be assigned the responsibility of maintaining the system.)

Limitations and Cost

A system of the kind described above is applicable within LC/LR manufacturing where the standard operation time, multiplied by the quantity within a production release, averages about an hour or longer. The technique can also be applied where nondirect manpower assignments are of similar length. For a plant with about three hundred operators, working on two shifts, there would be an add-on equipment cost in the range of $25,000, assuming that a computerized production control system was already functioning. The cost of necessary computer programming would depend on desired reporting functions and on the structure of the existing data base.

CONCLUSIONS REGARDING MPI APPLICATIONS

As was done in a previous chapter dealing with wage incentive applications, so should an attempt be made here to "separate the wheat from the chaff" (or facts from folklore) concerning the control plan usually referred to as measured day work. The problem in doing so, however, is that opinions about this system have not become so ingrained in the literature, or in the minds of individuals, as have the opinions concerning wage incentives. But various questions about the system are often raised, both by management personnel and by industrial engineers. An attempt is made below to identify typical questions and provide answers which are, in effect, a summary of material in this chapter and the one before it.

A fairly obvious conclusion is that the name itself is a handicap, for reasons that have been covered. The alternate name of Methods and Productivity Improvement, or MPI, was selected to avoid confusion in this book and for possible consideration by others.

The Focus of MPI Norms

Will labor problems be caused when operators are given definite performance targets, as has often been the case with wage incentive applications? The experience of various MPI plants within appendix-listed company K has been that those plants which closely monitor and control the performance level of operators in relation to norms do not have as many labor relations problems as tend to occur where performance discipline is lax. This may to some extent be due to more supervisory contact with operators in helping to eliminate problem conditions that cause low performance. However, it has been the overall observation that employee grievances in MPI plants are concerned more with labor-grade issues than with the validity of norms. (In wage incentives, the emphasis is reversed, because time standards affect take-home pay.)

If the failure to achieve norms by operators is not looked upon by management as a primary basis for disciplinary action, how can they be of any real value? The chief point to remember is that management-related problems are often the cause of failure to meet performance targets. A requirement that the real problem first be identified clearly, before any disciplinary action is taken, often serves to eliminate the need for taking further action. When specific operators do not achieve the norms on an average basis, this should alert the supervisor to focus on the cause of problems and their correction. That is why supervisors need the assistance of a routine reporting system which identifies the performance level of individual operators.

Will emphasis on meeting norms cause some operators to reduce the level at which they would otherwise perform? Emphasis should always be toward achieving work targets on an average basis, pointing out that the norms are not intended as a performance ceiling. It is true that the very high effort level of some incentive operators will not be observed where there is an MPI control plan. It is also true that just as many incentive operators work below the average level, largely without questioning by their supervisors, since a low-task point has been dignified and made acceptable by calling it normal. Getting low performers to meet the norms by correcting methods or other detracting conditions can offset what may be lost when others drop somewhat from a very high pace level. There are many who believe that their experience shows a well-managed MPI control plan to be the equal in performance level of a well-managed wage incentive plan. My experience indicates that to be the case. But there is an added gain caused by increased emphasis on methods improvement which the working climate within MPI tends to encourage. This is probably the most significant factor involved.

The Level of MPI Time Standards, or Norms

Should the MPI norm be established at the same methods/pace level as wage incentive normal? There is no valid industrial engineering theory or concept which would lead to this conclusion. Common sense would answer "no."

Should the MPI norm be established at the so-called "high-task" wage incentive level, which may also be referred to as average incentive pace? Again, there is no valid concept that applies. The level at which MPI norms are established is for staff and management groups within a plant to determine, after careful review. Considering the fact that the difference between average incentive pace and incentive normal is largely due to methods finesse and reduction of avoidable delays, there is little reason why the preceding question could not be answered with at least a "maybe."

Since the MTM–1 system of predetermined times is the most widely used basis for establishing time standards, other than direct time study, and since this system includes no basis for adjustment of its incremental values to correspond with the requirements of specific control plans, is this not evidence that the norms of MPI should be at the same level as wage incentive "normal?" No! The first predetermined time system (MTA) produces time values that are at a considerably higher task level than MTM. The same is said to be true of Work Factor, which is commonly adjusted to fit the requirements of whatever system is involved. 4M DATA—the computer-aided way to apply MTM–1—is adjustable by any designated factor. MTM was introduced long before there was reference within industrial engineering literature to the nonincentive version of measured day work. MTM produces low-task time values intended to serve as the wage incentive normal (Honeycutt, 1962). While it is used frequently in this way, there are also many variations of wage incentive normal, as shown in Figure 5. Despite theoretical concepts sometimes advanced by those who envision a single performance level recognized universally as the unquestioned basis for performance unless financial incentives are applied, the real world does not function that way.

Whatever the level of MPI norms, are they ever achieved on an average basis? The operators in a number of appendix-listed MPI plants did achieve established norms on an average basis. As noted previously, the operators' performance ratios in various departments of one large MPI plant were regularly above the 100 percent level. Operators' performance ratios at MPI plants with LC/LR operations were typically below the target level by 10–15 percent, except where there were reporting systems that identified the performance levels of individual operators in a reliable way.

The Question of Basic Wage Rates

Should the wage scale for comparable labor grades be higher in measured day work (MPI) than base rates in a wage incentive system, if it is assumed that similar types of work exist at each location? A theoretical case could be made for a "YES" answer here. On a practical basis, the answer would probably still be "YES" if the two plants were close together, since qualified employees would want to work where they could earn more. But there is no accepted concept that applies in either case, since job evaluation procedures are not enforced on a plant-wide basis. The list of variables that exist in the real world to affect wage rates would be too lengthy to enumerate here. Consider, for example, a muffler repair technician at a small shop adjacent to an automobile assembly plant. An operator with minimal skill at the latter plant might be earning much more than the pay of the trained muffler repairman.

How to Get Started

Should the application of norms in a new plant be delayed until ready to begin plant-wide? If a plant has been operated without time standards for a long period, can MPI be started with expectations of prompt results? Can a deteriorated wage incentive plan be converted to the MPI control plan? The longer there is a delay in applying and using norms as a basis for control, the greater will be the chance for resistance from some operators. Thus, do not delay, but begin section by section. If day work without time standards has been the practice for many years, getting operators to upgrade performance levels when norms are applied will clearly be more difficult than when operators know what to expect as they are hired. In such cases, the OSPE level of control shown by Figure 34 should be a minimum requirement, following careful explanation of the objectives. To apply MPI after wage incentives creates wage-rate questions, as previously discussed. Once negotiations have settled this point, the OSPE control level will also be needed for improvement. In all cases, the OSPE/SIS level, shown by Figure 34, should be a goal.

Possible MPI Savings and Overall Advantages

Can MPI control plans reduce overhead costs like well-managed incentive plans? Can they reduce direct labor costs, when incentive plans generally do not? How are nondirect functions affected by MPI applications in direct manufacturing? The question about the influence of MPI controls on nondirect functions is an easy one to answer. The effect is just the opposite of what can be expected when wage incentives are applied to direct operations. Instead of the inherent negative reaction caused by lack of bonus opportunity, the precedent set by MPI controls in the shop makes it easier to pursue similar objectives in nondirect departments. Since the ratio of nondirect to direct operators continues to increase in many plants, this point can be one of the most significant reasons favoring the MPI control plan.

Concerning the questions about direct labor and overhead costs, the first point to consider is whether an appreciable amount of paced or machine-controlled operations is involved, since there is little reason for wage incentives in such cases. For other kinds of work, let us assume that the application of either form of control plan would come after a period in which capable management had been active in cost-reduction efforts, but without time standards or performance evaluation based on standards. Let us also assume that the concept of wage incentive normal represents the methods/pace level of operators at the point of transition to an incentive control plan. And, although some may not agree, we will assume that MPI norms are established at about the same level as average incentive pace.

With these points in mind, a full-sharing incentive plan would not reduce direct labor costs. The MPI control plan has a chance to do so. Given the SPE level of MPI control, defined in Figure 34, an average ratio of 85 percent might be expected for operators' performance on LC/

LR work. This improvement in direct labor and overhead costs could well be less than the incentive system's initial reduction in overhead costs per product. However, there would not be a negative effect on nondirect work attitudes, and there would be less chance of future deterioration. And the "kicker" would be a better climate for continued emphasis toward methods improvement.

If higher levels of MPI control were applied, as also defined in Figure 34, experience would indicate that the 85 percent level could be improved upon. With the OSPE/SIS level of control, there is a fair chance of equaling wage incentive average performance levels, in which case the same overhead reduction per product would result, along with a direct labor cost reduction not possible with wage incentives.

There are many factors that influence expected results with either system of control. This and the preceding three chapters have attempted to explain them.

Summary of Conclusions

The symbol shown below can serve as a reminder of basic goals in the MPI control plan:

M&S ⇄ FDW

As the top arrow indicates, apply METHODS AND STANDARDS to define a FAIR DAY'S WORK. And, as the bottom arrow indicates, provide WORK-DONE FEEDBACK to SUPERVISORS AND MANAGEMENT.

15
Extending Labor Productivity Control to Nondirect Functions

In some manufacturing organizations, nondirect employees outnumber those performing direct operations. The purpose of this chapter is to describe how productivity control techniques can be applied successfully where nondirect work is involved. Variations in work of this kind at specific locations require that this coverage be on a somewhat general basis. Because maintenance labor and material costs are of particular significance, practical ways to control both the costs and effectiveness of this nondirect function will be discussed in more detail.

ADAPTING CONTROL TECHNIQUES TO FIT THE TYPE OF WORK

Listed below are categories of nondirect work in manufacturing. The groups within each category will seem at first glance to be unrelated, but there are similarities in the types of control that are applicable. Not all departments that are given the same name in different plants include the same activities, and there will be exceptions to the generalities noted here. For example, in response to a statement that work measurement standards are not economically feasible for repair maintenance work, one industrial engineering manager described a closely timed and semipaced group of a dozen mechanics that were utilized to overhaul individual vacuum units in a large plant where television picture tubes were manufactured. Other exceptions may come to the reader's mind as these nondirect functions are discussed. But there should be enough similarities for the comments that follow to have a useful meaning.

Maintenance, Toolroom, Model Shop, Engineering, Drafting

With the exception of some preventive maintenance jobs, the work in each of these departments is largely nonrepetitive. Not only would the man-hours to develop standard data and apply it for individual jobs be costly, but information required to derive time standards could be obtained only after the work is done. After-the-fact time values are of little use in such cases, and can lead to arguments and excuses. Estimates made in advance would be much more productive, and could be used to plan and schedule a full (and fair) day's work. That approach can properly be taken as a basis for control.

A following section discusses how estimates for the work done by maintenance personnel can be developed and used for daily planning and scheduling. To do that for any of the work categories listed above, two possible approaches can be considered. Where the sections involved are relatively small, the supervisor is logically the one to handle such functions. For larger groups, the use of an estimator/scheduler should be considered. There are potential problems either way. For effective results, fixed routines are essential in preliminary viewing of work requirements, developing estimates, preparation of a daily schedule, assignment of jobs to individuals, evaluation of performance, and denoting carry-over man-hours for the next day's schedule. If the supervisor does these things, the problem is getting him or her to adhere to a rigid time format in order to make the procedure accomplish its full potential. If an estimator/scheduler is utilized, the problems are: (a) to keep top management apprised that such a function is needed to reduce overall costs; and (b) to coordinate the supervisors' routines with what is prescribed by the scheduling system.

Work sampling typically shows high percentages of nonworking time in nondirect departments such as those listed. Experience has indicated that a properly managed estimating/planning/scheduling/supervisory function can reduce man-hour costs by 25–30 percent. But that will not happen without coordination, and management will not be convinced of savings in this range without solid evidence from time to time. It will be an unusual supervisor or manager in such groups who possesses the background, initiative, time, and determination to develop a successful control program and keep it going alone. Some staff coordination will almost invariably be required. Many organizations have relied on outside consultants to initiate such programs, but what happens when they leave? An alternate approach is for the industrial engineering department, or MPA group as we have referred to it in this book, to implement such applications and monitor them on a part-time basis. This requires sponsoring by management, and it also requires that MPA personnel have the background to realize that control functions of this kind may be quite different from techniques that have proved to be successful in direct manufacturing.

Once again, we are not talking here about establishing standard data or standards, but about setting up a microcosm of what the manufacturing organization refers to as job-order routing, manpower planning, production scheduling, material control, and performance reporting: not replicas of such functions, but specialized ways to accomplish the same results. Applications along this line should be developed only after careful analysis of what is justified.

MPA groups have not made the same headway in applying nondirect control plans as has been made in productivity control systems for manufacturing operations. A description of maintenance cost control functions, to follow in this chapter, will illustrate general ways in which the control techniques can be designed and put into effect

Manufacturing Inspectors, Plant Cleanup Personnel

As unrelated as these two work categories may appear to be, they are alike in that both can often be analyzed through direct time study, for purposes of methods analysis and to derive time standards. The standards can then be applied, though in somewhat different ways, as a basis for control.

Inspection requirements can be indicated on manufacturing route sheets as sequential operations. Although allowances may be required for delays or necessary discussions, time values can be developed and listed on the route sheets. If product inspections are on a percentage basis, this can also be noted. In the same way that manpower planning derives the number of production operators for planned work loads, so can the number of required inspectors be determined. If this is done carefully, and if supervisors are alert to see that production delays are not caused by substandard inspection performance, a basis for control will result.

Time standards for janitorial work are available commercially from various sources. The alternative, and perhaps a better one, is to determine the cleanup requirements and develop time standards internally. Use of adequate equipment is significant here, just as for manufacturing operations. The next step is to determine cleanup frequencies, establish regular schedules, make daily work assignments, and supervise to assure acceptable results.

Material Handling, Storeroom Attendants, Receiving Inspection, Order Service, Clerical Personnel

Similarities here lie in the fact that the personnel involved usually perform a mixed variety of work requiring manpower levels roughly in proportion to the manufacturing work load. Through careful MPA analysis, budget standards or "manning tables" can be developed that will serve as a basis for productivity control. This is not a simple procedure. Unless it is done carefully, unless there is full support by management, and unless the derivations are updated as methods or procedures change, the manning schedules that are set up will not be followed. But there is a chance here to extend productivity control into areas where it has been lax.

Methods Analysis. The first step is to analyze methods and procedures, one section at a time. Systematic questioning is needed. The previously described approach for questioning manufacturing methods can be revamped along the following lines:

- Question the purpose of each procedural step involved. First, is the overall objective actually required? If so, how can the steps to achieve the objective be reduced or simplified? With minimum steps defined, can specific operations to accomplish them be eliminated, combined, or simplified?
- Question basic methods and equipment. Can manual functions be automated to advantage? Can better equipment be justified? Can forms be eliminated, simplified, or the number of copies reduced? Is electronic data processing being used advantageously?
- Question the division of work between individuals. Is the work load balanced? Is there always a full day's work available? If not, can the regular crew size be reduced, transferring personnel from other work at fixed intervals?
- Question the workplace methods. Is the amount of walking minimized? Do inspectors and clerks have adequate lighting? Are the correct tools readily available? Is handling minimized between operations? Have provisions been made for effective use of both hands, for seating where practical, and for desk space where clerical entries are required?

Work Sampling, Combined with Transaction Counts. Only a general approach can be suggested here, to be modified as conditions warrant. After acceptable methods are in place, the next step might properly be a work sampling study, with a daily count made during the study of significant activity occurrences, or transactions. Examples are numbers of incoming order shipments inspected, numbers of shop orders for which material was issued, or numbers of orders processed by the order service group. The sampling will allow for an evaluation of net working time, particularly if performance rating is introduced into the study. By deriving this for time-span intervals, as can be done automatically with the microprocessor technique described in chapter 8, this would indicate whether manpower transfers at specified intervals should be considered.

The transaction counts can be used in several ways to supplement information provided by the sampling study. If there are variations in the transaction counts, without corresponding variations in the manufacturing load level, the analyst should determine whether there can be some leveling of the work load, or whether staffing must be such that load peaks can be handled. The net working time per transaction provides a basis for determining average time standards. In some cases, this has been used for performance reporting, not unlike the OSPE procedures for MPI, covered in the previous chapter.

Manning Tables. The overall objective of a sampling study could properly be the development of manning tables which show an acceptable number of employees for each nondirect group, at various manufacturing load levels. For analyses of this kind to be useful, they should be made by competent MPA engineers who are able to work cooperatively with managers of the groups concerned, and who are fully supported by plant management as the project is carried out. While it is not possible to list here all of the paths that such analyses should take, there must be included a determination of how the general methods should change as manning levels vary. At a high load level, for example, two fork-truck operators may be assigned on a full-time basis to move pallet loads from assembly lines to the shipping area. At intermediate load levels, one of the operators could divide his time between that activity and the loading of trucks. And at some lower level of activity, only one operator might be assigned for the movement of pallet loads to shipping.

At various plants within company K, an "engineered budget" program was developed along these lines, with manning tables used as a basis for adjusting crew sizes. Monthly budget statements were issued to specific department managers, comparing actual manpower costs and indirect material costs with budgeted amounts. This served to extend the concept of measured day work (referred to here as the MPI plan) from direct manufacturing to various nondirect departments.

Maintaining Nondirect Controls as Load Conditions Fluctuate

Through a selected combination of planning and scheduling of authorized work, time standards used for performance reporting, and manning tables with compliance reporting, it is possible to extend productivity control concepts to nondirect groups. Before going further in this discussion, there are two points that should be emphasized:

- A thorough MPA job must be done when initiating the control procedures, and plant management must be convinced of this. Otherwise, there may be arbitrary force adjustments taken from time to time that will act to block the effectiveness of systematic control procedures.
- There must be continued maintenance of what may be established initially along this line. When conditions or methods change, the time standards or manning tables must be revised. Planning and scheduling routines left entirely for section managers to administer are not likely to survive as effective control mechanisms.

In nondirect departments, such as maintenance and the toolroom, where highly skilled mechanics might be lost to the plant if laid off, it is particularly important to avoid unnecessary manpower fluctuations. There are ways to accomplish this. As will be further discussed in the section that follows, perhaps a third of the maintenance or toolmaking work load can be contracted during periods of heavy shop load. Then, as downturns occur in the manufacturing load, a maintenance or toolroom crew of minimum size can be retained by reducing or eliminating outside contracting. The same is true in some cases with engineering drafting. In janitorial functions, although potential layoffs are not so critical, many plants find that outside contracting is useful to some degree.

Maintenance Cost Control

This subject warrants further discussion. Within manufacturing, maintenance labor and material costs are typically the largest nondirect budget item. These costs continue to grow as direct labor becomes more mechanized. In process industries, maintenance manpower may equal or exceed the number of operating personnel. Over the years, control procedures have been developed that function to advantage in large maintenance departments. It is practical in such cases to establish small staff groups to coordinate the control systems, just as staff groups within manufacturing perform functions that are necessary for labor productivity control.

PROBLEMS OF PRODUCTIVITY CONTROL WITHIN SMALLER MAINTENANCE DEPARTMENTS

Principles of maintenance cost control remain the same for smaller craft groups in manufacturing as for large maintenance departments. The transition from principles to actual practice is more difficult, however. Some of the reasons for this may be worth noting, since it is only by finding ways to minimize the difficulties that control systems can be effective. After experience in developing maintenance control plans in some ten process plants, where maintenance crew sizes were as large as fifteen hundred, and in about twice that many manufacturing plants where the number of maintenance personnel ranged from twenty to several hundred, I would list the following reasons for a current lack of effective maintenance control within many manufacturing plants:

- A plant manager or manufacturing manager is not likely to be inherently supportive of what could be termed staff functions within nondirect groups. "You're just adding staff on top of staff" is a comment frequently voiced. While recognizing the need for manufacturing staff functions such as purchasing, production scheduling, material control, industrial engineering, etc., there is an understandable reluctance to expand such duties within nondirect groups.
- Industrial engineering managers, who should be in the best position to recommend and help establish control functions within maintenance departments, frequently do not realize what is needed. They may think of maintenance productivity control largely in terms of time standards for preventive maintenance jobs, or work sampling to identify nonworking percentages.
- Some maintenance managers and supervisors, like many of their counterparts in manufacturing, tend to resist outside "assistance" by those who do not share the responsibilities involved when repair work is not done properly or on time.

ANOTHER LOOK AT PRODUCTIVITY CONTROL PRINCIPLES

Under headings that follow, tested control concepts will be described. If the reader is in sympathy with views such as those noted above, an open-minded consideration of what follows may help change opinions somewhat. In order to present here a set of guidelines for maintenance cost control, and to do so in a way that shows their relation to other controls within manufacturing which are commonly accepted, it would seem logical to review again the list of productivity control principles in Figure 3. By examining them one at a time, the reader can form opinions as to whether they do or do not apply to maintenance cost control and, if they do apply, what general approaches can best serve to implement them.

Develop Clear and Fair Ideals

Maintenance personnel should be, and generally are, craftsmen who take pride in the skills they have acquired. They tend to be protective of those skills, sometimes in arbitrary and unfair ways. Aided by the influences that organized labor can exert, highly restrictive rules have been negotiated in many plants concerning prerogatives of the various crafts within a maintenance department. Examples of these restrictions include:

Narrowly Defined Craft Designations. In many cases, agreements have evolved concerning the boundaries of work that any specific craft can be asked to perform. At appendix-listed plants 61 and 67, for example, the maintenance department that serviced both locations included more than fifteen separate craft groups. The categories of work each group could be assigned to perform were rigidly defined, regardless of whether added work sequences were required to complete a job.

Unnecessary Helper Assignments. While some maintenance jobs require two or more individuals working together, many do not. It is fairly common, however, for the negotiated or implied rules within specific plants to say that a helper must go with each craftsman.

Varying Labor Grades within Crafts. There may be first-class and second-class electricians, or mechanics, or pipefitters, etc. There is some justification here, since it takes both experience and inherent skill to become a top-level craftsman. There may be elements of unfairness, however, in arbitrary restrictions concerning the type of work that can be assigned to those in different labor grades.

Limitations on Work That Can Be Contracted. There are frequent construction or repair jobs that could be handled more economically on a contractual basis, largely because of specialized skills or equipment not available within the plant maintenance organization. Objections by maintenance personnel to contracting of work are understandable when it is perceived that contracting practices threaten job security. But this does not have to be the case, as will be discussed, and restrictions on the contracting of work should be resisted strongly.

Steps Taken to Avoid Restrictive Practices. Current trends in relatively new plants listed in the appendix have been to establish only two designated craft groups—electrical and mechanical. To the extent that qualified craftsmen can be obtained, the same labor grade is applied. There is no helper category. Only when two men are needed on a job are two assigned. And, as in any new plant, there are no self-imposed restrictions against outside contracting when advantageous. Policies of this kind act to remove elements of unfairness often thrust upon maintenance management. There can be questions, however, as to whether such approaches are perceived by maintenance personnel to be fair from their standpoint. To a large extent, such questions would be answered by the way in which maintenance management recognizes requirements such as the following:

- If higher skilled employees are consistently assigned to perform work that requires such skills, the same basis for wage differential should exist that is commonly recognized throughout the plant in other types of work.
- Outside contracting of maintenance work will be perceived as unfair if there have been, or are likely to be, maintenance force reductions.
- On jobs requiring two or more men, the supervisor should make specific assignments to each, when practical, avoiding a drift toward regular helper assignments.

Elimination or reduction of arbitrary restrictions on how maintenance personnel can be utilized will help reduce costs. However, the productivity control techniques to be described under headings that follow are operable with or without restrictive rules for work assignment.

Select Qualified Personnel

This heading, from the list of principles in Figure 3, speaks for itself. When there are maintenance job openings, the required procedure may involve posting job vacancies so that employees who want to be upgraded can bid to fill such openings. If those who do so are without maintenance experience, and if qualified craftsmen are available from outside the plant, making the latter choice is a fair approach, and this right should not be allowed to slip away.

Provide Justifiable Staff

Although there are many possible organizational patterns, that shown in Figure 45 is typical of what might be found in a medium-sized manufacturing plant. The maintenance manager is likely to be a skilled professional who understands the need for cost control, but he will probably require some assistance in establishing and administering a comprehensive control plan. Such a program should also include getting manufacturing supervisors to recognize their responsibilities in avoiding equipment abuse, assigning some preventive maintenance (PM) jobs to operators, and minimizing emergency work requests. One of the staff groups shown at the right in Figure 45—the industrial engineering (MPA) department—could logically be expected to coordinate the implementation and periodic review of a maintenance control plan.

The fact that this does not happen very often—certainly not often enough—could be due to one or more of the reasons previously noted:

FIGURE 45.
Typical Manufacturing Organization, Medium-size Plant.

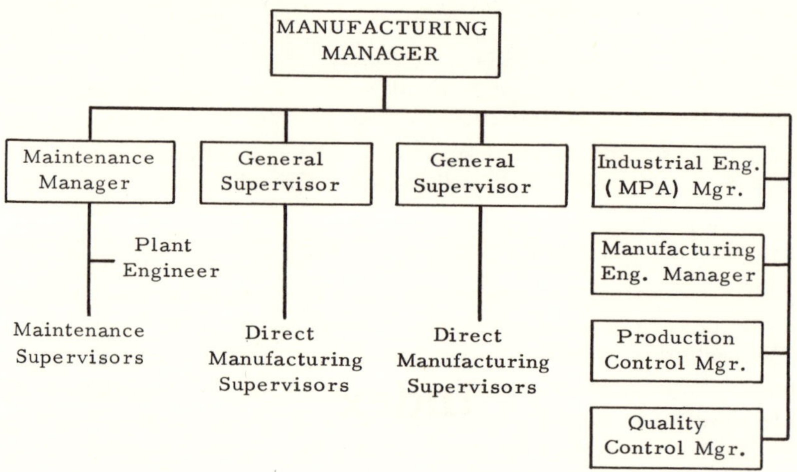

lack of top management's awareness of the need for such assistance, lack of MPA recognition of how to proceed, or resistance by maintenance to outside interference. The chances are that all three of these conditions do exist in most manufacturing organizations. At this point, it may help in understanding the message which this section of the chapter hopes to convey if several conclusions are listed next, before the discussion on which they are based. (The details that follow about other productivity control principles will provide logic to reinforce these conclusions.)

- A small estimating/planning/scheduling function, strongly supported by the maintenance manager and working closely with both maintenance and manufacturing supervisors, can pay big dividends in ways that will be described under headings to follow.
- For continuing effectiveness, the lead person in such an activity should report through the MPA manager. But there should be a clear understanding that the approaches involved must be tailored to the needs of the maintenance group and thus will be different from the control requirements for direct manufacturing. (Note: If the person(s) referred to report through the maintenance manager, past observations indicate that they tend to become part of the maintenance supervisory process, with diminishing effectiveness as a basis for productivity control.)

Standardize Working Conditions

Some equipment can be transported to a maintenance shop when repair work is required. There is as much reason for such areas to be kept clean, orderly, and well-lighted as plant operating areas. For repair or construction work at other locations in the plant, portable tool carts are often a good investment. With vise and table space, they serve to improve both working conditions and productivity.

Define Work Requirements

This is the starting point for maintenance cost control. Typically, there are four categories of jobs to be considered. It will help in defining these clearly, and in discussing how to control their costs, if we consider how they might apply to a piece of equipment with which everyone is familiar—the family automobile. It would be hard to find a single piece of equipment that includes as many of the potential repair requirements that could be encountered within an industrial plant: rotating, reciprocating, and belt-driven mechanisms; hydraulic controls; electrical and electronic systems; metal corrosion problems; repainting for appearance sake; etc. As we talk about automobile maintenance situations, please do not feel that this is being too elementary. There is not much about modern automobile design that could be termed simple. The categories of maintenance work on the automobile are as follows:

Preventive Maintenance. Included in this category are periodic inspections, lubrication and fluid changes, filter replacements, spark plug changes, etc. The car instruction booklet lists recommended PM functions at stated intervals, just as would normally be proposed by the suppliers of plant equipment. An experienced car owner would use judgment in deciding whether to follow blindly all of the recommended PM steps, realizing some may be listed to absolve the manufacturer of risk, rather than because they are known to be cost-effective.

Since much of the equipment in a manufacturing plant may not be provided with reliable PM lists, we might consider what a new-car owner—one who is mechanically inclined—would logically decide to identify as periodic preventive maintenance functions. From past experience, the owner would know about significant PM requirements—lubrication, spark plugs, filters, etc. If regular use of the car brought to light recurring problems, such as alternator belt slippage, brake disc scoring because of excess pad wear, or muffler corrosion, a maintenance-minded car owner would learn to check such conditions periodically. That is what the plant maintenance group should also do—determine through experience, based on repair records, the cost-effective inspections or repairs that need to be made at periodic intervals on plant equipment.

What the new-car owner without a service booklet should not do, of course, is to pay to have the engine or transmission disassembled at intervals to check for excessive wear. He or she will wait for definite

FIGURE 46.
Maintenance Work Order Format.

MAINTENANCE WORK ORDER — Request originator: Enter complete information in spaces at left of double lines.

Work order no. 8874

Equipment No.: 12593
Equipment Name & Location: Niagara punch press, Dept. 30
Charge: 587-30
Work Information: Prepare concrete floor area in Dept. 30, per drawing. Move press to new floor area. Repair flywheel guard.
Date of Request: 4/15/89
Requested start date:
Requested completion date (If critical): 6/15/89
Material required to start (List crafts): C
Non-stock mat'l required:
List drwg. nos.: J-1432
Requested by: W. Roberts
Approved by:
Approved for Maintenance: JRM
Crafts: C, EL, MW

performance symptoms before costly work is undertaken. And that is equally true in plant maintenance. Preventive Maintenance work can be overdone, driving up costs unnecessarily.

Nonemergency Maintenance Repairs. Most car repairs do not require emergency road service because the driver is alerted by substandard brake action, ammeter variation, engine sluggishness, lack of wheel balance, etc., and can get to a garage before the vehicle stops running or is damaged. In most cases, there is no rush to do this, and repair service can be scheduled ahead of time. The same thing applies in a manufacturing plant, provided operators and supervisors recognize that they have a shared responsibility in maintenance cost control. A desire to meet production schedules at all costs is the obstacle to overcome. Since both repair costs and production downtime are likely to be reduced by planning ahead, there is a clear reason for management to insist that direct supervisors initiate work orders promptly when equipment problems are spotted.

The usual way to do this is for the supervisor to issue a work request. The type of information required is shown by Figure 46. To avoid handling of carbon copies and to save time required for transmission by plant mail, the information can properly be phoned to the maintenance office for entry on the work order format. A work order number can then be obtained and noted in a sectional log book, for later reference if necessary.

Repair Work of an Emergency Nature. Turning again to the automobile as an example, we know that breakdowns do occur, despite preventive maintenance or attempts to spot problems before they become serious (or because of neglect along these lines). And we also know that emergency repairs are likely to cost more, not only for the repair work but because of personal delays. Often it is possible to arrange alternate transportation (rent a car, get a friend to help, or take the bus). In such cases, there is less delay time, and repair work can be scheduled by the garage. Similar situations apply in manufacturing. By shifting operators to other equipment, it may not be necessary to insist on immediate action. Maintenance supervisors need not interrupt work already in process, avoiding added cost that would otherwise be required. In any case, a work request should be made as early as possible, indicating reasons why prompt action may be essential.

Construction, Equipment Overhaul, or Equipment Installations. The personal car owner may decide it would be nice to have an automatic garage-door opener, a better car stereo system, or perhaps a specialized trailer-hitch installation. The first step would be to get a cost estimate. Perhaps the next step would be to get a budget OK from the owner's spouse. After that, the equipment involved can be ordered. In general, such installations could be scheduled far ahead if necessary.

Usually, about 20–30 percent of the work which a maintenance department must handle falls into this category. As noted previously, this is the kind of work that can either be contracted during busy periods or placed in the work backlog file for departmental handling during slack periods. Some of the PM jobs can also be scheduled to accomplish maintenance work-load leveling. By keeping the regular crew size just large enough to handle repair and some PM work during periods of peak load, it is often possible to avoid layoffs in maintenance when the plant work load drops appreciably. But this will be practical only if plant management understands the approaches necessary to accomplish this leveling of hard-to-replace manpower and is kept well informed of periodic load conditions.

Control Material Availability

The yearly cost of maintenance material and spare parts is often about equal to the cost of maintenance manpower. If spare parts that may be needed are kept on hand, some will remain in storage for years before being used, and some will eventually be discarded as specific equipment is replaced. It takes only a little arithmetic to conclude that inventory costs for an appreciable stock of spare parts can be very high. The alternative is to risk the cost of production delays when critical equipment is down for repair. Recommendations for spare-part stock orders can properly go to the maintenance manager, either from maintenance or manufacturing supervisors. In organizations such as that shown by Figure 45, it would be appropriate to require final approval by the manufacturing manager.

Expendable maintenance material can have a much higher turnover rate than that for spare parts. The maintenance manager's approval is normally sufficient for stock items in this category. For plants in or near large metropolitan areas, it is often possible to establish a basis for prompt delivery of selected material items needed for maintenance repairs, thereby reducing plant inventory requirements.

Getting material to maintenance men in time to avoid waiting, and without long walks on their part to and from a storeroom, is an objective that should be given careful consideration as part of a control program. In some cases, the storeroom housing maintenance material can be adjacent to the maintenance shop area. At appendix-listed plants 99 and 96—both large processing plants—there were hourly truck deliveries from the maintenance storeroom to delivery points throughout the plant. At plant 57, daily planning and scheduling of maintenance work included material delivery to specific plant areas before the day shift began.

Maintain Sound Performance Standards

As noted in chapter 3, time standards based on work measurement are not practical for most plant maintenance work. Estimates, based on experience and a review of job requirements, are preferable for the following reasons:

Infrequent Assignment of PM Work on a Full-time Basis. In manufacturing plants such as most of those listed in the appendix, PM functions that were repetitive in nature and known to be economically feasible ranged from about 10 percent to 20 percent of total maintenance man-hour requirements. Only a small portion of this amount was singled out for assignment on a continual basis to specific individuals such as oilers. The time required for other PM work could be estimated by supervisors closely familiar with the work involved. Based on the estimates, such work could be scheduled daily as fill-in jobs, along with repair and construction jobs which should also be estimated and scheduled. There would be no advantage in having 25 percent of a maintenance employee's daily work time covered by work measurement standards and the balance covered by estimates. However, when the nature of authorized PM work is such that it can be assigned to a specific crew on a full-time basis, work measurement can take the same approach as in manufacturing.

Practical Use of Estimates on Repair or Construction Work. It is possible to develop standard data, based on work measurement, for construction work and some repairs that recur at intervals. For example, the large maintenance department servicing plants 61 and 67 had accumulated volumes of such data on which several man-years of IE time had been expended. The data could be applied only after the work was completed and details recorded. Partly because of unreliable feedback information, and for various other reasons, the comparisons with actual time did not serve as a useful control technique.

Valid maintenance cost control comes through daily scheduling, in advance of work performance. This not only assures that a full day's work is targeted, but also permits planning ahead for material availability and equipment readiness. The schedule gives supervisors a practical way of knowing what results should be expected. It has been shown clearly that experienced estimators who review job requirements at the work site can establish believable work targets. Estimating skills are developed if the estimator reviews later the actual man-hours charged to each job. When tempered by observations of working effectiveness, this data can be used to prepare records for future reference. Estimating procedures are applied by large and small construction firms throughout the country which compete with each other for business. Example: If the reader's kitchen was remodelled in the past, the price quoted was undoubtedly based on someone's estimate, prepared after a preliminary survey.

Plan Manpower Requirements

It was previously noted that any system for manufacturing productivity control could be expected to function realistically only if the work force in each labor grade is in approximate balance with the planned work load. The same thing applies to plant maintenance. Two questions should be answered periodically, and soon enough to take action if there are negative answers: (1) Is there enough authorized maintenance work to provide a full day's work for each maintenance craftsman during an interval such as the next week? (2) Will the maintenance work force be sufficient to handle jobs that are required to be completed during that week?

Practical ways will subsequently be discussed for developing in advance the craft sequences and man-hour estimates illustrated in Figure 47. At this point, let us assume that the authorized work orders which can be planned ahead, and for which material is available, have been estimated as shown by the illustration. The total man-hours are then developed for each craft. From a tickler file of PM jobs scheduled for the coming week, or from the computerized file of such jobs if that arrangement of data is used, man-hour totals are also developed for each craft. A third source of manpower planning information can come from past records of average man-hours spent each week on rush jobs covered by work orders issued during the week. That amount of man-hour requirement might be high at the start of a control program, but it will

FIGURE 47.
Work Order Envelope, Showing Work Plan.

MAINTENANCE JOB ANALYSIS

WORK ORDER NUMBER 8874

SEQUENCE	CRAFT	PLANNED WORK STEPS	PLANNED MEN-X-HOURS	GET MAT'L	DATE SCHEDULED
1A	C	Prepare floor area, Dept. 30, per dwg.	2 × 12	✓	
1B	EL	Disconnect electrical, present loc.	1 × 2		
2	MW	Move press & repair guard	2 × 8		
3	EL	Make electrical connection	1 × 4	✓	

Work order no. 8874

Crafts C, EL, MW

become less with cooperative emphasis on planning ahead, and with increasing PM effectiveness.

The total man-hours from these three sources, for each craft, should be no less than the manpower expected to be available during the week, by craft. With records in order, manpower planning data of this kind can be put together quickly at the end of each weekly period, in time for action if the need is indicated.

Consider Whether Wage Incentives Are Justified

It is my firm conclusion that wage incentive applications should not be considered for typical plant maintenance functions, regardless of whether incentive plans are in effect for manufacturing operators. Even with extensive standard data, as in a preceding example, the opportunities for cheating in the reporting of work done are so obvious that maintenance wage incentives would quickly drift toward being just an expensive way to raise wage rates.

As mentioned in a previous chapter, there are applications from time to time in which maintenance incentives are based on an assumed relation between maintenance performance and the productivity of manufacturing departments. For example, if a fixed-size maintenance crew handles all repair requirements as manufacturing operators respond to wage incentives and produce more, the average bonus percentage earned by operators might then be applied as a bonus percentage for maintenance personnel. Serious administrative problems could be expected if this approach were taken. There are always changes in maintenance work requirements when equipment is added, taken out of service, or as it deteriorates. Arbitrary revisions in the incentive plan would continually be required.

Develop Methods Improvements

While detailed repair or construction methods are largely a function of the skill and experience possessed by maintenance personnel and their direct supervisors, the broader aspect of methods effectiveness can be directly influenced by establishing systematic ways to plan in advance the craft sequences involved. Figure 47 shows sequences for the work order of Figure 46. Through daily scheduling and supervisory coordination, the required work can proceed with minimum delay and without one craft waiting on another.

Other approaches to methods effectiveness can come by analyzing work sampling results, as suggested in chapter 8 for maintenance activities, or by a systematic analysis of ways to reduce the nonworking functions or delays that exist. Examples of the latter are:

- Walking or waiting to get material.
- Ineffective tools or equipment that cause lost time.
- Lack of adequate information about required tools or material.
- Lack of readily available information about equipment components.
- Lack of complete lubrication instructions.
- Equipment not available for repair after work order issued.
- Poor location of maintenance shop, or inadequate shop facilities.

Indicate Targets for Accomplishment

The need for estimating work targets has been noted above. To have a clear meaning and provide a basis for daily scheduling, estimates should be made for each craft sequence and should indicate optimum crew size as well as the estimated hours. The job plan of Figure 47 illustrates how this can be done in a simple way. The envelope in this illustration will hold both the work order copy and any material requisition copies that are required to order nonstock material, or for craft personnel to obtain from the storeroom before proceeding to the job site. Of course, the accumulation of records for daily planning and scheduling can be done in different ways. With electronic data processing used for manufacturing scheduling, questions would be expected as to whether maintenance work orders could be processed in somewhat the same way. As previously discussed, computerized priority lists for LC/LR manufacturing do not serve as a meaningful schedule. This is more emphatically the case in maintenance because of shorter lead times, the need to schedule jobs for specific individuals or crews, and the need to consider situations that can be determined only on the shop floor.

FIGURE 48.
Maintenance Scheduling Method.

MAINTENANCE WORK SCHEDULE — 6/6/89

W.O. no., craft, area, description			Original estimate man-hrs	Scheduled men-x-hrs	Man-hours remaining at end of shift: Planned	Revised	Requested next men-x-hrs
MILLWRIGHTS, DAY SHIFT - AVAILABLE TO SCHEDULE: (18)							
8561	2	Repair guard rails on platform	4	1 x 4	0		
8430	2	Repair heater vent	6	1 x 4	2		
8874	4	Move punch press to new location	16	2 x 4	0		
8452	4	Install new boring mill supports	80	2 x 4	72		
8443	3	Repair steel floor plates	24	1 x 6	0		
9061	3	Repair heater, I-8	16	1 x 2	14		
8963	4	Adjust drive mechanism	2	1 x 2	0		
8350	4	Install 2 turret lathe coolant guards	12	1 x 6	6		
8390	3	Install jib crane, C16W	80	2 x 4	0		
8732	3	Install jib crane, C15W	80	2 x 4	72		
8587				[illegible]			

Scheduling Methods. For a 200-man maintenance department at plant 73, listed in the appendix, the method of daily scheduling is illustrated by Figure 48. Hand-held load strips (a product of Acme Visible Records) were typed from the planning envelope shown in Figure 47. The strips were stored in a retainer file, by crafts, where they provided an instant view of all backlog man-hours. A file of the work orders within envelopes provided working information. Scheduling for the next day was done near the end of a shift. To schedule a specific work order sequence, the required load strip was removed from the retainer file and inserted into a similar retainer as shown in Figure 48. The scheduled men-times-hours and planned carry-over were entered in pencil. After completing preparation of the schedule, using about six of the retainers, copies were made with the header card shown in the illustration. Supervisors followed the schedule as closely as possible. About three hours before the end of the shift, they entered an estimated carry-over figure along with requested men-times-hours for scheduling the next day. Then they returned the copy to the central scheduler, discussing with him any significant points.

Preparation of the daily schedule, using this technique, required about two hours for the two-hundred-man crew. In another application involving shut-down maintenance at a large power generating station, less than one hour was required for schedule preparation covering about the same number of craftsmen. This technique would be applicable with smaller maintenance groups as well. Other quick-acting approaches that have been successful include the plan-rack technique shown by Figures 38–41 (plants 83 and 112) and Gantt-chart schedule boards of various kinds. To reemphasize the point made previously, simple procedures of this kind are more flexible than computerized scheduling techniques and require less time than would be involved with inputs to the computer of work-order data, repeated updating as conditions change, and entering commands to schedule suitable jobs for individual operators or crews.

Personnel for Job Planning. Having touched briefly on the fundamentals of maintenance planning and scheduling, it is time to consider who will do the preliminary job analysis, man-hour estimating, and daily schedule preparation. Remember that a 25–30 percent improvement has generally been obtained through systematic procedures of the kind described. A few possible approaches will be noted here for illustration, although it is recognized that careful analysis of existing conditions would be needed before taking steps of any kind.

Reference 27 discusses how a few area maintenance supervisors (think of them as coordinators/planners/estimators/supervisors) can handle job planning and estimating functions in large maintenance organizations The craft supervisors would assign manpower and supervise major jobs. In smaller groups, with perhaps three craft supervisors and maintenance crew of forty (assume two-thirds mechanical, one-third electrical), consider assigning the two mechanical supervisors according to plant areas, with each to plan job sequences, make estimates (getting assistance as required), and provide overall supervision. The electrical specialist would do electrical estimating and supervise such work plant-wide. Keep in mind that job sequences and estimates are not to be used as clubs to force compliance. Instead, they are for advance planning, so that scheduling of a full day's work becomes practical. If that is done systematically, improvement will result.

Personnel for Scheduling. Centrally, a scheduler would be required. He or she would be able to leave the office in the morning to review some jobs, analyze PM work, and help with estimating. The scheduler must be in the office during the afternoon for schedule preparation, after feedback from the supervisors. In large departments, consider two such persons centrally. As previously indicated, the lead scheduler can properly be a representative from the MPA staff. In effect, the scheduler would be loaned to the maintenance manager, with responsibilities for coordinating all phases of the planning and scheduling program.

Supervise to Achieve Productivity and Quality Objectives

A daily work schedule helps maintenance supervisors know where to make assignments so that their personnel can avoid waiting for material, waiting for access to equipment, waiting for another craft to complete work, or waiting for another job assignment. The schedule helps supervisors let their crew know in a routine way what is expected of them. Whether the activity of supervisors is specialized by craft or by plant area depends on several factors, including complexity of the work requirements and the supervisors' backgrounds. Area supervision promotes contact with manufacturing personnel, so that their service needs are recognized clearly. With sound backup provided in the department for plant engineering, daily scheduling and material procurement, the number of people that one supervisor can properly direct, while participating actively in job-planning functions, is generally considered to be in the range of twelve to fifteen. There is much back-and-forth travel required on the part of maintenance supervisors. In medium or large-sized plants, a small, battery-powered vehicle for each can often be a good investment.

Evaluate Individual Performance

In the absence of work measurement standards, and considering the difficulties of precise time reporting for maintenance work assignments, the evaluation of individual performance ratios is not usually justified except for PM assignment to a specific crew. However, a written daily schedule, along with estimates shown on the work orders, helps maintenance supervisors monitor performance and make their own evaluations. Where estimating steps have been refined and time reporting is done reliably, regular comparisons between work-order estimates and actual man-hours for specific crafts can serve a useful purpose. In plants 73 and 98, for example, the maintenance manager reviewed daily such comparisons for jobs completed the previous day. Questions were asked in specific cases.

Evaluate Sectional Performance

An important requirement in the approach to maintenance productivity control is for all work done by maintenance personnel to be covered by an approved work order. At plant 73 and others listed in the appendix, it was found that assigning sequential numbers having no more than four digits reduced chances for error in accumulating man-hour and material charges to work orders. At the end of each shift, maintenance personnel entered on weekly record cards the man-hours of time spent on specific work order numbers. The supervisors initialed these record cards daily. Then, at the end of the week, data processing entries were made from the cards to provide the following information:

- Budget charges to accounts previously listed on work orders.
- Maintenance man-hours spent on each work order, by craft.
- Cumulative man-hours worked on specific equipment numbers, for equipment repair records.

When work orders were completed, it was possible to compare actual times with estimated times, by craft, as noted above. Since emergency jobs were seldom estimated in advance, a performance evaluation system of this kind is not all-inclusive or foolproof. But as the man-hours spent on rush work are reduced through the effects of preventive maintenance and cooperative action by manufacturing supervisors, these comparisons become more effective as an aid in cost control.

Provide Management Coordination

As previously emphasized concerning productivity control functions for manufacturing operations, the systematic steps that form the basis for control will tend to drift and lose effectiveness unless there is continued management interest and support. If the MPA group is represented in a maintenance control system, as should be the case, the MPA manager and maintenance manager should cooperatively make sure that their superior is aware of how key aspects in the control program are accomplishing cost-saving objectives.

CONCLUSIONS

The principles of labor productivity control are just as applicable in nondirect functions as in direct manufacturing, but different techniques are generally required to apply the principles in a practical manner. Three groups of nondirect functions were listed. A different system for applying the control principles is preferable for each of these groups. The systems are:

- Job planning, estimating, and scheduling, with possible use of outside contracting to level work loads.
- Methods analysis, followed by time standards and manpower planning.
- Methods analysis, followed by the development of manning tables that correspond with various manufacturing load conditions.

The first of these systems is applicable within plant maintenance, which usually is the nondirect function involving highest cost. Specific techniques for maintenance cost control can be developed through analyzing how each of the control principles can best be implemented. A number of illustrations were shown to indicate how this has been done successfully in the past.

For a nondirect control system to be effective on a continuing basis, one of the primary requirements is for a management staff group, such as MPA, to be actively involved both in its implementation and continued operation.

16
Managing the Interactions between Control Functions

This short chapter will discuss interactions between labor productivity control functions and other control or service objectives that are typically part of the management process. The purpose is to show both the interdependence involved and the ease with which some objectives can veer off course if not managed carefully. Because the general area of quality control has been receiving so much attention nationwide, in part due to the perception of current Japanese excellence in this field, particular attention will be given to interactions between labor productivity control and quality control.

TYPICAL FUNCTIONS INVOLVED

A set of principles in which labor productivity can properly be rooted has been noted in Figure 3. These principles are embodied in the following list of typical functions. Groups which provide essential data or services are also included.

- Production Scheduling and Control
- Material and Inventory Control
- MPA Group (An acronym for Methods and Productivity Awareness, used in this book to designate the category of industrial engineering that is concerned with analysis of manual methods, preparation of routing information, development and application of time standards, analysis of performance data, and ways of upgrading performance. The MPA functions to assist in nondirect cost control are noted in chapter 15.)
- Quality Control
- Financial Control

- Design Engineering
- Marketing and Order Service
- Manufacturing or Production Engineering
- Purchasing
- Plant Maintenance
- Data Processing
- Transportation and Warehousing
- Personnel Relations

Direct supervisors, guided and aided by other levels of management, are key implementers of the control procedures. Requirements along this line which are imposed on supervisors must not monopolize their time. Operators must be able to understand how to respond to certain procedural details without the need for supervisory intervention except when there are unusual problems.

The above listing of various control, staff, and service functions as separate groups does not rule out combinations that may be justified. In some cases, direct supervisors can perform the duties involved. An example was previously noted in which operators and their supervisors handled all product inspections. In appendix-listed plant 95, a large ship-repair business, supervisors effectively handled what would otherwise be done by manufacturing engineers and inspectors.

INTERDEPENDENCE AND COMPETITIVE TENDENCIES

Most of the listed groups are dependent on each other for effectiveness, requiring cooperation; yet there are also competitive tendencies that could cause friction to develop. This is not news to any manufacturing manager, whose responsibility it is to see that these tendencies are channeled in a constructive way.

With quality control drawing increased attention in the United States at the time this book was prepared, it may be of interest to examine some of the interactions between the group having that primary objective and other functions noted above.

Design Engineering

Certainly the design of many products has a significant effect on the probable quality that will result, particularly when there are limitations in available equipment or related manufacturing experience. Whether a design is as simple as practical, or overly complex, enters into the picture. The total number of parts involved to accomplish the purpose of a designed product is significant. Tolerances, materials specified, machining requirements, the design of load-bearing components, the finish called for, and many other considerations combine to influence resulting product quality.

It was standard practice at a number of appendix-listed plants for specified MPA or manufacturing engineers to "sign off" on engineering drawings before their issuance, to guard against unwarranted specifications that would adversely affect production methods, equipment and tooling costs, or quality considerations.

Purchasing Policies

Evidence points to the finesse involved when Japanese companies purchase material. High quality standards are said to be commonly specified and enforced. Within the United States, valid questions have arisen in some cases as to whether competitive bids should be the rule for parts acquisition, with lowest price being the chief criterion, or whether the past history of a supplier's workmanship is more significant.

Manufacturing Engineering

Is a complex piece of automated equipment clearly justified when calculated to pay off in relation to simpler methods, even though there is a strong chance the skills to operate or maintain it may not be readily available? For new products just out of the design stage, should highly automated equipment be specified when the parts involved have not yet been produced, and potential quality problems have not been determined?

Production Scheduling and Control

Even after considering the potential costs of work-in-process inventory, should central scheduling of completion dates be so tight that supervisors cannot wait for operators to be available who have had prior training on hard-to-perform operations?

Methods and Productivity Awareness Group

Have needed operator instructions been provided, either on the route sheets or together with them? Has the sequence of listed operations been carefully screened to allow for inspection points where justified? Are specified assembly methods suitable to warrant the probability of zero defects in later operation of the assembly? Have time standards considered requirements for self-inspection by operators at critical points?

Plant Maintenance

Have valid preventive maintenance steps been planned for, to avoid foreseeable malfunctioning of equipment? Are planned PM jobs being scheduled and performed regularly? Do manufacturing supervisors stress to operators the fact that equipment must be operated so as to avoid preventable damage? Does excessive downtime of equipment force the use of other equipment unlikely to assure quality?

Direct Supervisors

Do unnecessary clerical routines, or perhaps frequent meetings, take up time that should be used to train operators or spot quality problems? Has a cooperative attitude been developed with inspectors toward the requirements of both quality and productivity? Does the labor productivity control system in effect allow for a climate of cooperation by operators toward quality objectives? Are the reasons for defects identified clearly and followed up promptly?

Marketing

Is there a routine feedback of quality problems that have been spotted in the field? Is this done without undue delay?

AVOIDING ONE-SIDED CORRECTIVE ACTION

When pressures arise to correct a condition which has become evident, there are temptations to take a one-sided approach. With overall budgetary constraints, for example, staff personnel may simply be shifted to concentrate on the problem condition, allowing other significant control projects to drift or be discontinued. There is no need to go further in discussing this point, as the potential hazard from neglect of necessary controls is evident to experienced managers.

Published Material

There may be a reason, however, to point toward some of the one-sided viewpoints that are seen in technical literature, suggesting how management should proceed along certain lines. Excerpts from published material about quality control may be taken as a case in point. A popular current book about the automobile industry states that one of the men credited with introducing quality control principles to Japanese industry during the 1950s has listed some fourteen "points for management transformation" in U.S. automobile manufacturing (see Maryann Keller, 1989). Two of these points were as follows:

- "Eliminate work standards (quotas) on the factory floor. Substitute leadership."
- "Eliminate management by objective. Eliminate management by numbers, numerical goals. Substitute leadership."

And in one section of a current handbook on quality control, considerable emphasis is placed on the concept that workers will be more likely to develop a desire and willingness to control quality by their work practices if they are not encumbered with detailed instructions, but are allowed to develop their own methods and procedures. There would, of course, be supervisory leadership here also.

Discussion of the Concepts Listed Above

There is potential confusion in the use of the word "quota." If it is taken to mean no more nor less than time standards (or norms in the MPI system), previous chapters have stressed the need to use the norms for evaluating *average* performance by individual operators. Defining the expected average performance level is a necessary step in providing direct supervisors with a way to manage effectively. How they use such information is of course critical for MPI effectiveness. A typical discussion in chapter 13 between the supervisor and a new operator gives an example of how norms should be viewed by operators. But inherent problems remain with the two objectives listed above and in the suggestion that operators develop their own methods.

One of the operational sequences that I have observed in which the principles noted above would probably work smoothly is described as follows: A large commercial bakery transports pans of a fruitcake mix down a conveyor belt where about a dozen operators place pecan halves to fully cover the cake dough prior to baking. It would be understandable that these operators and their supervisor could determine themselves how this should be done. They might well decide that each person should work independently to completely cover one unit, off the conveyor (as an industrial engineer would probably decide also). And the supervisor could certainly tell whether the performance level was acceptable on this operation of ultimate simplicity.

Instead of a job like that, however, consider an automotive engine assembly line, or perhaps a refrigerator assembly line involving a hundred operators. Personnel with the necessary skill to develop valid assembly methods and line combinations would not be available for hire on such work at the going rate. Nor would their supervisor be able to help develop effective methods combinations unless he or she devoted the preliminary analysis time that industrial engineers would require. With automobile parts fabrication equipment being determined and the layout rearranged prior to model changes, it is clear that planned general methods within that industry must be followed with little variance.

What seems to be implied in the several points listed above is that it might be OK to develop time-based analyses for planning purposes, but not to let the operators know either the time values or the methods details on which they are based. As noted in previous chapters, such an approach involves elements of unfairness, and it is known to be an unsound basis for control that soon leads to lack of time standards maintenance and low productivity levels. Since supervisors have other duties that obviate their functioning as timekeepers, there would be no effective way to evaluate or control productivity. Conditions of this kind are what various reference sources have in mind when day-work performance levels are referred to as being in the range of 60–70 percent.

We do not mean to be facetious here, or to denigrate serious attempts to raise quality levels when this is called for. But my observations have been that sound quality control is more likely to be achieved when labor productivity levels are acceptable, concurrent with intelligent supervision, than when overly permissive leadership is in the picture. Perhaps the previous quotes will illustrate the kind of one-sided approach to productivity control that should be avoided.

QUALITY CIRCLES

At this point, it seems appropriate to discuss briefly a technique that is helping to generate cooperative employee attitudes. Some background is needed to assist in drawing conclusions.

During the early 1940s, when maximum production for wartime needs was essential, there was a concerted effort in the United States to promote the recognition by management of workers' ideas for improvement. In one large aircraft plant (appendix plant 107), employee suggestions which could be implemented received cash awards based largely on yearly savings. Separate from this program, a "Labor-Management Production Drive Committee" was initiated, with rotating members, following a pattern established nationwide. At biweekly intervals, the labor group met separately to discuss current problems. Then, during the following week, that same group met with top management representatives to present their ideas and to reach conclusions. A coordinator attended both the labor and combined meetings, to see that action was taken on decisions reached. Both the suggestion follow-up and production drive coordination were handled as an industrial engineering function.

A close look at these two programs leads to the conclusion that their value consisted primarily of improvements in employee relations, with identifiable savings being less significant. Unfortunately, suggestion award plans in U.S. plants have dwindled, and employee support for meetings about increased production, per se, would be hard to generate. That is one reason why "Quality Circles" seems a welcome idea. Scheduled meetings are involved in which ideas are exchanged between labor and management representatives. This concept, which was transplanted after being observed in effective use within Japanese industry, has spread broadly through U.S. companies since about 1980.

The subjects discussed in circle meetings that I have observed were not limited to matters affecting product quality, and management representatives attending them included IE and ME staff members, as well as supervisors and QC personnel. With the basic theme of quality, however, there is a valid framework for employee interest, and continued participation is more solidly based than would likely be the case with production output themes.

INDIRECT FINANCIAL INCENTIVES

Perhaps the reader may already have questioned why this book has not explored the subject of financial incentives based on overall performance levels, or perhaps the subject of profit-sharing as a basis for motivating operators toward productivity goals. These topics will be addressed briefly here, because they can influence employee attitudes toward other control functions, including quality control as well as other aspects of labor productivity control. Of course, the effect on attitudes may be negative rather than positive when there are no profits to share, or if the net results of a large group's performance does not reflect the way an individual has viewed his or her own performance during the same period.

Broad-based Cost-saving Plans

The Scanlon and Rucker plans, named for their originators, are cost-saving plans that usually function on a plant-wide basis. They involve a comparison between total wage cost and what may be termed the total normal wage cost. In the Scanlon plan, the latter cost is established as a percentage of sales, which must be developed for each major product. In the Rucker plan, the normal wage cost is calculated by applying a formula, derived through analysis, which determines the value added by the manufacturing process rather than from sales. In both cases, there is a partial distribution of saving during a specific period, with the balance credited as a reserve to guard against periods of deficit balance.

Another plan of this general type involves a more definitive measure of normal wage cost, derived by the accumulation of standard hours for manufactured products. When improvements are made through the introduction of new equipment or revised methods, calculations are then made to account for such changes. If the plan were extended to nondirect groups, a basis for their performance evaluation would be necessary. In effect, this becomes a massive group incentive plan.

Profit-sharing and Bonus Plans

Since the accounting process to establish the profit earned by a corporate entity is always a necessary function, the allocation to employees of a percentage of profits becomes the simplest way to provide an indirect financial incentive, where this is considered to be appropriate after comparing possible morale improvements against potential disadvantages. Among the factors that may be considered in the distribution of funds are relative salary levels, years of service, and prior decisions concerning groups eligible to participate.

Bonus plans, or incentive compensation plans, are normally restricted to specified groups, with distribution of funds based on achievement of goals and objectives. Bonus plans are more likely to have some relation to payments made in prior years than to objectives clearly specified in advance.

Potential Advantages and Disadvantages

The anticipated advantage from indirect financial incentive plans is that of improved morale, which would lead to improved cooperation toward productivity and quality objectives. In-depth analysis of results achieved by companies that have taken such approaches is outside the scope of this book. However, it would seem fair to list the following disadvantages or limitations that could be expected:

- The obviously remote relation between an individual's effort and a large group's result would tend to make valid productivity control dependent on having other forms of control in effect. Ford Motor Company provides an example. With a day-to-day control plan based on time standards without wage incentives, its hourly workers were paid yearly profit-sharing amounts averaging $1900 during a recent seven-year period.*

* As noted in the *Wall Street Journal*, March 5, 1990

- When the specified calculation of incentive payments causes them to be reduced appreciably,* despite the perception by employes that their work level has not dropped, a negative effect on morale could result.
- Past experience with group wage incentives suggests that profit-sharing plans based on standard hours would engender resistance toward time standards maintenance.

* Example: A reduction in such payments by Kodak was reported in the *Wall Street Journal*, January 29, 1990.

17
Summary of Conclusions

> Science is built up with facts, as a house is with stones, but a collection of facts is no more a science than a heap of stones is a house.
>
> —Jules Poincaré

This quotation not only makes a crystal-clear point but almost asks for extension to other related areas. The commonly used phrase, "scientific management," has about the same meaning as labor productivity control. Try substituting that phrase for "science," along with the word "functions" to replace "facts." The statement that results still has a valid meaning. The point to be emphasized is that scientific management (or productivity control) must be comprised of functions that are required for specific purposes, and which are fitted together to form a working entity. In chapter 2, we referred to the required functions as "productivity control principles." Harrington Emerson called them "principles of efficiency," but his more precise word has become a bit distasteful over the years because of the so-called "efficiency experts" who took too many shortcuts.

This book has tried to emphasize that basic principles for productivity control cannot be omitted without the management process being weakened, perhaps even collapsing. Figure 3 lists a slightly revised version of Emerson's original list, brought up to date with the help of wording used in one large company. One change made was to insert the word "consider" in front of "wage incentives." Two chapters in the book serve, in effect, to explain why this de-emphasis of wage incentive concepts seems appropriate today.

FIGURE 3.
Resultant Principles for Labor Productivity Control.

1. Develop CLEAR AND FAIR IDEALS.
2. Select QUALIFIED PERSONNEL.
3. Provide JUSTIFIABLE STAFF.
4. STANDARDIZE WORKING CONDITIONS.
5. DEFINE WORK REQUIREMENTS.
6. CONTROL MATERIAL availability.
7. Maintain SOUND PERFORMANCE STANDARDS.
8. PLAN MANPOWER REQUIREMENTS.
9. CONSIDER whether WAGE INCENTIVES are justified.
10. Develop METHODS IMPROVEMENTS.
11. INDICATE TARGETS for accomplishment.
12. SUPERVISE TO ACHIEVE PRODUCTIVITY AND QUALITY OBJECTIVES.
13. EVALUATE INDIVIDUAL PERFORMANCE.
14. EVALUATE SECTIONAL PERFORMANCE.
15. Provide MANAGEMENT COORDINATION.

The purpose of preceding chapters has been to analyze various techniques and systems currently available to implement the control principles in Figure 3, which is reprinted here for emphasis. We have tried to sort "facts from folklore." On the one hand, there are ideas and techniques for which there is considerable evidence of practical use. On the other hand, there are concepts that have been publicized or widely applied which seem to lack substance. To imply that there is a clear separation between the two areas is not always conclusive, because of wide differences that exist in personnel, policies, and types of work. In the summary that follows, the reader will find comments that are in opposition to other published material, established practices, or well-known beliefs. The reasoning involved in these differences of opinion can be found in preceding chapters. Also included are references to various new developments that have a bearing on conclusions in this chapter.

CONCEPTS AND ORGANIZATION

How multiplant companies seek to promote productivity results must differ according to the type of work in respective plants. When manufacturing functions are similar at different locations, there is a basis for increased corporate staff involvement in aspects of the control process such as the derivation of standard time data. When plant functions are dissimilar, corporate staff activities are more likely to be aimed at training and reviews of control functions. In general, corporate management seems locked into viewing short-term profits as a key element of decentralized control, somewhat to the detriment of longer-range productivity planning. When a profit downturn leads to arbitrary nondirect force reductions, as may often be the case, there can be tendencies toward overstaffing during normal years, lack of cooperation by nondirect management with productivity control plans, and greater difficulty in maintaining such plans.

Labor union involvement in multiplant organizations can have a strong effect on the success with which control plans are managed. Because of inevitable perceptions of unfairness that occur at intervals in wage incentive administration, decisions to follow this path toward productivity control should include provisions for corporate reviews to assure consistent maintenance of the systems at all locations. The key role of direct supervisors as management representatives in a successful control plan—whether wage incentive or measured day work—calls for careful consideration of both the span of supervisory control and the question of whether group leaders or assistant supervisors should be utilized.

Reasons were noted in Chapter 2 why the staff group involved in labor productivity control should be given a more definitive name than "Industrial Engineering." Although this is not particularly significant within a specific plant, use of the more general term throughout this book would have been misleading. The name "Methods and Productivity Awareness" (MPA) has been applied as a descriptive term, to avoid confusion in these chapters. Attempts to combine MPA duties with those of manufacturing engineering in larger plants have often proved counterproductive, for reasons noted. A list of needed MPA abilities required to handle duties normally assigned to this group shows that there can properly be a mixture of experience and training, and there can be paths for career specialization. Ways to inhibit undue turnover within the group were noted, as were the typical ways of assigning individual responsibilities. The interaction between MPA personnel and direct supervisors involves a combination of assistance in methods improvement along with maintaining a framework for sectional performance evaluation, which requires some finesse on the part of the engineers. In all cases, it is essential that the MPA group keep plant management informed concerning net savings from cost improvements related to productivity control functions.

WORK MEASUREMENT CONSIDERATIONS

Four primary uses of time standards in the labor control process were noted in chapter 3. These applications would be ineffective unless the time values were reasonably precise and consistent. Eight additional uses were also listed in which precision of time values would be desirable but not imperative. When the past experience of a manager has been largely in functions where the latter uses of standards were predominant, that individual may not realize the need for careful maintenance of time values if a control system is to be worthwhile.

For direct time study to produce sound time values, experience in methods analysis and training in performance rating are required. To get reliable results from predetermined time applications, only the basic systems should be used. And since different systems vary in time content derived for any specific operation, a careful study is required to verify consistency of results and to select an adjustment factor for the control plan which is in effect. The most-used system is MTM–1, which produces low-task time values generally considered appropriate as a definition of wage incentive "normal." The concept of normal serves as a promotional aid in wage incentive applications but has no place in a measured day-work control plan. Several large companies have made detailed studies which indicate that a multiplier of 0.83 or 0.84 is appropriate to adapt MTM–1 results for use as measured day work target standards with short-cycle, repetitive (SC/R) operations. Whatever the technique used for work measurement, the cost-effective approach is to develop standard time data as an intermediate step in deriving time values before shop orders are issued. When standard data is not available in specific cases, estimates based on comparisons with previously developed standards may be necessary. They should be identified as temporary values.

A number of condensed predetermined time systems are available. In most cases, they were developed by combining hand motions to derive Get or Place aggregates or the equivalent. Because the choice of such aggregates is both limited and approximate, and because these systems provide no way to analyze simultaneous motion interactions, their application involves large plus-or-minus errors. Claims that these errors will "average out" on longer job cycles should be viewed with skepticism, since the motion content of industrial operations is not randomly put together.

Despite a marked shift in recent years from wage incentive control plans to forms of measured day work, some industrial engineering terminology pertaining to work measurement remains keyed to wage incentive thinking. The definition for "normal" and references to day work as a low-task performance level must be disregarded in nonincentive control plans.

While the older S.A.M. performance rating films are still of value in defining incentive normal, they make no reference to the target standards for measured day work. This is a matter for individual plants to determine subjectively. Available evidence suggests that measured daywork target standards can be set at about the same level as average incentive pace in a well-managed incentive plan. Both predetermined time systems and the basis for training in performance rating should be adjusted to decisions made along this line at specific plants. In performance rating, any of several published guidelines can be used, after appropriate adjustment to the system involved and after training. A basic but simple concept is described in chapter 3, for use as a rating guide.

The way that general allowances are applied in a wage incentive plan may differ somewhat from the approach often followed in measured day work. For time values to be meaningful as a basis for daily scheduling, the "unavoidable" delay allowances not likely to occur on a daily basis can properly be omitted in the latter system. When such delays do occur, downtime can be credited in the reporting process. In this way, follow-up to correct delaying conditions is more likely to occur. If performance rating training is appropriately developed, the rating process can serve to replace the need for most fatigue allowances. On jobs where excessive effort is still a requirement, added allowances are justified.

A FRESH LOOK AT DIRECT TIME STUDY

Although the concept of direct time study has remained essentially unchanged over many years, new techniques are available that eliminate most of the postanalysis clerical functions and reduce by at least a third the total analysis time. A battery-powered, hand-held microprocessor with internal timer can be used to store the usual notations for element identification and times. When stored data is transmitted through a computer terminal, a simple program produces a printed time study that is the equivalent of manual studies except for element and foreign element descriptions. The elements are described manually, for attachment to the computer printout. Procedures involved are described in chapter 4. While a three-watch system with clipboard costs less and eliminates subtractions on the data format, its appearance is a step backward in some respects.

The need for competent methods analysis prior to and during time study requires training and experience. The analyst should know how to construct standard data and be able to apply predetermined time analysis when appropriate. Perhaps the primary advantage of direct time study, in relation to predetermined time applications, is its believability (at least in cases where performance rating does not greatly affect the net result). Among the disadvantages are tendencies to neglect methods refinement, a possible masking of later methods changes, potential errors in performance rating, and the requirement for job performance before a study is made.

ANALYSIS WITH PREDETERMINED MOTION TIMES; COMPUTER-AIDED APPLICATION OF BASIC MTM

Whether because of its demonstrated validity, the availability of training material, or for less tangible reasons, the Methods-Time Measurement system (MTM–1) has become the most-used of several basic predetermined time systems. Fundamental concepts in its application are described in chapter 5. Three MTM–1 analyses, in graphic form, are shown by Figures 12–14 to illustrate how significant methods improvements can be pictured and checked for time content through use of the technique.

Because manual applications of MTM–1 are tedious, slow, and costly (as is also true of the other basic systems), there has been a proliferation of condensed systems that require less time to apply because their "building blocks" are larger and the procedures involved are simpler. Most of these are said to be "based on MTM–1." That is misleading, since how the larger blocks of time were derived is of no consequence. As previously noted, use of these systems to develop motion times involves a hoped-for but doubtful averaging out of large positive and negative errors. They cannot be used rationally on short, SC/R operations where the application of predetermined times is most needed.

The recent development of 4M DATA (Micro-Matic Methods and Measurement Data) serves to make the precise application of MTM–1 simpler and much faster to apply. This system retains the methods analysis capabilities of MTM–1, adding to that through the derivation of four "improvement indices" which evaluate the motion effectiveness of a specific analysis and point out where to look for improvement. Data retrieval capabilities allow elements previously analyzed to be used again for other analyses. Chapter 6 describes how the system functions, and logic diagrams in the appendix show for the first time how 4M motion aggregates are interpreted to apply basic MTM.

The portable microprocessor pictured in Figure 7, which is being used widely for direct time study, has been applied within one company for 4M DATA analysis. Entries can be made on the microprocessor keyboard at a job site, with less structuring of notations in motion sets than would otherwise be required. After direct transmission of stored data through a computer terminal, a front-end program converts the data into a 4M input, to be handled like any other. Figure 21 illustrates the procedure, and a logic diagram in the appendix section shows how the front-end program functions. As illustrated by Figure 22, analysis time is minimized with this approach.

A number of advantages can be achieved through predetermined time applications, provided the basic systems are used with adequate training and experience. The advantages include improved methods analysis capabilities, precise methods definition for later recognition of changes, elimination of performance rating inconsistencies, and reduced costs for standard data development. These advantages will be most apparent for SC/R operations. For methods/time analysis of longer-cycle, less repetitive (LC/LR) work, the best approach would involve selected applications of computer-aided predetermined times or direct time study, used for the development of standard time data.

DEVELOPING AND APPLYING STANDARD TIME DATA

As noted in chapter 7, the synthesis of work measurement results to develop standard data for a specified category of operations can be through logical arrangement by the analyst, mathematical analysis, or through identification of elements for later selection. The end product may be in the form of tabular information, formulas, or coded elements. Techniques for easy application of the data include reference to pick-off sheets, computerized derivations from data inputs, or computerized selection of coded elements. Illustrations of these various approaches are found in chapter 7. Their development requires analysts with skill, ingenuity, and common sense.

In the development of standard time data, making provisions for easy maintenance as methods are revised later is an important requirement. Computerized applications involving special programs are a disadvantage from this standpoint, because the need to revise programs makes it unlikely that this will be done promptly. An automated technique for data maintenance can be applied when specific elements are used to build larger data blocks. Current adaptations of the 4M DATA system include this capability. There will inevitably be a gradual loosening of standard data and time values, as methods are improved, unless a procedure is set up for standards auditing. Taking such a step is a basic requirement.

THE WORK SAMPLING TECHNIQUE AND ITS USES

As stated in chapter 8, work sampling utilizes brief and randomly spaced observations of selected work functions to determine activity percentages. Statistical mathematics can be applied to derive the number of random samples required for a desired percentage of accuracy, assuming that the observations are made without bias of any kind. Use of the alignment chart in this chapter facilitates doing so. A number of observations are typically made during each randomly selected tour of an area. This is not the equivalent of randomness for individual observations, as explained in the chapter. Obtaining numerous samples during a single tour introduces bias to disrupt the statistical theory. Other forms of bias typically involved in most work sampling studies include worker anticipation of sampling tours, abnormal conditions that occur only on a periodic basis, the inability to account for operators who may be in rest rooms or elsewhere outside a section, and the difficulty in identifying some categories of operators or their activities.

Statistical theory can be only an approximate guide to the reliability of sampling results, because of bias introduced in these and other ways. But work sampling remains a quick and economical way to obtain a wide variety of pertinent data that supplement control functions based on work measurement. Steps for planning and making studies of different kinds are described in chapter 8. Work sampling studies are not the equivalent of work measurement controls and do not substitute for them. Reasons include the following: Operators' work methods are not evaluated; only group activity is covered; and the evaluation of working pace at a glance—though sometimes attempted during sampling studies—is inherently unreliable. In cases where performance rating is applied during work sampling, results without considering the ratings are normally reported along with results that do include the ratings.

Sampling studies made in the usual way involve a clerical routine after each tour, to summarize and review the data. This can be simplified through use of the microprocessor pictured in Figure 7 to record the observations. A computer program required to accomplish this could normally be developed by MPA personnel. One company used such an approach to provide for multicategory work sampling. In effect, this permitted making several different studies during the tours required for a single study. Since the microprocessor that is pictured will record time-of-day automatically, it was possible to develop a segment of the computer program that would summarize each individual study and also provide time-span summaries of activity percentages during specified blocks of time throughout a shift interval. Chapter 8 describes how this was done.

Supervisory personnel and others who are not familiar with work sampling tend to doubt the validity of results from such studies. It is worthwhile to develop a short training program that demonstrates and explains how the technique functions. A description is given of films used within one company for that purpose.

IMPROVEMENT CURVES—EMPIRICAL, CONFUSING, QUESTIONABLE, USEFUL

Figure 30 illustrates the parabolic shape of curves developed from historical data of man-hour cost per production unit versus cumulative production quantity. Also shown is the way that such curves become straight lines on logarithmic coordinates, with man-hours decreasing at a fixed rate for each doubling of cumulative production quantity. The rate of cost decrease is referred to as the slope of the curve. Simplicity of cost representation is the primary reason why this concept has been widely applied for cost estimating. Most of the applications have been in defense-related industries.

The estimating process often involves derivation of a standards intercept point on the logarithmic curve. This is where the work measurement time standards are supposedly achieved. Developing man-hour cost estimates at other points on the curve can be done routinely, once the slope, intercept point, and total time value are known. Chapter 9 illustrates and explains the steps involved. Also explained is a procedure that some plants use in accounting for the added cost resulting from breaks in production.

What this book calls "improvement curves" are commonly referred to as "learning curves." The latter phrase has long been applied with relation to the operator-learning process, but learning by operators is only a part of the overall man-hour improvement process. The theory of improvement curves is entirely empirical, although various published articles have confirmed original observations about the parabolic shape of curves as defined above. There is evidence, however, that some companies are applying this theory to their own work without first deriving slopes, standards intercepts, or other key factors. As illustrated in chapter 9, big differences in estimating results can occur if incorrect improvement-curve parameters are applied. There is also much that is vague and obscure about the concept of a standards intercept point, as Figure 31 helps to bring out.

Chapter 9 illustrates possible ways in which the slope of improvement curves can be derived. Obtaining data for this purpose may be difficult, but that should be a first step before application of the theory for estimating purposes.

OPERATORS' LEARNING

A distinction is made in chapter 9 between what has been called threshold learning and reinforcement learning. It is the latter process in which learning curves are applicable. Such curves follow a parabolic shape, as noted for improvement curves, although there is clearly some point at which the learning process ends for a specified method. Reasons are noted in the chapter as to why it is not considered helpful to apply learning allowances in most control plans, with group wage incentives being one exception. This should not alter the recognition that learning time is costly and should be minimized to the extent practicable. Various training aids can shorten the process of threshold learning, but supervisory attention is the most basic requirement. Supervisors require some flexibility in selecting jobs for specific operators, if learning time and other delaying conditions are to be minimized.

SELECTING AND PREPARING FOR A PRODUCTIVITY CONTROL SYSTEM

Determining how to apply the labor productivity control principles listed in Figure 3 is the suggested way to prepare for installing a control system. Chapter 10 discusses typical approaches for implementing each of these. Examples are noted where wage incentive plans could properly be considered, and where they would clearly be impractical. Following these examples is a list of questions which can assist in drawing conclusions along this line.

WAGE INCENTIVE CONCEPTS

While there have been numerous forms of wage incentive payment plans over the years, the most common form is the "full sharing" plan described by Figure 32. The primary cost-improvement objectives in a wage incentive application are methods-upgrading prior to and during the installation, and reduction in overhead costs per unit of product. There will inevitably be some downgrading of work effort on the part of those not covered by the incentive plan (direct operators remaining on day work and nondirect employees such as those within maintenance and the toolroom).

For the system to function as intended, it will be necessary to guarantee that time standards will not be changed unless methods are revised. This sets up a condition not easy to administer without causing grievances, since improvements are expected to be no less frequent than would be the case without the incentive plan. How to apply wage incentives for machine-controlled operations is often a matter of concern. If there is a preponderance of such operations, incentive systems would not be practical.

Individually applied wage incentives generally bring a more positive response toward improved output. Group wage incentives have frequently been utilized in the past. In such cases, a working group leader makes job assignments, checks material availability and may assume other responsibilities normally considered to be supervisory functions. A third form of wage incentives has illogically been called "measured day work." This has no relation to the control plan which this book refers to by that same name within chapters 1–12. To minimize confusion, the term "step incentives" has been used within the book when referring to this method of wage payment. It involves bonus earnings in steps of 5 or 10 percent, applied during a specified period such as a one-month interval. Wage incentives may be applied to operators on paced lines without invoking the formalities of group wage incentives. This is not likely to offer advantages that cannot be achieved with measured day work, provided the measured day-work application is not within a plant where incentives are applied to other work.

WAGE INCENTIVE LIMITATIONS AND PROBLEMS

One reason given for wage incentive applications is that day-work performance is inherently low. While this is likely to be true for day-workers within an incentive plant, day work performance in a plant with an advanced form of measured day work can approach average incentive performance levels.

Assuming that average incentive pace is about 25 percent above that which may have existed without any control plan, observations have indicated that increased work pace is usually a minor contributor to this amount. The balance of improvement tends to come from operator-controllable methods and/or reductions in avoidable downtime. This helps to explain why equivalent improvement can often be obtained without wage incentives, as covered in chapters 13 and 14.

There are numerous reasons why wage incentive plans may begin to deteriorate. A number of these reasons are listed in chapter 12. They are difficult for the MPA/management team to counter on a long-term basis. Group wage incentive systems are particularly subject to decay. A major reason for this is the fact that both the performance level of individual operators and the performance level on specific operations is hidden because of the group reporting system. The overriding reason lies in the fact that management's influence and control becomes diluted, and group leaders have a strong interest in helping operators camouflage true working conditions. Case histories are given in which numerous plants with this form of control plan were shut down, moved to another geographical area, or sold. In all such cases, high labor costs were a significant factor.

Examples are noted in which deteriorated incentive plans were revitalized in a systematic manner. This becomes more difficult in a multi-plant corporation with strong labor unions at incentive locations. An example is also given of successful conversion from wage incentives to measured day work. Another example described how one large plant resisted repeated challenges concerning revisions in standards by using films of previous operations to show that changes had indeed been made.

MEASURED DAY-WORK CONCEPTS

Reasons are noted in chapter 13 as to why the term "measured day work" should be discarded and replaced with something else that avoids confusion with step incentives (called measured day work in IE literature). In chapters 13 and 14, the term "Methods and Productivity Improvement" (MPI) has been utilized when referring to forms of this control plan.

Recognizing that "normal" has long been used as a good "public relations" name for the low-task performance level in wage incentives (even though this is not the normally expected average performance, but about 20 percent below such a level), and recognizing also that no word defining a low-task level would be useful in the measured day work (MPI) control plan, another term has been used in the final chapters of the book when referring to the target standards of MPI. The word "norm" was applied instead of "time standard" or its equivalent.

Within MPI, continued emphasis on methods improvement is a primary concept, and the system promotes such emphasis because there is not the inherent resistance by operators to change that may affect opportunities for bonus. A systematic questioning procedure for methods upgrading is noted in this chapter.

There is no valid industrial engineering concept for relating MPI norms in any way to wage incentive normal. The performance level for norms is a matter for individual plants to determine subjectively. It is probable that this will in most cases result in levels which are about the same as that of average incentive pace. Direct supervisors within an MPI control plan should be authorized to review and check standard data and norms, although this would in most cases evolve into occasional questions about specific norms.

MPI supervisors are in direct contact with operators, without group leaders. Operators may be assigned as justified for setup, material handling, training, etc. The operator/supervisor ratios should be such as to make close supervisory contacts practical.

Figure 34 defines three different MPI categories, with specific functions noted for each. The category referred to as Sectional Performance Evaluation (SPE) involves the approximate reporting of sectional performance ratios and is a minimal approach, not calculated to accomplish much more for LC/LR work than sound management could do, without norms. The second category, Operators' and Sectional Performance Evaluation (OSPE), provides supervisors with records concerning individual operators' performance, and this helps in knowing where some problems exist. The third category, OSPE/SIS, brings short-interval scheduling into the picture and can provide effective productivity control.

There will inevitably be questions as to how a supervisor should proceed when norms are not met by an operator on a continuing basis. The recommended approach is to investigate carefully the conditions that exist, so as to identify the real problem. Appropriate action to correct the problem is the next step. There is an important difference between such an approach and that of taking action specifically because of the failure to meet established norms. Performance reporting principles are discussed in chapter 13. Three significant performance ratios are defined as a basis for weekly reporting.

Administration and careful follow-up of the MPI control plan is generally a function of the MPA manager. For the plan to succeed, there must be strong support from the plant or manufacturing manager.

HOW TO UPGRADE RESULTS FROM MPI (MEASURED DAY WORK)

With paced lines or equipment, the short-interval scheduling concept noted in Figure 34 is automatically applied. What is said in chapter 14 is primarily applicable to nonpaced SC/R or LC/LR operations. To implement the OSPE category of MPI control, a reliable record of individual operators' performances is required. Various ways to accomplish this have been tried. One involves electronic data collection equipment, but this has disadvantages of high cost, lost time walking to the recording units, and frequent errors despite the use of error-screening programs. The primary disadvantage of this method is that supervisors are not informed when electronic records about work status go to a central location.

When operators at their work stations record manually what has occurred, supervisors have a chance to observe the records, but there is a clerical cost and no assurance that supervisors will stay current in the review of what has happened.

"Short-interval scheduling" is a name given to a procedure that has been applied many times, often with consulting groups handling the implementation. The objective is to force the planning of work completion targets, along with records of progress in relation to the work plan. In typical previous applications, supervisors are required to do this manually, with massive paperwork passed up the line to make sure it is done. There is follow-up for correction of delaying conditions, with paperwork to enforce such steps. This technique secures positive results while it continues, but the paperwork and confrontations with operators are distasteful to all concerned. The process usually collapses when the outside policing crew has left.

A system known as PLANACODE has been developed and tested to apply short-interval scheduling without the serious disadvantages referred to. Bar-coded tabs applied to cards identify specific job assignments. A unique type of card-rack retains the assigned job cards to show each operator's work schedule and job-completion status. The supervisors are required to update the plan at intervals, which should always be part of their job normally, but this can be done with a minimum of paperwork. At end of shift, a portable bar-code reader is used by one individual to collect pertinent data from the plan-racks. This serves not only to update central scheduling information but also to provide inputs for computerized weekly reports concerning both sectional performance and individual operator's performance. The completed job cards are the basis for notations required to establish follow-up for correction of detracting conditions. Data collection costs are minimized. This is a new approach. In its test at one location, performance results were positive, supervisory responses positive, and operators' responses clearly without the negative attitudes that were seen with short-interval scheduling in the past.

A number of questions are asked and then answered at the conclusion of Chapter 14 regarding MPI advantages and disadvantages. It seems fair to say that this control plan, when well managed, can accomplish desired results without the serious potential disadvantages that come with wage incentives, provided the OSPE or OSPE/SIS categories are implemented (defined in chapter 14). If MPI controls are allowed to drift through neglect, there could be fewer problems in revitalizing them than would be the case with wage incentives.

EXTENDING LABOR PRODUCTIVITY CONTROL TO NONDIRECT FUNCTIONS

In chapter 15, a number of nondirect service or staff functions commonly found in typical manufacturing plants have been sorted into three groups, according to the types of productivity control functions that have been applied within them and observed to be successful. For groups such as plant maintenance, the toolroom, and engineering drafting, control procedures can begin with planning and estimating work-order sequences. After this can come the daily scheduling of work targets for individuals or required crews to handle. Work measurement standards can properly be developed for nondirect functions such as inspectors and janitors, with scheduling in appropriate ways. For a number of other functions, systematic methods analysis is a first step, followed by the careful development of manning tables that can be the basis for flexible budgets which conform with production load levels.

The largest and most costly nondirect function is usually plant maintenance. Chapter 15 analyzes steps that have proved successful for maintenance cost control. The productivity control principles of Figure 3 are utilized in describing steps to consider.

MPA staff personnel have historically specialized in direct labor control functions. In many cases the development and application of nondirect controls are left to the managers involved. There are perhaps three reasons for this: (1) plant management may not be convinced that staff assistance is needed to develop and help maintain nondirect control functions; (2) MPA analysts may not understand that the control functions required in such areas are usually quite different from the approaches based on work measurement which are applicable to direct labor; and (3) the managers within such areas may tend to resist what they regard as outside interference. The discussions in chapter 15 emphasize that MPA engineers should be involved closely with nondirect cost control.

MANAGING THE INTERACTIONS BETWEEN CONTROL FUNCTIONS

Management staff and service functions involved in labor productivity control can properly be assigned to assist in the implementation of principles previously noted in Figure 3. There can be a selected combination of functions for handling by specific groups. Since the functions are interdependent, cooperative action between the groups involved is essential. There tends to be a certain amount of competition in some cases, requiring management coordination to avoid a one-sided approach.

Because of current emphasis on finding ways to improve the quality of U.S. manufactured products, a number of examples were given in this chapter showing how each of the interrelated functions can have a strong influence on quality control effectiveness. Through overemphasis on quality control aspects, there could be tendencies to neglect needed productivity controls. While plant management is generally aware of potential problems along this line, some current literature contains one-sided proposals directed toward ways of upgrading quality control. This chapter points out several examples which recommend that time-tested productivity control functions be dropped in order to help engender an atmosphere of quality awareness by operators. Since many examples can be found in which productivity control and product quality go hand-in-hand, such advice can be grouped with other one-sided viewpoints and set aside.

A fairly recent trend, which is aimed at helping to promote an atmosphere of quality awareness and interest by operators, is the widespread application of what has been called Quality Circles. Borrowed from Japan, this concept can fill a void that has been extant in most companies since Labor-management Production Drive Committees were popular during a wartime period. By promoting the interchange of constructive ideas between labor and management groups, Quality Circle meetings can help fill another void that seems to be increasing as suggestion award plans become less prevalent.

There are several forms of indirect financial incentive plans that could be considered as possible ways to influence the attitudes of employees toward productivity and quality goals. These include the Scanlon and Rucker plans, which depend on derived formulas to identify normal labor cost, or the use of standard hours on a plant-wide basis for this purpose. Also in the category of indirect financial incentives are broad-based profit-sharing plans and more specialized bonus or incentive compensation plans. The scope of this book does not provide for in-depth analysis of results from prior applications along these lines. While the incentive pull of such plans toward productivity improvement by individuals would be minimal, and potential disadvantages are listed, they could be considered in combination with MPI control concepts.

Appendix

LIST OF COMPANIES AND PLANTS

In preceding chapters, reference has been made to various companies and plants in which detailed observations and analyses of labor productivity control applications have been possible. The plants are listed below, with information as to their size, type of work, and type of control system. For manufacturing plants, the control systems listed include wage incentive, measured day work, and day work. When both incentive and measured day work are checked, a change was made to the latter. When the process category is checked, analyses within the plant primarily involved maintenance control functions.

	EMPL.	LCLR	SCR	TYPE OF WORK	INC.	MDW	DW	Proc.
1	200	x		Electrical wire mfg.		x		
2	300	x	x	Electrical components, instr.		x		
3	500	x		Electrical controls		x		
4	800		x	Transformers		x		
5	5000	x		Specialized electronic mfg.		x		
6	2000		x	Electrical control equipment	x			
7	300		x	Electric motors	x	x		
8	400	x		Specialty metals		x		
9	800		x	Small electrical products	x			
10	500	x		Generating equipment repair				x
11	2000	x		Large electric motors	x	x		
12	500	x		Electrical apparatus		x		
13	300	x		Electrical apparatus service		x		
14	1500	x		Large power equipment		x		
15	500	x		Specialized equipment		x		
16	400	x		Electronic equipment		x		
17	800	x		Specialized metal products		x		
18	3000		x	Major appliances	x	x		
19	400	x		Electrical products		x		
20	300		x	Ceramic products	x			
21	400		x	Wood products		x		
22	500	x	x	Electronic products		x		
23	400		x	Fluorescent lamps	x	x		
24	500	x		Mechanical equipment		x		
25	500		x	Office equipment		x		
26	400	x		Electrical equipment		x		
27	800		x	Major appliances	x	x		

	EMPL.	LCLR	SCR	TYPE OF WORK	INC.	MDW	DW	Proc.
28	1000	x		Large power equipment	x	x		
29	400		x	Plastic materials		x		
30	250	x		Electrical & electronic equ.	x			
31	800	x		Specialized electronics		x		
32	800	x		Large mechanical equipment	x	x		
33	400			Research laboratory				x
34	250		x	Information systems		x		
35	100			Trucking distribution ctr.			x	
36	1000	x	x	Transformers		x		
37	400	x		Energy systems		x		
38	4000	x		Large mechanical equipment	x	x		
39	300	x		Electrical equipment	x			
40	400		x	Electric motors	x			
41	300		x	Electrical products	x	x		
42	200		x	Electrical equipment		x		
43	400	x	x	Refrigeration equipment		x		
44	150	x		Electronic equipment		x		
45	150			Insulating materials				x
46	1500		x	Major appliances	x			
47	1500		x	Electronic products		x		
48	500	x	x	Refrigeration equipment		x		
49	1000	x		Large transformers		x		
50	200		x	Specialty watches		x		
51	500	x		Electrical equipment	x			
52	800	x	x	Air conditioning equipment		x		
53	300		x	Heating equipment	x			
54	200		x	Electrical products	x	x		
55	600	x		Electrical distrib. equip.		x		
56	1000	x		Large generating equipment		x		
57	500			Research laboratory			x	
58	400	x		Electronic equipment		x		
59	200	x		Transportation equipment			x	
60	100			Plastics				x
61	4000	x		Large generating equipment	x			
62	250			Research laboratory			x	
63	200			Marketing group			x	
64	160		x	Printing & office supplies	x			
65	600	x		Electrical apparatus	x	x		
66	300	x		Renewal parts center	x			
67	2000	x		Electrical apparatus	x			
68	800			Research laboratory				x

	EMPL.	LCLR	SCR	TYPE OF WORK	INC.	MDW	DW	Proc.
69	1500		x	Electrical products		x		
70	800	x		Mechanical equipment		x		
71	400	x		Electrical apparatus		x		
72	400	x		Electrical equipment		x		
73	3000	x		Transformers	x			
74	500	x		Transformers		x		
75	400	x		Electrical appliances	x			
76	600	x	x	Air conditioning equipment		x		
77	300	x		Electrical equipment		x		
78	800	x		Aerospace equipment		x		
79	400	x		Industrial equipment		x		
80	1000	x		Large generating equipment		x		
81	300		x	Electric motors	x	x		
82	250		x	Electric motors		x		
83	300		x	Lighting fixtures		x		
84	500	x	x	Components, pwr. gen. equip.		x		
85	400		x	Electronic parts		x		
86	400	x	x	Electrical apparatus		x		
87	200	x		Electrical products			x	
88	400	x	x	Electrical products	x			
89	200		x	Electrical apparatus		x		
90	200		x	Mechanical products		x		
91	150		x	Office equipment		x		
92	100		x	Specialty watches		x		
93	2000	x	x	Wide range of electr. prod.		x		
94	350		x	Electric materials	x			
95	2000	x		Ship repair & shipbuilding		x		
96	1200			Petroleum refining				x
97	600			Sugar refining				x
98	1400			Petroleum refining				x
99	1400			Petroleum refining				x
100	1500			Petroleum refining				x
101	250			Petroleum refining				x
102	350			Petroleum refining				x
103	500		x	Paper products		x		
104	250		x	Paper products	x			
105	8000			Petro-chemical (multiplant)			x	x
106	1000			Chemical processing				x
	20,000	x		Aircraft manufacturing		x		
	10,000		x	Automobile parts manuf.		x		
109	300			Petroleum products distrib.			x	
110	300	x	x	Transportation equipment		x		

The companies which include one or more of the previously listed plants are shown below, along with their principal business and location.

A. Automobile manufacturing, Michigan
B. Aircraft manufacturing, California
C. Electric materials manufacturing, Pennsylvania
D. Petroleum prod., refining, distrib., New Jersey
E. Petroleum prod., refining, distrib., Oklahoma
F. Petroleum prod., refining, distrib., California
G. Petroleum prod., refining, distrib., Arkansas
H. Paper production and fabrication, Florida
J. Sugar refining, California
K. Electrical & other manufacturing, U.S. and abroad
L. Ship repair and shipbuilding, Alabama

Other companies specifically referred to in this book are as follows:

M. Equipment manufacturing, Illinois
N. Technological products and SC/R manuf., Ohio

LOGIC FOR THE 4M DATA COMPUTER PROGRAM

Motion times stored within the 4M program are listed in Figure 15. The Get or Place notations, which comprise over 90 percent of the typical 4M input data, are defined by Figure 16. Other notations are listed in Figure 15. The simultaneous motion rules of Figure 17 are embodied within the program. How the program recognizes a "set" of motions was described in chapter 6. As noted, the motions identified by entries on a single line of the input format are always considered a motion set, to be fitted together according to the MTM–1 chart for simultaneous motions. Actions which cannot be performed simultaneously because of physical barriers or other limitations should be entered on separate lines. Unless there is a physical requirement for one action to be completed before another takes place (such as a washer placed before a nut is placed), a number of adjacent lines can be identified as a continuing motion set. This allows the program to overlap certain motions when MTM–1 rules permit. A motion set is identified by entering code B in a designated column of each line. (Code C serves the same purpose when two sets are adjacent to each other.)

The primary logic segments of the program were described in Chapter 6 and are diagrammed on pages that follow. Definition of symbols used in the logic charts are listed below:

- *1L, 2L, 1R, 2R = first and second motions within Get or Place aggregates or other motion entries, on the left or right sides of the analysis format.*
- *1A, 2A, 1B, 2B = same as above, except that A and B may be designated as either the left/right or the right/left motions. (This is done to reduce the length of certain logic sequences.)*
- $1A_{LC}$ *= the lower Case of first motion, side A. Examples: The lower Case of a C-Reach is an E-Reach. The lower Case of a C-Move is a B-Move.*
- *RMCD = Case C or D Reach or Move.*
- *RMXC = Case C Reach or Move, distance X, where X is the length of a C Reach or Move that extends beyond the lower Case motion which overlaps a C motion of the other hand.*
- *RMFC = fractional Reach or Move, Case C. The time is 20 MU. This is the required motion that follows a lower Case Reach or Move, per MTM-1 procedures. Use of the figure 20 in procedural charts has this meaning.*
- *TL, TR, or TA, TB = times for left or right-hand motions within a motion set of one line. These times are utilized in the calculation of improvement indices by the 4M program.*
- *TN = net time for motion set of one line. Total time for an element is a summation of the net times.*
- *NS = "next simo" motion. This is the motion category, within a set of one line, which remains to be considered for interaction with motions on the next line of a continuing set.*
- *TS = time for that part of the NS motion which has not already been overlapped within the motion set*

of one line. This amount of motion time is available for interaction with motions on the next line of a continuing set.

- *= less than or equal to. (Used as a question within the program logic.)*

- *S = "simo." (Used as a question, such as "Can motion 1A be considered simultaneous with motion 1B, after application of MTM-1 procedural rules?)*

- *Code L or code R, in "lead hand" column of input format: Indicates that either the left or right hand is required to lead the other during Reaches or Moves that could be simultaneous if lowered in Case. (This method detail is seldom required. When neither code is applied, the logic program takes an optimum approach.)*

- *NSTS = the next to be considered for simultaneous action, having a time value of TS as derived in a preceding step of the logic chart.*

AN ILLUSTRATION OF HOW THE LOGIC CHARTS ARE APPLIED

Shown in Figure 49 is a graphic diagram of the element covered by Figures 18–21 in chapter 6. Motion analysis within the diagram differs from that in Figure 19 only by the inclusion of Release times within Grasp times, as previously noted. The symbols listed are taken from the chart of Figure 15. They will be seen to differ somewhat from the MTM–1 symbols in Figure 19. It is not necessary to learn the MTM–1 symbols to apply 4m DATA, although adequate training is necessary. A review of the logic steps that follow should be a part of such training. Understanding when to denote continuing motion sets is of particular significance.

A step-by-step application of logic charts 1–4 to derive the net time for this element is given below. Although short, the element involves several complex procedural steps which are seldom handled correctly or consistently by analysts performing a manual application of MTM–1. The purpose of material that follows is to show how 4M logic may be reviewed by those who want to check its validity for any combination of motions.

FIGURE 49.
Graphic Diagram of Element in Figures 18–21.

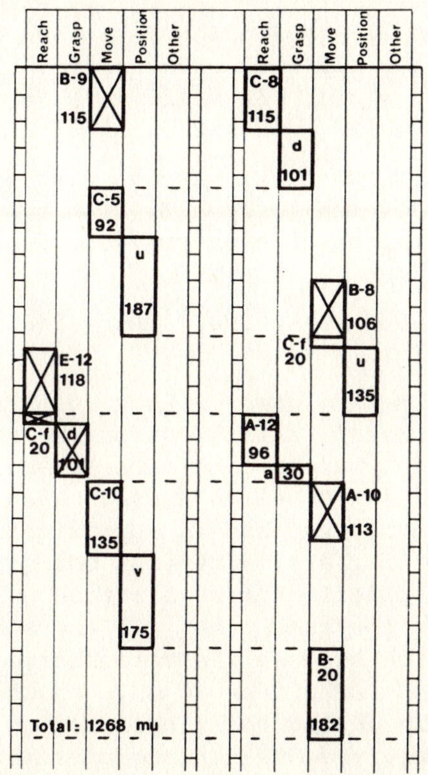

ANALYSIS OF FIRST LINE: Apply chart 1, as in all cases except for continuing lines within a designated motion set. 1L = MC14, 1R = RC8. (The 4M notations enable the computer program to recognize MTM-1 motion categories and times, although some motions will be reduced in case to conform with MTM-1 procedures.) Both of the motions involve Case C, and 1R is less than 1L. Thus, apply chart 3, designating A = left-hand motions and B = right-hand.

3/1: *Is 1L (MC14) simo with 1R (RC8)? NO.*
3/3: *Is* $1L_{LC}$ *(MB14) simo with 1R? YES.*
3/5: *Is (MB14 = 146) less than or equal to (RC8 = 115)? NO.*
3/15: *Is there 2R? YES, 2R = G42 = 101.*
3/16: *Is MB14 simo with G42? NO. Find maximum dis-*

tance, D2, for motion Y, like MB14. RC8 = 115. MB9 = 115. D1 - D2 = 14 - 9 = 5. Thus, X = 5, Y = MB9.

3/18: Is there 2L? YES, 2L = Position, code u = 187. Thus, TN = 115 + 92 + 187 = 495. TL = 115 + 92 + 187 = 394. TR = 115 + 101 = 216. NS = MC. TS = 187 + 92 = 279.

ANALYSIS OF SECOND LINE: Apply chart 4, since lines 1 and 2 are bracketed by code B. Chart 1 is not used at this point, since this is the second line of a continuing motion set.

4/1: TN_1 = 495. TL_1 = 394. TR_1 = 216. NS_1 = MC. TS_1 = 279.

4/2: Is (TS_1 = 279) greater than 30? YES. As previously noted, this question is asked to conform with what is considered standard practice by qualified MTM-1 analysts. When the time for a motion by one hand is approximately equal to the time for a simultaneous motion by the other hand, completion of each motion will tend to occur at the same time. If there is enough difference between the motion times (assumed within 4M DATA to be 30 MU), another motion can begin during the longer motion of the other hand, provided MTM-1 procedures indicate that simo action is possible.

4/4: Is (NS_1 - MC) on left? YES.

4/9: 1L = $NSTS_1$ = MC, time 279. 2L = 0. 1R = MC8. 2R = Position, simo code u, time 135.
The purpose here is to determine whether there are right-hand motions that can be simo with the left-hand MC motion. Within a continuing motion set, the 4M program continues with this left-right-left-right analysis process, applying MTM-1 rules precisely in doing so.
Is 1R a Case C motion? YES. Apply chart 3, with A = R, B = L.

3/1: Is (1R = MC8) simo with (1L = MC)? NO.

3/3: Is ($1R_{LC}$ = MB8) simo with 1L? YES.

3/5: Is there 2L? NO. (2L = 0, as specified in 4/9.)

3/7: Is there 2R? YES. TN = 279 + 135 + 20 = 434.

TR = (MB8 = 106) + 135 + 20 = 261. TL = 279. NS = Position, simo code u. TS = 135 + 20 = 155.

4/12: TN_{2x} = 434. TL_{2x} = 279. TR_{2x} = 261. NS_{2x} = Position, code u. TS_{2x} = 135.

4/13: Is NS_{2x} on left? NO.

4/14: 1R = (Position, code u = 155). 2R = 0. 1L = RC12. 2L = G42. Is 1L a Case C motion? YES.

4/16: Apply chart 3, with A = L, B = R.

3/1: Is 1L simo with 1R? NO.

3/3: Is ($1L_{LC}$ = RE12) simo with 1R? YES.

3/5: Is ($1L_{LC}$ = RE12 = 118) less than or equal to (1R = 135)? YES.

3/6: Is there 2R? NO.

3/7: Is there 2L? YES, 2L = G42. TN = 155 + 101 + 20 = 276. TS = 118 + 101 + 20 = 239. TR = 155. NS = G42. TS = 101 + 20 = 121. Go to chart 4, step A.

4/A: TN_2 = 276. TL_2 = 239. TR_2 = 155. NS_2 = G42. TS_2 = 121. Go to step N.

4/N: For lines 1 and 2 of the continuing set, TN_2 = 495 + 276 = 771. TL_2 = 394 + 239 = 633. TR_2 = 216 + 261 = 477. NS_2 = G42. TS_2 = 121. Go to 4/33.

ANALYSIS OF THIRD LINE: Above values will have their labels changed so that the logic chart can be applied again. The motions on line 3 will now be referred to as if this were the second line in the set.

4/33: YES, line 3 has code B. Relabel the values TN_1, TL_1, etc.

4/2: Is (TS_1 = 121) greater than 30? YES.

4/4: Is (NS_1 = G42) on left? YES.

4/5: Is there $1R_2$? YES, $1R_2$ = RA12 = 96.

4/9: 1L = G42 motion, time 121. 2L = 0. 1R = (RA = 96). 2R = (Grasp a = 30). Is 1R a Case C/D motion? NO.

4/10: Apply chart 1. Find corresponding YES/NO answers in column 6. Thus, go to chart 2. Is there 2L? NO. Is there 2R? YES. Is 1L simo with 1R? YES. Is 1L simo with 2R? YES. Is 1L 1R? NO. Is 1L 2R? NO. Is 1L 1R +2R? YES. Part of set? YES. (Other ques-

tions do not apply, since 2L = 0.) From line 9 on chart 2: TN = 1R + 2R = 96 + 30 = 126. TL = 1L = 121. TR = 1R + 2R = 126. NS = Grasp, code a. TS = 1R + 2R - 1L = 96 + 30 - 121 = 5.

4/12: TN_{2x} = 126. TL_{2x} = 121. TR_{2x} = Grasp a. TS_{2x} = 5.

4/13: Is NS_{2x} on left side? NO.

4/14: 1R = Grasp a, 5. 2R = 0. 1L = 0. 2L = 0.

4/15: Apply chart 1. Find corresponding YES/NO answers in column 5. Thus, TN = TR = 1R = 5. TL = 0.

4/A: TN_2 = TR_2 = 5. (This refers to line 3, as noted above.)

4/N: TN_{set} = TN_1 + TN_2 = 771 + 5 = 776. TL_{set} = TL_1 + TL_2 = 633. TR_{set} = TR_1 + TR_{2x} = 477 + 126 = 603.

4/33: Does next line have same set-code? NO. (This concludes the analysis of lines 1-3.)

ANALYSIS OF FOURTH LINE: Apply chart 1. 1L = MC10 = 135. 2L = Position, code v, time 175. 1R = MA10 = 113. 2R does not exist. Find corresponding YES/NO answers in column 8. Go to chart 3, A=L, B=R.

3/1: Is 1L simo with 1R? YES. Apply chart 2. Is there 2L? YES. Is there 2R? NO. Is 1L simo with 1R? YES. Is 2L simo with 1R? YES. Is 1L   1R? NO. Is 2L   1R? NO. Is 1L + 2L   1R? NO. From line 6, TN = 1L + 2L = 135 + 175 = 310. TL = 1L + 2L + 135 + 175 = 310. TR = 1R = 113.

ANALYSIS OF FIFTH LINE: From 4M DATA procedures, P02T (T for "toss") is a Case B Move, treated as Case A for simo application. Apply Chart 1. From column 5, TN = TR = 1R = P02T,20" = 182.

TOTAL ELEMENT TIME: 776 + 310 + 182 = 1268 MU.

DERIVATION OF MOTION ASSIGNMENT INDEX: LH motion time = 633 + 310 = 943. RH motion time = 603 + 113 + 182 = 898. MAI = (943 + 898)/(2 x 1268) = 0.73, or 73 percent.

DERIVATION OF OTHER IMPROVEMENT INDICES: The computer program identifies and obtains a percentage *value for the following motion groups: RMB = Reaches, Moves & Body motions; GRA = Grasps, Releases, Apply Pressures; POS = Positions; PROC = Process times not overlapped by specified motions.*

4M DATA LOGIC CHART 1

First Step in the Analysis of Data on one Input Line

ASK THESE QUESTIONS	1	2	3	4	5	6	7	8	9	10	11	12
Is there 1L?	N	Y	Y	N	N	Y	Y	Y	Y	Y	Y	Y
Is there 2L?		Y	N	–	–							
Is there 1R?	N	N	N	Y	Y	Y	Y	Y	Y	Y	Y	Y
Is there 2R?		–	–	Y	N							
Is 1L a C/D motion?	–			–	–	N	Y	Y	Y	N	Y	Y
Is 1R a C/D motion?	–	–	–			N	N	Y	Y	Y	Y	Y
Is 1R less than 1L?	–	–	–	–	–				Y			N
Is code L applied?*								N	N		Y	N
Is code R applied?*								Y	N		N	N
Action	GO TO LOGIC CHART 5.	TN=TL=1L+2L. TR=0	TN=TL=1L. TR=0	TN=TR=1R+2R. TL=0	TN=TR=1R. TL=0	GO TO LOGIC CHART 2.	GO TO LOGIC CHART 3. A=L, B=R			GO TO LOGIC CHART 3. A=R, B=L		

If –, omit question, since no values exist.
If blank, may be either Y or N.

* In 1-line analysis, or on either line of 2-line analysis.

4M DATA LOGIC CHART 2

For Analysis of Data on One Input Line, without Case C or D Motions

	Is there 2L?	Is there 2R?	Is 1L S 1R?	Is 1L S 2R?	Is 2L S 1R?	Is 2L S 2R?	Is 1L ≤ 1R?	Is 1L ≤ 2R?	Is 2L ≤ 1R?	Is 2L ≤ 2R?	1L ≤ 1R+2R?	1L+2L ≤ 1R?	1L+2L≤1R+2R?	Part of Set?	TN	TL	TR	NS	TS
1	N	N	N	-	-	-		-	-	-	-	-	-		1L+1R	1L	1R	1R 1L	1R or * 1L
2	N	N	Y	-	-	-	Y	-	-	-	-	-	-		1R	1L	1R	1R	1R-1L
3	N	N	Y	-	-	-	N	-	-	-	-	-	-		1L	1L	1R	1L	1L-1R
4	Y	N	N	-	N	-		-	-	-	-	-	-		1L+2L+1R	1L+2L	1R	2L	1L+2L
5	N	Y	N	N	-	-			-	-		-	-		1L+1R+2R	1L	1R+2R	2R	1R+2R
6	Y	N	Y	-		-	N	-		-	-		-		1L+2L	1L+2L	1R	2L	1L+2L-1R
7	N	Y	Y		-	-	Y		-	-		-	-		1R+2R	1L	1R+2R	2R	1R+2R-1L
8	Y	N	Y		Y		Y	-		-	-	N	-		1L+2L	1L+2L	1R	2L	1L+2L-1R
9	N	Y	Y	Y	-	-	N		-	-	Y	-	-		1R+2R	1L	1R+2R	2R	1R+2R-1L
10	N	Y	Y	N	-	-	N		-	-		-	-		1L+2R	1L	1R+2R	2R	2R
11	Y	N	Y	-	N	-	Y	-		-	-		-		1R+2L	1L+2L	1R	2L	2L
12	Y	N	Y	-	Y	-	Y	-		-	-	Y	-		1R	1L+2L	1R	1R	1R-1L-2L
13	N	Y	Y	Y	-	-	N		-	-	N	-	-		1L	1L	1R+2R	1L	1L-1R-2R
14	Y	Y	Y		Y	Y	Y					N	Y		1R+2R	1L+2L	1R+2R	2R	1R+2R-1L-2L
15	Y	Y	Y	Y		Y	N				Y	N	N		1L+2L	1L+2L	1R+2R	2L	1L+2L-1R-2R
16	Y	Y	Y	Y		Y	N				Y	N	Y		1R+2R	1L+2L	1R+2R	2R	1R+2R-1L-2L
17	Y	Y	Y		Y	Y	Y					N	Y		1L+2L	1L+2L	1R+2R	2L	1L+2L-1R-2R
18	Y	Y	Y		N	N	Y								1R+2R+2L	1L+2L	1R+2R	2L	2L
19	Y	Y	Y	N		N	N								1L+2L+2R	1L+2L	1R+2R	2R	2R
20	Y	Y	Y		Y		Y				Y				1R+2R	1L+2L	1R+2R	2R	1R+2R-1L-2L
21	Y	Y	Y	Y			N			N					1L+2L	1L+2L	1R+2R	2L	1L+2L-1R-2R
22	Y	Y	Y	Y		N	N			Y					1R+2R+2L	1L+2L	1R+2R	2L	2L
23	Y	Y	Y		Y	N	Y				N				1L+2L+2R	1L+2L	1R+2R	2R	2R
24	Y	Y	N	N	N	N									1L+2L+1R+2R	1L+2L	1R+2R	2R 1L	1R+2R or * 1L+2L
25	Y	Y	Y		N	Y	Y			N					1R+2L	1L+2L	1R+2R	2L	2L-2R
26	Y	Y	Y	N		Y	N			Y					1L+2R	1L+2L	1R+2R	2R	2R-2L
27	Y	N	N	-	Y	-		-		-	-		-	N	1L+1R	1L+2L	1R	1R	1R-2L (=0)
28	N	Y	N	Y	-	-				-	-		-	N	1L+1R	1L	1R+2R	1L	1L-2R (=0)
29	Y	N	N	-	Y	-		-		-	-		-	Y	1L+2L+1R	1L+2L	1R	1L	1L+2L
30	N	Y	N	Y	-	-			-	-		-	-	Y	1L+1R+2R	1L	1R+2R	1R	1R+2R
31	Y	Y	N	Y	Y		Y								1L+1R+2R	1L+2L	1R+2R	1R	1R
32	Y	Y	N	Y	Y		N								1R+1L+2L	1L+2L	1R+2R	1L	1L
33	Y	Y	N	N	Y										1L+1R+2R	1L+2L	1R+2R	2R	1R+2R-2L
34	Y	Y	N	Y	N										1R+1L+2L	1L+2L	1R+2R	2L	1L+2L-2R

If -, omit question, since no values exist.
If blank, may be either Y or N.
** - Test for minimum TN when following line coded B or C.*

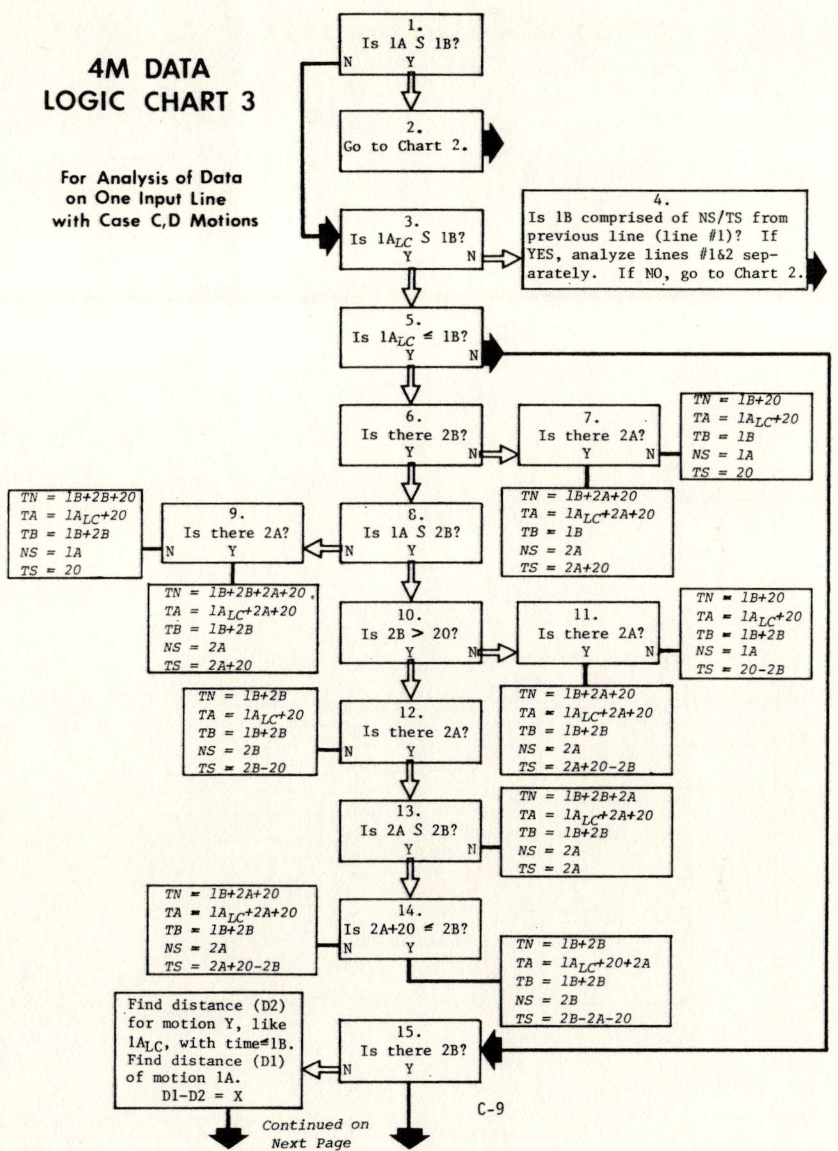
4M DATA
LOGIC CHART 3
For Analysis of Data on One Input Line with Case C,D Motions
1. Is 1A S 1B?
2. Go to Chart 2.
3. Is 1ALC S 1B?
4. Is 1B comprised of NS/TS from previous line (line #1)? If YES, analyze lines #1&2 separately. If NO, go to Chart 2.
5. Is 1ALC ≤ 1B?
6. Is there 2B?
7. Is there 2A?
TN = 1B+20
TA = 1ALC+20
TB = 1B
NS = 1A
TS = 20
TN = 1B+2A+20
TA = 1ALC+2A+20
TB = 1B
NS = 2A
TS = 2A+20
8. Is 1A S 2B?
9. Is there 2A?
TN = 1B+2B+20
TA = 1ALC+20
TB = 1B+2B
NS = 1A
TS = 20
TN = 1B+2B+2A+20
TA = 1ALC+2A+20
TB = 1B+2B
NS = 2A
TS = 2A+20
10. Is 2B > 20?
11. Is there 2A?
TN = 1B+20
TA = 1ALC+20
TB = 1B+2B
NS = 1A
TS = 20-2B
TN = 1B+2A+20
TA = 1ALC+2A+20
TB = 1B+2B
NS = 2A
TS = 2A+20-2B
12. Is there 2A?
TN = 1B+2B
TA = 1ALC+20
TB = 1B+2B
NS = 2B
TS = 2B-20
13. Is 2A S 2B?
TN = 1B+2B+2A
TA = 1ALC+2A+20
TB = 1B+2B
NS = 2A
TS = 2A
14. Is 2A+20 ≤ 2B?
TN = 1B+2A+20
TA = 1ALC+2A+20
TB = 1B+2B
NS = 2A
TS = 2A+20-2B
TN = 1B+2B
TA = 1ALC+20+2A
TB = 1B+2B
NS = 2B
TS = 2B-2A-20
15. Is there 2B?
Find distance (D2) for motion Y, like 1ALC, with time≤1B. Find distance (D1) of motion 1A. D1-D2 = X
Continued on Next Page
C-9

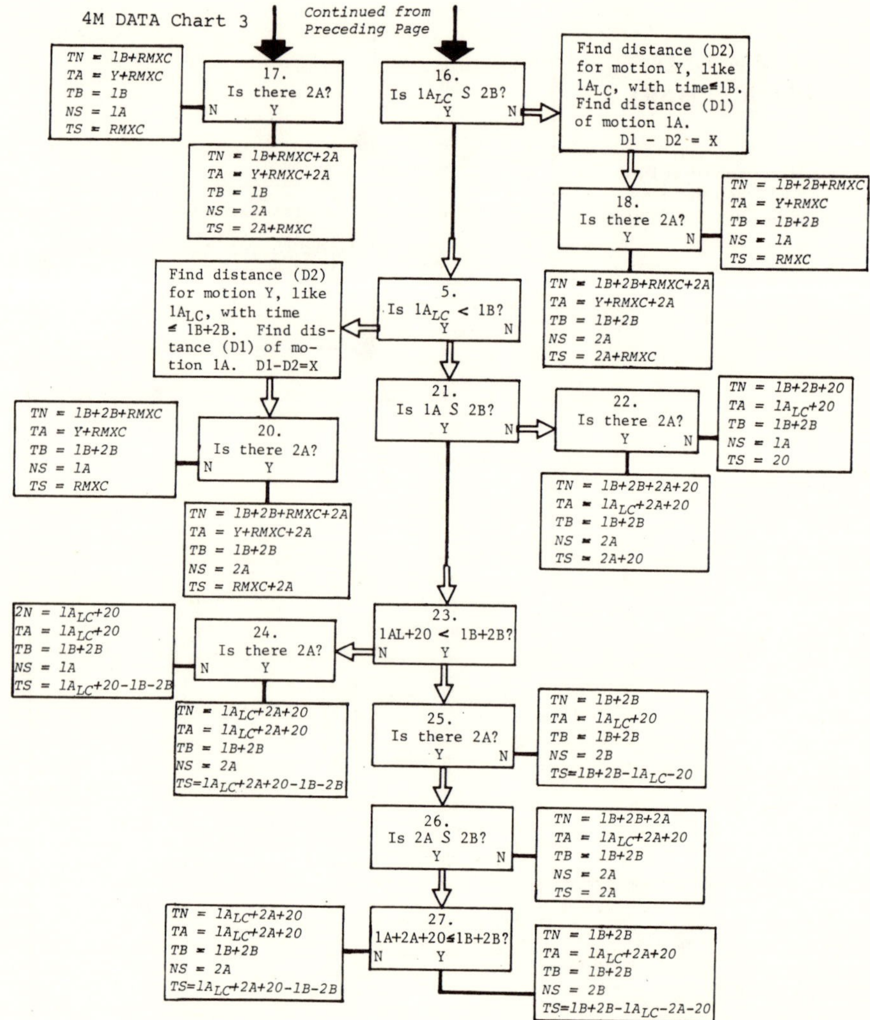
4M DATA Chart 3
Continued from Preceding Page
TN = 1B+RMXC TA = Y+RMXC TB = 1B NS = 1A TS = RMXC
17. Is there 2A? N Y
16. Is 1A_LC S 2B? Y N
Find distance (D2) for motion Y, like 1A_LC, with time≤1B. Find distance (D1) of motion 1A. D1 - D2 = X
TN = 1B+RMXC+2A TA = Y+RMXC+2A TB = 1B NS = 2A TS = 2A+RMXC
18. Is there 2A? Y N
TN = 1B+2B+RMXC TA = Y+RMXC TB = 1B+2B NS = 1A TS = RMXC
TN = 1B+2B+RMXC+2A TA = Y+RMXC+2A TB = 1B+2B NS = 2A TS = 2A+RMXC
Find distance (D2) for motion Y, like 1A_LC, with time ≤ 1B+2B. Find distance (D1) of motion 1A. D1-D2=X
5. Is 1A_LC < 1B? Y N
21. Is 1A S 2B? Y N
22. Is there 2A? Y N
TN = 1B+2B+20 TA = 1A_LC+20 TB = 1B+2B NS = 1A TS = 20
TN = 1B+2B+RMXC TA = Y+RMXC TB = 1B+2B NS = 1A TS = RMXC
20. Is there 2A? N Y
TN = 1B+2B+2A+20 TA = 1A_LC+2A+20 TB = 1B+2B NS = 2A TS = 2A+20
TN = 1B+2B+RMXC+2A TA = Y+RMXC+2A TB = 1B+2B NS = 2A TS = RMXC+2A
2N = 1A_LC+20 TA = 1A_LC+20 TB = 1B+2B NS = 1A TS = 1A_LC+20-1B-2B
24. Is there 2A? N Y
23. 1AL+20 < 1B+2B? N Y
TN = 1A_LC+2A+20 TA = 1A_LC+2A+20 TB = 1B+2B NS = 2A TS=1A_LC+2A+20-1B-2B
25. Is there 2A? Y N
TN = 1B+2B TA = 1A_LC+20 TB = 1B+2B NS = 2B TS=1B+2B-1A_LC-20
26. Is 2A S 2B? Y N
TN = 1B+2B+2A TA = 1A_LC+2A+20 TB = 1B+2B NS = 2A TS = 2A
TN = 1A_LC+2A+20 TA = 1A_LC+2A+20 TB = 1B+2B NS = 2A TS=1A_LC+2A+20-1B-2B
27. 1A+2A+20≤1B+2B? N Y
TN = 1B+2B TA = 1A_LC+2A+20 TB = 1B+2B NS = 2B TS=1B+2B-1A_LC-2A-20

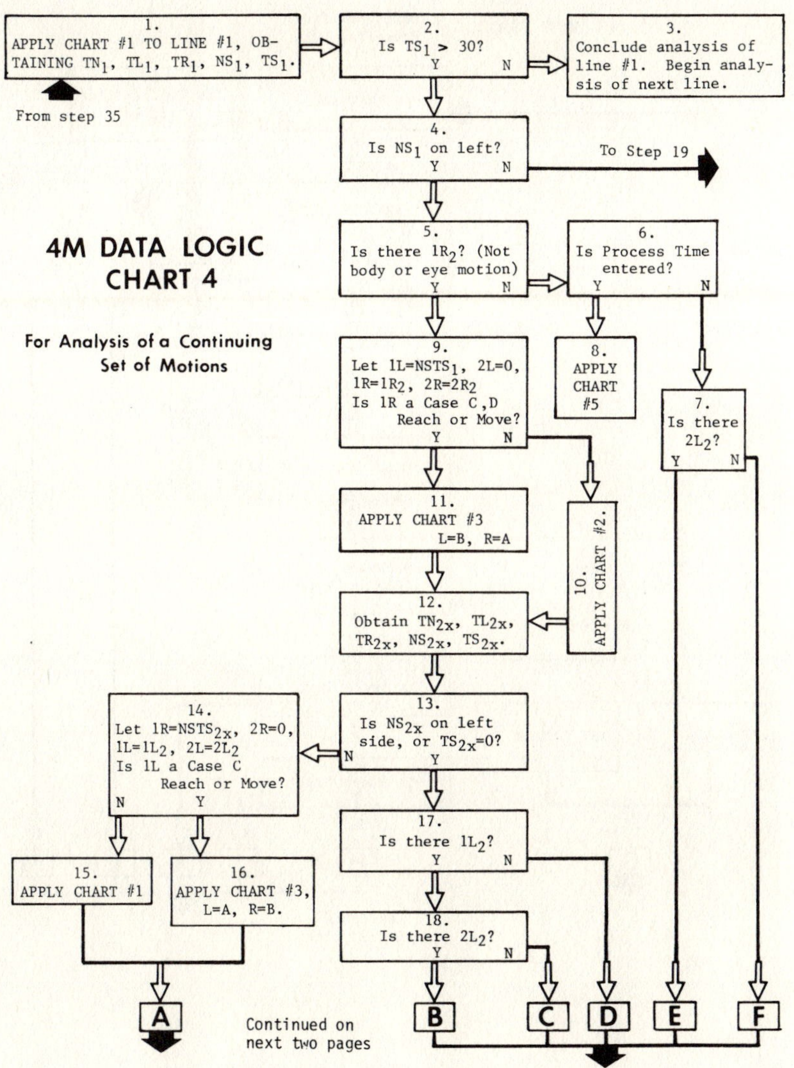
1.
APPLY CHART #1 TO LINE #1, OBTAINING TN1, TL1, TR1, NS1, TS1.
From step 35
2.
Is TS1 > 30?
Y N
3.
Conclude analysis of line #1. Begin analysis of next line.
4.
Is NS1 on left?
Y N
To Step 19
5.
Is there 1R2? (Not body or eye motion)
Y N
6.
Is Process Time entered?
Y N
4M DATA LOGIC CHART 4
For Analysis of a Continuing Set of Motions
9.
Let 1L=NSTS1, 2L=0, 1R=1R2, 2R=2R2
Is 1R a Case C,D Reach or Move?
Y N
8.
APPLY CHART #5
7.
Is there 2L2?
Y N
11.
APPLY CHART #3
L=B, R=A
10.
APPLY CHART #2.
12.
Obtain TN2x, TL2x, TR2x, NS2x, TS2x.
14.
Let 1R=NSTS2x, 2R=0, 1L=1L2, 2L=2L2
Is 1L a Case C Reach or Move?
N Y
13.
Is NS2x on left side, or TS2x=0?
N Y
17.
Is there 1L2?
Y N
15.
APPLY CHART #1
16.
APPLY CHART #3, L=A, R=B.
18.
Is there 2L2?
Y N
A
Continued on next two pages
B
C
D
E
F

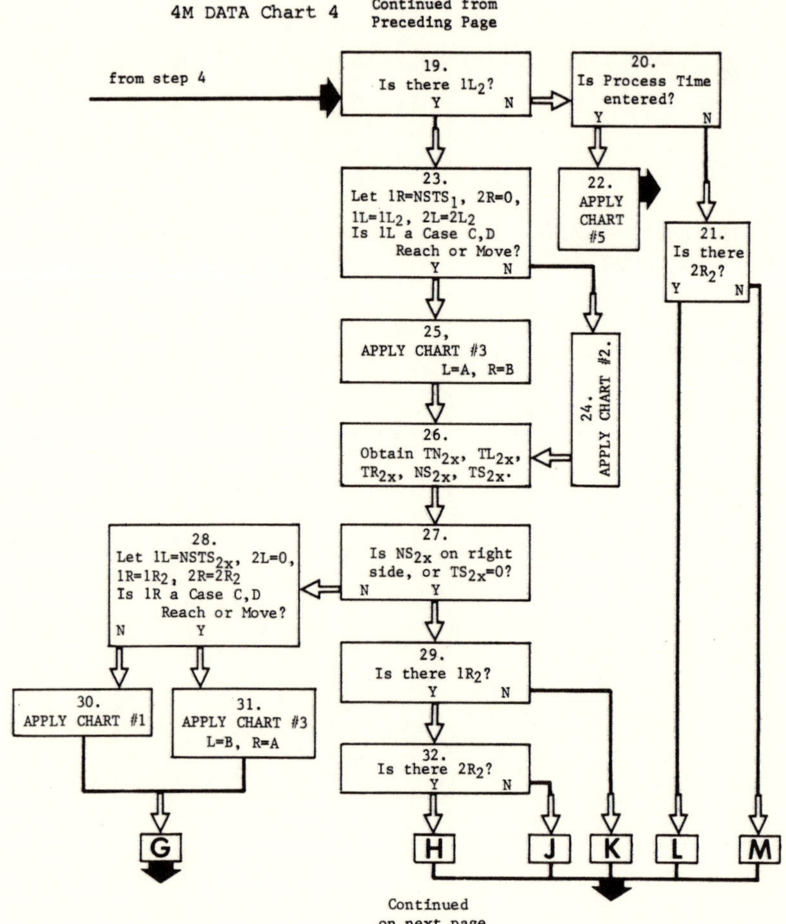
4M DATA Chart 4
Continued from Preceding Page
from step 4
19. Is there 1L2? Y N
20. Is Process Time entered? Y N
23. Let 1R=NSTS1, 2R=0, 1L=1L2, 2L=2L2 Is 1L a Case C,D Reach or Move? Y N
22. APPLY CHART #5
21. Is there 2R2? Y N
25, APPLY CHART #3 L=A, R=B
24. APPLY CHART #2.
26. Obtain TN2x, TL2x, TR2x, NS2x, TS2x.
28. Let 1L=NSTS2x, 2L=0, 1R=1R2, 2R=2R2 Is 1R a Case C,D Reach or Move? N Y
27. Is NS2x on right side, or TS2x=0? N Y
29. Is there 1R2? Y N
30. APPLY CHART #1
31. APPLY CHART #3 L=B, R=A
32. Is there 2R2? Y N
G
H
J
K
L
M
Continued on next page

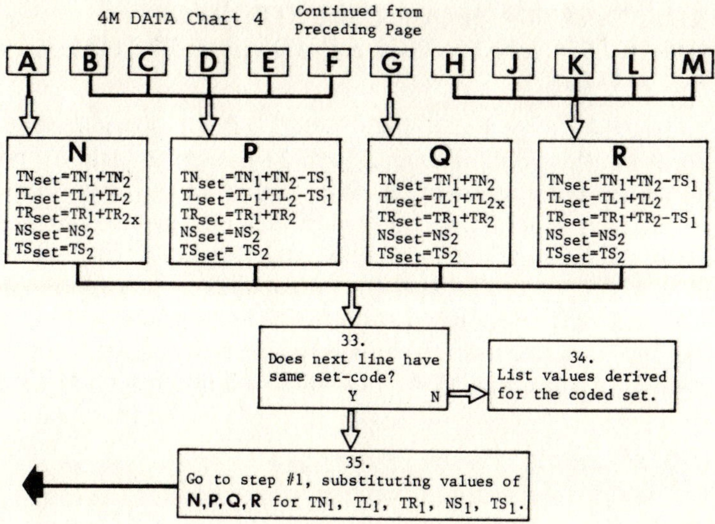

4M DATA Chart 4
Continued from Preceding Page
A B C D E F G H J K L M
N
$TN_{set}=TN_1+TN_2$
$TL_{set}=TL_1+TL_2$
$TR_{set}=TR_1+TR_{2x}$
$NS_{set}=NS_2$
$TS_{set}=TS_2$
P
$TN_{set}=TN_1+TN_2-TS_1$
$TL_{set}=TL_1+TL_2-TS_1$
$TR_{set}=TR_1+TR_2$
$NS_{set}=NS_2$
$TS_{set}= TS_2$
Q
$TN_{set}=TN_1+TN_2$
$TL_{set}=TL_1+TL_{2x}$
$TR_{set}=TR_1+TR_2$
$NS_{set}=NS_2$
$TS_{set}=TS_2$
R
$TN_{set}=TN_1+TN_2-TS_1$
$TL_{set}=TL_1+TL_2$
$TR_{set}=TR_1+TR_2-TS_1$
$NS_{set}=NS_2$
$TS_{set}=TS_2$
33. Does next line have same set-code?
Y
N
34. List values derived for the coded set.
35. Go to step #1, substituting values of N,P,Q,R for TN_1, TL_1, TR_1, NS_1, TS_1.

RESULTS FOR STEPS A-M
IN CHART 4 ANALYSIS

A	B	C	D
From Chart #2 or Chart #3, Obtain TN_2, TL_2, TR_2, NS_2, TS_2.	$TN_2=TN_{2x}+1L_2+2L_2$ $TL_2=TL_{2x}+1L_2+2L_2$ $TR_2=TR_{2x}$ $NS_2=2L_2$ $TS_2=TS_{2x}+1L_2+2L_2$	$TN_2=TN_{2x}+1L_2$ $TL_2=TL_{2x}+1L_2$ $TR_2=TR_{2x}$ $NS_2=1L_2$ $TS_2=TS_{2x}+1L_2$	$TN_2=TN_{2x}$ $TL_2=TL_{2x}$ $TR_2=TR_{2x}$ $NS_2=NS_{2x}$ $TS_2=TS_{2x}$
E	**F**	**G**	**H**
$TN_2=TS_1+1L_2+2L_2$ $TL_2=TS_1+1L_2+2L_2$ $TR_2=0$ $NS_2=2L_2$ $TS_2=TS_1+1L_2+2L_2$	$TN_2=TS_1+1L_2$ $TL_2=TS_1+1L_2$ $TR_2=0$ $NS_2=1L_2$ $TS_2=TS_1+1L_2$	From Chart #2 or Chart #3, Obtain TN_2, TL_2, TR_2, TS_2.	$TN_2=TN_{2x}=1R_2+2R_2$ $TL_2=TL_{2x}$ $TR_2=TR_{2x}+1R_2+2R_2$ $NS_2=2R_2$ $TS_2=TS_{2x}+1R_2+2R_2$
J	**K**	**L**	**M**
$TN_2=TN_{2x}+1R_2$ $TL_2=TL_{2x}$ $TR_2=TR_{2x}+1R_2$ $NS_2=1R_2$ $TS_2=TS_{2x}=1R_2$	$TN_2=TN_{2x}$ $TL_2=TL_{2x}$ $TR_2=TR_{2x}$ $NS_2=NS_{2x}$ $TS_2=TS_{2x}$	$TN_2=TS_1+1R_2+2R_2$ $TL_2=0$ $TR_2=TS_1+1R_2+2R_2$ $NS_2=2R_2$ $TS_2=TS_1+1R_2+2R_2$	$TN_2=TS_1+1R_2$ $TL_2=0$ $TR_2=TS_1+1R_2$ $NS_2=1R_2$ $TS_2=TS_1+1R_2$

HOW TO CONVERT A SEQUENTIAL STRING OF MICROPROCESSOR NOTATIONS INTO A VALID MTM–1 MOTION ANALYSIS

This subject may be of limited interest because of its specialized nature. It is included in this book, however, because it seems to define a path of ultimate simplicity for achieving the consistency and accuracy of motion and time analysis which a basic predetermined time system can provide. The details given below will be somewhat generalized. They can be expanded by a competent analyst to fit the capabilities of a specific microprocessor and any revisions in the 4M DATA format. A "front-end" computer program was used to convert the microprocessor output into a correct 4M DATA input format. A summarized description is given below.

MICROPROCESSOR INPUT NOTATIONS: It is necessary to devise easy-to-remember codes, using available microprocessor keys, to simulate the 4M notations and provide certain directions needed by the front-end pro gram. In the unit pictured by Figure 7, there could be entered an asterisk, comma, letters C,F,H, and any desired numerals. This was sufficient to provide usable codes along the following lines:

**5: Element number 5 begins, and continues until another element number is denoted in the same way. Entered by computer program in columns 6-7, along with code E in column 80.*

C42,12: 4M DATA notation G42, for right hand, entered in columns 41-44. Distance of 12", entered in 45-46.

CC42,12: Same, but for left hand. Entered in 32-35 and 36-37.

F123,16: Place notation for right hand, P123, entered in 41-44. Distance of 16", entered in 45-46.

FF123,16: Same, for left hand. Entered in 32-35 and 36-37.

FFF123,16: Same, for both hands, entered in 32-35, 36-34, 41-44, 45-46.

CF500: Process time of 500 TMU, entered in 71-74.

901 through 919: Codes for body motions, entered in 41-44. (While the most-used body-motion codes can be remembered, a pocket card may be needed for those which are seldom used. The Turn, Disengage, Apply Pressure, and Eye Motions involved codes beginning with 921, 951, 961, and 971.)

A listing of the several other codes used for microprocessor application of 4M DATA would not be helpful, since it is outside the scope of this book to cover all material related to the 4M system. The illustrations noted above are sufficient to explain references to columnar locations in the flow chart that follows. While microprocessor codes, in themselves, enable the front-end computer program to assign correct 4M notations within the columnar locations, other directions are needed for placing the various notations on specific lines. The logic chart that follows does that. It will be possible to follow steps in the chart by referring to the sequential microprocessor notations of Figure 21, and observing how the flow chart directs their arrangement vertically in accordance with Figure 18.

There are newer models of the microprocessor pictured in Figure 7, which allow the input of alphabeticals. Since a shifting action is needed to accomplish this, the simpler technique noted above was found to be preferable. Either type of unit could be adapted for this purpose, however, as well as for other uses described in previous chapters.

If it is necessary to apply the somewhat more detailed 4M input format, utilized with recent 4M programs issued by the MTM Association, columnar numbers noted above would of course be changed to fit.

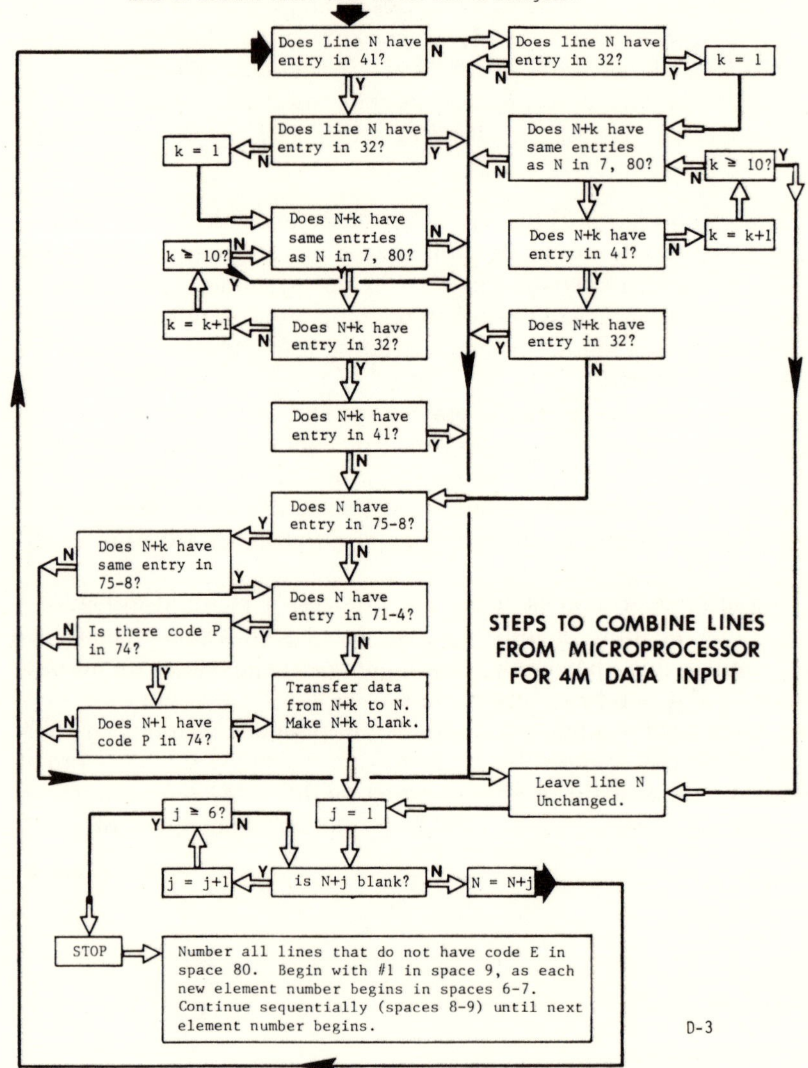
After assigning sequential lines of microprocessor output to the columnar format of Figure 18, begin here to combine lines into format for 4M analysis.
Does Line N have entry in 41?
Does line N have entry in 32?
k = 1
Does line N have entry in 32?
k = 1
Does N+k have same entries as N in 7, 80?
k ≥ 10?
Does N+k have same entries as N in 7, 80?
k ≥ 10?
Does N+k have entry in 41?
k = k+1
k = k+1
Does N+k have entry in 32?
Does N+k have entry in 32?
Does N+k have entry in 41?
Does N have entry in 75-8?
Does N+k have same entry in 75-8?
Does N have entry in 71-4?
Is there code P in 74?
Transfer data from N+k to N. Make N+k blank.
Does N+1 have code P in 74?
Leave line N Unchanged.
j ≥ 6?
j = 1
j = j+1
is N+j blank?
N = N+j
STOP
Number all lines that do not have code E in space 80. Begin with #1 in space 9, as each new element number begins in spaces 6-7. Continue sequentially (spaces 8-9) until next element number begins.
STEPS TO COMBINE LINES FROM MICROPROCESSOR FOR 4M DATA INPUT
D-3

Bibliography

Books A-E are wide-ranging in scope and would be found in many libraries. Listings that follow provide information along specific lines, as noted.

A. Barnes, R. M. *Motion and Time Study*. 7th ed. New York: Wiley, 1980.

B. Karger, D. W., and F. H. Bayha. *Engineered Work Measurement*. 4th ed. New York: Industrial Press, 1987.

C. Maynard, H. B. (ed.) *Industrial Engineering Handbook*. 3rd ed. New York: McGraw-Hill, 1971.

D. Salvendy, Gavriel (ed.) *Handbook of Industrial Engineering*. New York: Wiley, 1982.

E. *Computerized Work Measurement* —A compilation of articles published in *Industrial Engineering,* prior to 1985. Norcross, Georgia: Institute of Industrial Engineers.

PREDETERMINED TIME SYSTEMS

Brisley, C. L and Karl Eady. "Predetermined Motion Time Systems." Reference D, Chapter 4.5

"Computer-aided Predetermined Time Systems." Reference B, Chapter 19.

Honeycutt, J. M. Jr. "Comments on an Experimental Evaluation of the Validity of Predetermined Elemental Time Systems." *Industrial Engineering*. May-June, 1962.

Martin, J. C. "The 4M DATA System." *Industrial Engineering*. March, 1974.

Martin, J. C. "Practical Advantages Through Application of 4M DATA." *MTM Journal*. Vol. 1, No. 4.

Martin, J. C. "Program, Portable Microprocessor Allow Direct On-site Input of 4M (MTM–1) DATA." Reference E.

Mishra, Davendra. "Computerized Work Measurement." Reference D, Chapter 4.7.

TIME STUDY AND PERFORMANCE RATING

Anderson, C. A. "Performance Rating." Reference C, Sec. 3, Chapter 3.

Martin, J. C. "A Better Performance Rating System." *Industrial Engineering*. August, 1970.

Mundel, M. E. *Motion and Time Study*. 4th ed. Englewood Cliffs, N.J.: Prentice-Hall, 1960.

A and B references, noted above.

WORK SAMPLING

Barnes, R. M. *Work Sampling*. 2nd ed. New York: Wiley, 1957.

Brisley, C. L. "Work Sampling." Reference C, Sec. 3, Chapter 2.

WAGE INCENTIVE APPLICATIONS

Fein, Mitchell. "Wage Payment Plans." Reference C, Sec. 6, Chapter 2.

Maynard, H. B. "Group System of Wage Payment." Reference C, Sec. 6, Chapter 4.

MEASURED DAYWORK APPLICATIONS

Fein, Mitchell. "Short-interval Scheduling: A Labor Control Technique." *Industrial Engineering*, February, 1972.

Martin, J. C. "PLANACODE—Graphic Short-interval Scheduling with Bar-code Data Collection." *MTM Journal*. Vol. XI, No. 4, 1985.

O'Donnell, P. D. "Measured Daywork." Reference C, Sec. 6, Chapter 3.

DATA COLLECTION METHODS

Smith, W. A. Jr. "Data Collection Systems—Part I: Characteristics of Errors." *Industrial Engineering*. December, 1967.

Smith, W. A. Jr. "Data Collection Systems—Part II: Environmental Effects on Accuracy." *Industrial Engineering*. January, 1968.

WAGE SYSTEMS AUDITS

Martin, J. C. "Standards and Wage Systems Audits." Reference C, Sec. 6, Chapter 9.

IMPROVEMENT AND LEARNING CURVES

Anderlohr, G. "What Production Breaks Cost." *Industrial Engineering*. September, 1969.

Cochran, E. B. *Planning Production Costs, Using the Improvement Curve*. San Francisco: Chandler Publishing Co.

Hancock, W. M. and F. H. Bayha. "The Learning Curve." Reference D, Chapter 4.3.

Nanda, R. and G. L. Adler. *Learning Curves: Theory and Application*. Inst. of Ind. Engineers, Norcross, Ga.: Engineering and Management Press, 1982.

NONDIRECT COST CONTROL

Bacci, G. J. "Indirect Operations: Measurement and Control." Reference D, Chapter 4.9.

Hodson, W. K. "Fundamentals of Indirect Labor Measurement." Reference C, Sec. 4, Chapter 3.

Lewis, B. T. and J. P. Marron (eds.) *Facilities and Plant Engineering Handbook*. New York: McGraw-Hill, 1973. (Martin, J. C. "Maintenance Cost Control Systems." Sec. 8, Chapter 2.)

MATERIAL CONTROL

D'Ovidio, G. J. and R. L. Behling. "Material Requirements Planning." Reference D, Chapter 11.6.

QUALITY CONTROL

Garvin, D. A. *Managing Quality*. New York: The Free Press, 1988.

Juran, J. M. et al. *Quality Control Handbook*. New York: McGraw-Hill, 1988.

HISTORICAL

Carson, Gordon B. (ed.) *Production Handbook*. 2nd ed. New York: Ronald Press, 1958. (Section 15, "Wage Plans and Controls."

Emerson, Harrington. *The Twelve Principles of Efficiency*. J. R. Dunlap, 1911.

Hammond, Ross W. "The History and Development of Industrial Engineering." Reference C, Sec. 1, Chapter 1.

Keller, Maryann. Rude Awakening. New York: William Morror and Co., 1989.

Index

About the Author

JOHN C. MARTIN is a retired Registered Professional Engineer with over 40 years experience in industrial engineering and manufacturing.